SURVIVANCE, SOVEREIGNTY, AND STORY

SURVIVANCE, SOVEREIGNTY, AND STORY

Teaching American Indian Rhetorics

Edited by
LISA KING
ROSE GUBELE
JOYCE RAIN ANDERSON

with a foreword by Resa Crane Bizzaro

UTAH STATE UNIVERSITY PRESS
Logan

© 2015 by the University Press of Colorado

Published by Utah State University Press
An imprint of University Press of Colorado
5589 Arapahoe Avenue, Suite 206C
Boulder, Colorado 80303

 The University Press of Colorado is a proud member of
The Association of American University Presses.

The University Press of Colorado is a cooperative publishing enterprise supported,
in part, by Adams State College, Colorado State University, Fort Lewis College,
Metropolitan State College of Denver, Regis University, University of Colorado,
University of Northern Colorado, Utah State University, and Western State College of
Colorado.

Cover design by Daniel Pratt
Cover art: "Rainbow Crow" by Robert J. M. Latora

Supplementary material is available at http://www.survivancesovereigntystory.org.

ISBN: 978-0-87421-995-1 (paper)
ISBN: 978-0-87421-996-8 (e-book)

Library of Congress Cataloging-in-Publication Data

Survivance, sovereignty, and story : teaching American Indian rhetorics / edited by Lisa
King, Rose Gubele, Joyce Rain Anderson.
    pages cm
  Includes bibliographical references and index.
  ISBN 978-0-87421-995-1 (paper) — ISBN 978-0-87421-996-8 (e-book)
1. Indians of North America—Study and teaching (Higher) 2. Rhetoric—Study and
teaching (Higher)—United States. 3. Sovereignty—Study and teaching (Higher)—
United States. 4. Cultural pluralism—Study and teaching (Higher)—United States.
5. Survival—Study and teaching (Higher)—United States. 6. Government, Resistance
to—Study and teaching (Higher)—United States. I. King, Lisa (Lisa Michelle) II.
Gubele, Rose. III. Anderson, Joyce Rain.
  E76.6.S87 2014
  970.004'9707—dc23
                              2014044778

CONTENTS

ACKNOWLEDGMENTS

To begin, we wish to honor the story of the Rainbow Crow, who carried the fire from the heavens to the freezing Peoples below. Though Crow's voice and appearance changed from the smoke and soot, they remain as the evidence of this journey. So, too, do our stories fly through both good and hard times: not the same as they were in the beginning, now changed by flame and urgency, but still with us like the flicker of the rainbow in Crow's feathers today. These stories are always with us.

This collection emerged from workshops at the Conference on College Composition and Communication (CCCC). As editors, we hope that the book and supplemental website will encourage those who wish to teach American Indian rhetorics responsibly. As with any scholarship, we stand on the shoulders of those who have broken ground in rhetoric and composition, particularly in areas that have struggled for inclusion in the canon.

The names we call out here are among many, but these are the people who have influenced, encouraged, and otherwise been supportive. They are, in no particular order, Victor Villanueva, Jacqueline Jones Royster, Gerald Vizenor, Scott Lyons, Joy Harjo, and Thomas King. Most importantly, we appreciate the constant support of the members of the American Indian Caucus at CCCC, and we especially thank Resa Crane Bizzaro, who was always there to help and listen.

Individually, we have been supported by our families. For Lisa, her family includes her husband and son, Thorsten and Julian. For Rose, her partner, Ida Merrick, and her brother, Dahle Gubele. For Joyce Rain, her daughter and son, Rebecca Rain Frew and Robert Latora; grandchildren, Hunter, Robert, Hayden, and Helana Rain; her parents, Jim and Anna Anderson; and her cousins, Donna Mitchell and Kerri Helme.

And always, we wish to thank and honor our ancestors and elders who continue to guide us. We take responsibility for any mistakes.

WAKING IN THE DARK

Janice Gould

Waking in the dark, I lie in bed near the open window
and stare at the sky.
The stars pass by like migrants,
each one bent with a burden of light,
each one murmuring a little song
remembered from childhood.
The road they tread is long, their feet dusty,
hardened by the persistence
and permanence of passage.
The night wind rushes past
cool as velvet, smelling faintly
of lilac and sand.
It nudges the stars along,
and when they begin to wane,
whispers encouragement, explaining
the necessity of movement,
proposing a purpose: how simple relativity
sustains us, that the force of gratitude
connects us on our journey, watchers
of skies and stars. Waking in the dark,
I lie in bed near the open window
and stare at the sky.

FOREWORD

ALLIANCES AND COMMUNITY BUILDING
Teaching Indigenous Rhetorics and Rhetorical Practices

Resa Crane Bizzaro

As an indigenous scholar, I have often been contacted by those who want to learn more about native peoples in the United States. Many who ask are non-native teachers who struggle to provide unbiased portrayals and culturally appropriate explanations of indigenous ways of viewing the world and our relationships to it. Just last week, I found a message in my inbox, which asked me for advice on bridging the gaps among urban high school students and contemporary indigenous peoples. The veteran English teacher who communicated with me noted that she had raised awareness among her students of the "Tonto Syndrome," or what Hank Stuever (2004) identifies as "heap-big stereotypes—the residue of racism that has transfixed American Indian[s]" as absent or culturally extraneous in American society. But this teacher was at a loss for how to get students to stop talking about indigenous peoples in the past tense, as if we no longer exist.

Indeed, this problem is persistent among many, particularly those who rarely—if ever—come into contact with "real, live Indians" or only see depictions of indigenous peoples in movies and popular culture. Based on my observations of the media's coverage of a variety of indigenous issues—ranging from using native names for sports mascots to drilling for natural gas and oil on indigenous lands without permission—many Americans are unaware that native peoples still exist and thrive. And, unfortunately, the stereotype of the proud warrior as "representative Indian" persists in American culture—along with other oversimplified portrayals, including the noble savage; the wasp-waisted, buckskin-clad maiden; the heroic guide; and—more recently—Tonto himself, who has become the "Indian of the mind," according to Stuever (2004). And that Indian of the mind is typically juxtaposed, as Cutcha Risling Baldy (2012) points out, against the "strong, valiant, white character."

These misappropriations of culture and stereotypical portrayals are what this book aims to quash, while simultaneously providing evidence of indigenous peoples' historical, cultural, and political contributions in an ever-diversifying United States. Several challenges exist for native peoples in this country today. One of the biggest is determining who speaks about us and how—what Scott Lyons (2000) calls rhetorical sovereignty. Another challenge is how to talk about and teach others about our survival of and resistance to (what Anishinaabe scholar Gerald Vizenor [1999] calls survivance) the assimilation tactics of the dominant culture since first European contact and which continue to this day. We also must continue to insist upon the U.S. honoring treaties and respecting indigenous nations as sovereign groups with our own systems of government within the territorial boundaries of the United States. Additionally, we seek to discuss these matters—and more—without essentializing native peoples, who come from oftentimes radically diverse communities and locations.

The past fifteen to twenty years has seen the publication of a number of articles discussing rhetorical practices and strategies, representing a variety of indigenous nations, and a developing discipline within English Studies. Within the past few years, we have seen a few books on indigenous rhetorics published, including Stromberg's (2006) *American Indian Rhetorics of Survivance* and Baca and Villanueva's (2010) *Rhetorics of the Americas*. However, in my discussions and correspondence with teachers who would like to present more accurate, legitimate, and representative histories—including the cultural continuance—of native peoples in this country, I have not had an opportunity to refer them to one source that will help them devise specific strategies for their classrooms.

With the publication of this collection, that lack begins to be remedied. Addressing key concepts, such as rhetorical sovereignty, historical and contemporary colonization, relationships among peoples, and the use of new technologies by indigenous peoples, this book demonstrates methods of teaching such information to non-native peoples, while affirming the practices of those native peoples among them. This book also addresses the purposes and uses of story to make meaning of both our places in the world and our understanding of those places. This text allows teachers to demonstrate indigenous ways of knowing and habits of mind that permit the development of an integrated psyche, focusing on mind, heart, body, and spirit. This book is the one I will recommend to others—and use in my own classes—as we all work toward a more realistic and sensitive portrayal of native peoples and their knowledge, history, and culture.

References

Baca, Damián, and Victor Villanueva. 2010. *Rhetorics of the Americas: 3114 BCE to 2012 CE.* New York: Palgrave MacMillan.

Baldy, Cutcha Rising. 2012. "The Lone Ranger and Tonto Movie: Could This Ever Be a Good Idea?" CutchaBaldy.weebly.com. March 20. http://www.cutcharislingbaldy .com/1/post/2012/03/the-lone-ranger-and-tonto-movie-could-this-ever-be-a-good -idea.html.

Lyons, Scott. 2000. "Rhetorical Sovereignty: What Do American Indians Want from Writing?" *College Composition and Communication* 51 (3): 447–68. http://dx.doi.org /10.2307/358744.

Stromberg, Ernest. 2006. *American Indian Rhetorics of Survivance: Word Medicine, Word Magic.* Pittsburgh: University of Pittsburgh Press.

Stuever, Hank. 2004. "The 'Tonto Syndrome': Indian Stereotypes Ignore the Diversity of Modern Native People." Brainerd Dispatch. *Washington Post.* September 27. http:// brainerddispatch.com/stories/092704/opi_0927040014.shtml.

Vizenor, Gerald. 1999. *Manifest Manners: Narratives of Postindian Survivance.* Lincoln: University of Nebraska Press.

1. RHETORICAL SOVEREIGNTY

2. HISTORICAL + CONTEMPORARY COLONIZATION

3. RELATIONSHIPS

4. NEW TECHNOLOGY

SURVIVANCE, SOVEREIGNTY, AND STORY

Introduction

CAREFUL WITH THE STORIES WE TELL
Naming Survivance, Sovereignty, *and* Story

Lisa King, Rose Gubele, and Joyce Rain Anderson

> *So you have to be careful with the stories you tell. And you have to watch out for the stories that you are told. But if I ever get to Pluto, that's how I would like to begin. With a story. Maybe I'd tell the inhabitants of Pluto one of the stories I know. Maybe they'd tell me one of theirs. It wouldn't matter who went first. But which story? That's the real question. Personally, I'd want to hear a creation story, a story that recounts how the world was formed, how things came to be, for contained within creation stories are relationships that help to define the nature of the universe and how cultures understand the world in which they exist.*
>
> —*Thomas King,* The Truth about Stories

STORIES ABOUT BEGINNINGS

In *The Truth about Stories: A Native Narrative,* Cherokee author Thomas King presents the reader with a framework for stories that both affirms indigenous storytelling traditions—past and present—and undermines the larger cultural narratives that get told about indigenous peoples. Past a feel-good cheering for storytelling in the once-upon-a-time sense that dismisses stories as the place for children, King is arguing something much bigger: the stories we tell about ourselves and about our world frame our perceptions, our relationships, our actions, and our ethics. They change our reality. The stories we tell each other tell us who we are, locate us in time and space and history and land, and suggest who gets to speak and how.

WHO GETS TO SPEAK

One might therefore say stories are highly rhetorical. One might also say indigenous epistemologies, framed thusly, are also therefore powerfully rhetorical, drawing on persuasive and reality-shifting language practices as old as time immemorial and just as applicable now as they have ever been. They might even help suggest a way out of the colonial

DOI: 10.7330/9780874219968.c000

stories that have blocked vision for so long, privileging some rhetorical storytelling traditions and silencing others.

Such a call for challenging the colonial stories that framed the discipline of rhetoric and composition are not new, and the last twenty years have seen rhetoric and composition scholars such as Victor Villanueva, Keith Gilyard, Jacqueline Jones Royster and Jean C. Williams, Catherine Prendergast, Gwendolyn Pough, Scott Richard Lyons, Malea Powell, and others call for a rethinking of the discipline that challenges the Greco-Roman tradition in rhetorical analysis and composition teaching as the primary or only appropriate framework. It is past time, as Villanueva (1999, 659) has argued, to "break precedent" with the stories that silence so many of our scholars and our students. A growing awareness of the exclusion of American Indian[1] voices has led to an increasing classroom focus on American Indian rhetorics and literature, and although this trend is notable, some of the potential for progress is thwarted by the unintentional perpetuation of stereotypes and appropriation of American Indian cultures. Complicating this process is the discipline's tendency to prioritize so-called objective approaches to knowledge and Euro-American narratives of rhetorical practice, a tendency that discourages the inclusion of American Indian voices or misrepresents them. As a result, even the best intentions can result in damaging consequences for American Indians (Lyons 2000, 458–62; Powell 2002, 397–98).

We therefore echo and reinforce the call for critical evaluation of where we are as scholars and teachers in rhetoric and composition and the call for alliance among communities to work through the complexities of what breaking precedent with the master story would entail, particularly with American Indian and indigenous rhetorics. If we are to reset the terms of the story of our discipline, how shall we do that? What new terms and practices and stories can we draw from to better inform our scholarship and our teaching practices? How do we use our stories and the stories of our students—and *story* here reaches to the very foundations of how we frame our knowledge—to teach communication? Persuasion? Alliance building? Rhetoric? Writing?

LOCATING PEDAGOGICAL STORIES, THEORY, AND PRACTICE

This collection is an endeavor to provide some answers to these questions as they have developed out of the American Indian Caucus (AIC) at the Conference on College Composition and Communication (CCCC), especially with the development of the AIC teaching workshop series of the past seven years. It is not meant as a final answer to how pedagogical practice should be changed, but it is an ongoing endeavor to explore and present the work of indigenous teacher-scholars and allies as an alternative frame for how we might go about our classroom practice.

The exigence for the collection came out of this continued need for discussion concerning indigenous rhetorics in the classroom as the caucus has become a steady presence at CCCC. The American Indian Caucus, founded in 1997 by Malea Powell and Scott Lyons as the Caucus for American Indian Scholars and Scholarship, was intended to be a space for Native scholars and non-Native allies to meet and create a community within the larger CCCC framework (Elder, Hidalgo, and Pinkert 2011). As the caucus has grown and maintained its presence under the joint leadership of Powell, Resa Crane Bizzaro, and Joyce Rain Anderson, it has also been seeking ways to broaden the conversation about indigenous rhetorics and writing outside caucus conversation, especially as interest has grown among allies who wished to support indigenously oriented scholarship and pedagogies but were not sure how. In what ways could pedagogical and scholarly work be shared? What other venues could be tapped or created to support the conversations?

With this exigence in mind, members of the caucus proposed the first teaching workshop, "Survivance, Sovereignty, and Story: Teaching American Indian Rhetorical Texts," for the 2008 CCCC, which brought caucus members forward to present critical sources, pedagogical practices, teaching demonstrations, sample units and assignments, and other materials on indigenous rhetorics and writing. The result was a small but effective workshop that has steadily increased its following at subsequent CCCC gatherings, and caucus members provided six additional workshops between 2009 and 2015.

This collection, then, is a moment to collect ourselves and the stories we have been telling, stories that have begun to reshape the discipline of rhetoric and writing and its pedagogical practices, and find ways to set new precedent. The essays in this collection are a result of the work of the past workshops and in reality are the work of the caucus since its founding. The collection makes available the sources, critical theorizing, and pedagogical practices caucus members have presented in past workshops and includes extended and updated examinations of praxis and discussion of American Indian rhetorics in the rhetoric and writing classroom. More specifically, the overall goals of the collection are (1) to develop a deeper understanding of the role of American Indian rhetorics in writing classrooms, (2) to situate the workshop within current literature, understandings, and practices of teaching American Indian rhetorics, and (3) to provide teachers with models they may adapt for their own classroom use.

[handwritten margin notes: "AMERICAN INDIAN CAUCUS"; "WORKSHOP → GREW TO PEDAGOGY"]

While there are already-existing texts on how to teach American Indian and indigenous literatures, none have yet considered how to teach American Indian rhetorics. It is relatively easy now for teachers to find resources on how to teach well-known, individual indigenous authors such as N. Scott Momaday, Louise Erdrich, or Sherman Alexie, or even less widely known but important indigenous writers. The Modern Language Association publishes resources on several indigenous writers (all three of the above, to begin with), and the National Council for the Teaching of English also has support resources for teaching literature.[2] Furthermore, the Association for the Study of American Indian Literatures as well as its journal, *SAIL*, supports a much broader range of pedagogical and analytical discussion on indigenous writers and literary production.

As just noted above, however, American Indian *rhetorics* and their potential impact on the rhetoric/writing classroom are not subjects that have received much extended discussion or exploration. To be sure, Ernest Stromberg's 2006 edited essay collection, *American Indian Rhetorics of Survivance: Word Medicine, Word Magic*, began drawing attention to historical and contemporary analyses of American Indian writers/speakers/rhetors, and Baca and Villanueva's 2010 edited collection *Rhetorics of the Americas: 3114 BCE to 2012 CE* presents essays that explore the array of rhetorical traditions of the indigenous Americas precontact and their historical and contemporary manifestations. In addition, scholars such as Scott Richard Lyons, Malea Powell, Joyce Rain Anderson, Resa Crane Bizzaro, Angela Haas, Qwo-Li Driskill, Rose Gubele, and Lisa King have published work in the last twelve years that has begun building a body of work elaborating on and extending the discussion of American Indian rhetorics and pedagogies, frequently citing Lyons's (2000) germinal essay "Rhetorical Sovereignty: What Do American Indians Want from Writing" and building on his concept of indigenous "rhetorical sovereignty." This collection therefore represents the accumulation of pedagogical theorizing and curriculum development that has developed alongside and in tandem with this scholarly work, from many of the same scholars named above and specifically through the CCCC American Indian Caucus workshops and their presenters.

CAREFUL WITH THE STORIES WE TELL: NAMING *SURVIVANCE, SOVEREIGNTY,* AND *STORY*

As noted in the epigraph, "Contained within creation stories are relationships that help to define the nature of the universe and how cultures understand the world in which they exist" (King 2005, 10). The very terms in which a story is told shape the story, shape the epistemologies of the world glimpsed there, and draw a listener/reader's understanding in particular directions. Call it Kenneth Burke's "terministic screens," or Chaïm Perelman's "presence," or Lyons's (2000, 452) observation that "he who sets the terms, sets the limits," but the terms we use here are significant and have been adopted with purpose. The study of American Indian texts (alphabetic, visual, digital, performative, oral, and material) requires an understanding of the importance of sovereignty to American Indian nations as well as the diversity of cultures and subject positions that exist under the umbrella term *American Indian.* Most importantly, the introduction of American Indian texts requires cross-cultural understanding. Knowing that power of naming the originating terms as a way to set the framework, in the following we offer a discussion of the terms that first shaped the original AIC teaching workshop in 2008 and how we understand them to connect to rhetoric, composition, and pedagogical practice.

Survivance, Rhetoric, and Pedagogy

I. (SURVIVANCE
SURVIVE
GENOCIDE
+
RESISTANCE
TO ASSIMILATION

Coined by Gerald Vizenor as a key term in describing his vision of Indigenous nations, *survivance* is survival and resistance together: surviving the documented, centuries-long genocide of American Indian peoples and resisting still the narratives and policies that seek to marginalize and—yes, still now—assimilate indigenous peoples. As he puts it, "Survivance is an active sense of presence, the continuance of native stories, not a mere reaction, or survivable name. Native survivance stories are renunciations of dominance, tragedy, and victimry (Vizenor 1999, vii). Survivance is resisting those marginalizing, colonial narratives and policies so indigenous knowledge and lifeways may come into the present with new life and new commitment to that survival.

In terms of indigenous rhetorics, *survivance* can mean many things. It can refer to the survival and perpetuation of indigenous communities' own rhetorical practices, it can refer to indigenous individuals' and communities' usage of Euro-American rhetorical practices, and it can refer to all the variations and nuances in between. It has to do with the spoken word, the written text, material rhetorics, and contemporary technology. It is the recognition of how, when, and why indigenous peoples communicate, persuade, and make knowledge both historically and now.

Teaching survivance is therefore an act of recognition: acknowledging the ongoing presence and work of indigenous peoples, particularly the way indigenous communities negotiate language and rhetorical practice in a paracolonial[3] world. For educators and students to fully appreciate—or even to begin appreciating—indigenous rhetorics and what can be learned from them, students must understand American Indian rhetorical practices as survivance.

SOVEREIGNTY

Sovereignty, Rhetoric, and Pedagogy

With the coinage of "rhetorical sovereignty," Scott Richard Lyons (2000) has provided scholars and teachers of American Indian rhetorics with a powerful frame through which to read those rhetorical practices and a challenge to find ways to recognize that sovereignty by incorporating indigenous rhetorics into the classroom. Political sovereignty is, in many respects, what sets indigenous nation-peoples apart from being only another "minority" in the United States or anywhere on their homelands (Grande 2008). Though a layered and sometimes-contested concept given the word's Euro-American roots, *sovereignty* has become a touch-stone for any discussion of indigenous rhetorics because inherent in that discussion will be indigenous rhetors', rhetoricians', communities', and peoples' inherent "right and ability . . . to determine their own communicative needs and desires in this pursuit [of agency, power, and community renewal], to decide for themselves the goals, modes, styles, and languages of public discourse" (Lyons 2000, 449–50). It points to indigenous always-existing rights to exercise speaking, to refuse to be silenced. And it continues to point to the exigencies of oppression, unequal power, injustice, and land rights that prompt the need for indigenous peoples to speak, again and again, locally, globally, and even in our classrooms.

As a result, invoking indigenous sovereignty as part of a pedagogical framework calls attention to the fact that American Indian peoples are nations and have recognized rights. Labeling indigenous rhetorics as simply the study of another minority community within the United States commits the error of erasing those nations and those rights; recognizing indigenous sovereignty as part of rhetorical practice recognizes both an American Indian nation's rights as a nation and the nation's and its rhetors' rhetorical choices as part of that frame, and lays the groundwork for appropriate, respectful, and historically accurate discussion of American Indian texts.

STORY

Story, Rhetoric, and Pedagogy

Though the Euro-American canonization of texts has historically drawn a sharp line between "literature" and all other writing, that designation

does not necessarily exist in indigenous rhetorics: all literature, all theorizing, all writing are part of the stories, or as Thomas King suggests
above, the connected narrative that tells us who we are in relationship
to one another. Within this framework, it should be only natural that
indigenous voices are heard, especially as they have not been recognized or listened to before. Furthermore, as Craig Womack asserts,
indigenous voices should not be thought of as an addition to the canon
but rather as the foundational voices, the foundational stories on and
of these lands (Womack 1999).

Story and rhetoric, then, go hand in hand. Indigenous stories (theorizing, speaking, writing, making) are the rhetorical turns that reorient
the framework that so long has pointed back toward the Greco-Roman
tradition, even as Euro-American epistemologies have received and
given that tradition new birth. Indigenous rhetorics are the memories,
the memoria, so to speak, of this land, its original logos and the means
through which relationships among all communities on this land can be
restored. Recognizing and engaging indigenous rhetorics is in part how
we begin to reason together. One place this work starts is in our classrooms: by recognizing story as a meaningful, theory-full practice, we can
responsibly engage indigenous rhetorical practices as we find them, not
only as the genres Euro-American education might validate.

Together, *survivance, sovereignty,* and *story* create a frame, or perhaps
more properly a web of associations and meaning making that guides
pedagogical practice. We hope this collection therefore serves to continue the discussion of pedagogical practice, decolonization, and the
place of indigenous rhetorics in the classroom—thus serving as our own
contribution to indigenous survivance, sovereignty, and story, even as we
continue to build relationships within the wider community of instructors and students.

AMERICAN INDIAN RHETORICS: ALPHABETIC, VISUAL, DIGITAL, PERFORMATIVE, ORAL, AND MATERIAL

In sum, this collection of essays is meant as a starting place to talk about
the teaching of indigenous rhetorics, especially in classrooms where the
instructors and students are non-Native. It comes out of a community
effort and alliances among Native and non-Native scholar-allies at the
CCCC American Indian Caucus and an understood need to assist interested instructors in their efforts to do this kind of teaching. Covering
a range of topics, including sovereignty, decolonial practices, community building, local knowledge, and specific examples of working with

indigenous texts, the essays theorize pedagogical practice and help frame both the why-teach and the how-to-teach of indigenous rhetorics as part of a rhetoric and/or writing classroom. The essays range in topic from teaching rhetorical sovereignty, indigenous languages, indigenous rhetorical practices, history, music, and land to collective rhetorical practices, American Indian digital rhetorics, code-switching, and challenging the literary/rhetorical canon. While any one essay can stand alone as a discussion, the overlaps, reiterations, and elaborations on these concepts and themes also serve to form a conceptual web that builds through these essays' relationship with each other. As Leslie Marmon Silko observes of Pueblo storytelling and spiders' webs, there are "many little threads radiating from the center, crisscrossing one another. As with the web, the structure emerges as it is made, and you must simply listen and trust . . . that meaning will be made" (Silko 1997, 48–49). So it is here: the center comes from survivance, sovereignty, and story, and the following chapters build the web of related concepts.

As a beginning point, chapter 1, "Sovereignty, Rhetorical Sovereignty, and Representation: Keywords for Teaching Indigenous Texts," endeavors to work through the significance of the term *sovereignty* with respect to indigenous nations and communities. While the well-intentioned instructor might include an indigenous text for the sake of multicultural inclusion, Lisa King argues that if the instructor does not know the key concepts—especially sovereignty—that shape indigenous discourses, these concepts will likely be misrepresented. By providing a brief history of the term *sovereignty* to illustrate its resonance in Indian country as well as link it to historical representations and misrepresentations of American Indians, this essay offers a framework to better equip instructors to work through the rhetorical exigencies and ramifications of a given indigenous text. As a result, the pedagogical strategies for teaching the recognition of sovereignty, adapted to a particular institutional context, assist teachers in helping their students make connections among the representations of indigenous peoples students may have already seen, why those representations are significant as texts, and how those representations may be addressed and reflected in indigenous texts.

But decolonizing classroom practice and the study of rhetorics does not end with the recognition of sovereignty. In chapter 2, "Socioacupuncture Pedagogy: Troubling Containment and Erasure of Indigeneity in the Composition Classroom," Sundy Watanabe draws particular attention to teaching in a first-year composition classroom and in doing so focuses on a pedagogy of socioacupuncture to address the problems inherent in a tradition of composition that privileges only the Euro-Western vantage point. Instead of fixing indigenous peoples in the past as static entities, as traditional pedagogies often do, Watanabe argues that a socioacupuncture method of pedagogy allows instructors and students to trouble institutionally sanctioned boundaries and power structures, upending traditional conceptions of containment and erasure in at least one local academic community they study. The chapter defines and explains socioacupuncture, provides interpretation based on specific examples from field research, and then utilizes the concept to explore the degree to which instructor and students as a scholarly community are able to produce texts that conform to academic conventions while incorporating a sense of indigenous voice and community.

Chapter 3, "Decolonial Skillshares: Indigenous Rhetorics as Radical Practice," extends both the critique of academic institutions and "texts" and proposes further ideas for how indigenous rhetorics can be taught in order to reshape classrooms and pedagogical practice. Here, Qwo-Li Driskill asserts that the colonization of classrooms continues through an exclusive focus on the Greco-Roman tradition; the counter to colonial practices then becomes the recentering of the classroom on indigenous rhetorics. In Driskill's classroom, students do not learn only about indigenous rhetorics—students also begin learning the rhetorics themselves through linguistic, embodied, and material practices. Drawing on the idea of the skillshare from hir experiences with activism in trans and two-spirit movements and within indigenous craft circles and language groups, Driskill uses the idea of decolonial skillshares as a guiding pedagogy in the classroom to counter the destruction of indigenous cultural memory, to transform cultural memories for both indigenous and non-indigenous people, and to create spaces for Native people to learn and teach embodied rhetorical practices as a tactic of decolonization.

Continuing the theorizing of indigenous rhetorics and pedagogy in the first-year classroom, Gabriela Raquel Ríos observes in chapter 4, "Performing Nahua Rhetorics for Civic Engagement," that writing and rhetoric pedagogies traditionally understand the written text as the central framework for civic or public rhetorical practice when that may not necessarily be the case. Using her work with the Nahuatl difrasismo *in ixtli in yollotl* to enact a rhetorical framework for inquiry in a first-year writing course designed in conjunction with the Ford Foundation's Difficult Dialogues Initiative, Ríos articulates how *in ixtli in yollotl* combines the act of acquiring knowledge with what it means to be human—learning about the world and Nature around us as a necessary means for becoming fully human and understanding ourselves as relatives who are in turn related to the cosmos that surrounds us. From her research and pedagogical experience, Ríos demonstrates how helping students incorporate *in ixtli in yollotl* into their rhetorical repertoire both challenges students to understand civic participation as human responsibility and provides a land-based framework for inquiry beyond Aristotelian logic or social constructivism.

Chapter 5, "Un-learning the 'Pictures in Our Heads': Teaching the *Cherokee Phoenix*, Boudinot, and Cherokee History," provides a different turn in analyzing indigenous texts with its emphasis on history and primary texts, and here Rose Gubele examines the use of primary print texts from indigenous authors. By taking these kinds of texts as her primary focus, Gubele illustrates a method to bring written indigenous histories forward as legitimate histories as well as to explore the continued formation of written indigenous rhetorics as they changed and developed through contact with European-American forms of literacy. This chapter provides a case study in nineteenth-century Cherokee written rhetorics from the Cherokee and English-language newspaper, the *Cherokee Phoenix*, and in doing so Gubele uses materials that touch on some of the most difficult and pivotal times in Cherokee history—the encroachment of the United States and state governments onto Cherokee land, ending ultimately in Cherokee removal—in order to assist students in reexamining history and rhetoric from a written Cherokee perspective.

Kimberli Lee provides another angle for pedagogical practice and student participation in revisiting her work with contemporary indigenous musicians in the classroom.[4] While noting that the musicological and anthropological work done on traditional or ceremonial songs and chants is important work, in chapter 6, "Heartspeak from the Spirit: Songs of John Trudell, Keith Secola, and Robbie Robertson," Lee argues for the value of using contemporary indigenous artists' music as exemplars of rhetorical practice. Citing the wide thematic range of contemporary indigenous music, including resistance to oppression, cultural continuance, and indigenous historical viewpoints, Lee illustrates how text and music interact in rhetorically powerful ways for both Native and non-Native students and prompt discussion concerning the rhetorics of music and how music can function as a language unto itself. Thus, contemporary indigenous musicians draw on multiple rhetorical practices in the production of their music, making the study of that music an opportunity to learn about both the music of living indigenous artists and communities and music as indigenous rhetorical practice.

Indigenous rhetorical practices do not belong only in undergraduate education, however, and chapter 7, "Making Native Space for Graduate Students: A Story of Collective Indigenous Rhetorical Practice," theorizes how indigenous pedagogies and the practice of indigenous rhetorics can inform work at the graduate level. Malea Powell and Andrea Riley Mukavetz present their experience of collaboratively teaching a graduate seminar, American Indian Rhetorics, focusing especially on the stories of their collective struggles in accumulating an indigenous rhetorical practice that lives in balance with the demands of the academy. This is, they argue, the space from which their theorizing arises—the intersection of their experiences as both teachers and learners in the shared space of the course. The result is a course outline that is more suggestive than comprehensive and that follows the advice of Lisa Brooks to map Native space over/into/around/under academic and other dominant spaces. Together, Powell and Riley Mukavetz weave stories about indigenous rhetorical practices and theoretical/methodological frames from specific indigenous locations into both their own practices as scholars and teachers within the academy and within the various exigencies of their own lives.

Joyce Rain Anderson reinforces this connection to Native space and indigenous knowledge tied to land in her affirmation of bringing local Native knowledge into the classroom as a means to reconnect students with the land they walk on, to break the primacy of colonial stories, and to reassert the living presence and knowledges of local Native communities. Using her own classroom and university as a case study of creating a "common pot" that sustains all communities and knowledges, in chapter 8, "Remapping Colonial Territories: Bringing Local Native Knowledge into the Classroom," Anderson demonstrates the pedagogical importance and vitality of foregrounding indigenous ways of knowing that connect and educate the mind, heart, body, and spirit in how she links local indigenous material practices and rhetorics. As examples, Anderson highlights a Three Sisters Garden; a visiting Wampanoag artist who teaches quilling; student activities that include making corn-husk dolls, beading, and pottery; and the how-to of building indigenously based campus-wide initiatives. In this way, Anderson argues that working with local, land-based indigenous knowledges in the classroom contributes to a deeper student understanding of material and rhetorical relationships to land and to Native communities.

Focusing on rhetorical practices of survivance in language and literature, chapter 9, "Rhetorical Sovereignty in Written Poetry: Survivance through Code-Switching and Translation in Laura Tohe's *Tséyi'/Deep in the Rock: Reflections on Canyon de Chelly*," makes the case that by studying how American Indians use written language—particularly through code-switching and the decision to translate or not translate terms or ideas in their works—students will begin to understand how American Indians articulate intellectual and cultural sovereignty, as well as rhetorics of alliance and survivance, and their significance. Jessica Hoover observes that colonial educational systems have endorsed problematic ways for both non-Indians and American Indians to engage with literatures and rhetorics authored by, for, and about American Indians. Thus, making students privy to texts that display said rhetorical moves is imperative because many students do not understand, or even acknowledge, that American Indians struggle for sovereignty. By using Diné writer Laura Tohe's *Tséyi'/Deep in the Rock: Reflections on Canyon de Chelly* as an example, Hoover encourages students to discuss the importance of language, the reasons for how/why shifting languages is critical, and how different American Indian nations may use language in various ways to affirm their cultural and intellectual sovereignty.

Chapter 10, "Toward a Decolonial Digital and Visual American Indian Rhetorics Pedagogy," brings the collection full circle as Angela Haas makes the case for employing a decolonial pedagogy specifically aimed at digital and visual rhetorics in the teaching of American Indian literatures. Providing an array of examples for teaching at the undergraduate and graduate levels, Haas works simultaneously to demonstrate the "perpetuation of a colonial rhetorical assemblage" that places American Indian peoples' intellectual traditions outside the accepted narrative of (post)modern society and to affirm American Indian peoples' always-ongoing relationship with technology. In doing so, she demonstrates that this pedagogy interrogates the "rhetorical velocity" (Ridolfo and DeVoss 2009) of colonial rhetorical tropes that shape digital and visual representations of Indian-ness, privileges evidence of indigenous digital and visual survivance, supports a digital and visual rhetorical sovereignty, and holds non-Native students accountable as allies to American Indians. Such a pedagogy functions to decolonize habits of mind and practice that have historically shaped how we understand American Indians and indigenous rhetorical and technological traditions.

Together, these essays of survivance, sovereignty, and story in the rhetoric and writing classroom and their accompanying sample materials (http://www.survivancesovereigntystory.org) provide a decolonized vision of what teaching rhetoric and writing can be, and they give us a foundation to talk about what rhetoric and pedagogical practice can mean when examined through American Indian and indigenous epistemologies and contemporary rhetorics. They recognize and honor the intellectual work of indigenous thinkers and rhetoricians who have carried this knowledge into the present. They bring the discussion of breaking precedent in the discipline forward to show how the balance that never was there might be established and how decolonizing the ways we think about rhetoric and writing might proceed. Ultimately, this work continues the call for alliance among Native and non-Native scholars, teachers, and students to transform the discipline for the benefit of all.

Notes

1. We have chosen to discuss the work here in terms of *American Indian* rhetorics; while *Native American* as a term has recently been privileged in indigenous studies, because the following work comes out of the American Indian Caucus at CCCC, we have retained *American Indian* as the broad descriptor.

2. One example is Dorthea M. Susag's (1998) *Roots and Branches: A Resource of Native American Literature*, for use at the middle-school and high-school level. Also available are individual lesson plans such as Read-Write-Think: Native Americans Today for grade-school levels at http://rwtverio.ncte.org/lessons/lesson_view3221.html?id=63. Additionally, some author-specific materials have been published, such as the pedagogical essay collection on Sherman Alexie: *Sherman Alexie in the Classroom: "This is not a silent movie. Our voices will save our lives"* by Heather E. Bruce, Anna E. Baldwin, and Christabel Umphrey (Bruce, Baldwin, and Umphrey 2008). At the same time, there is no comprehensive discussion of American Indian rhetorics and little published on their pedagogical use or ramifications.

3. For more on *paracolonial*, see Gerald Vizenor (1999 77); within rhetoric and composition studies, see Malea Powell (2002).

4. Reprinted from *Studies in American Indian Literatures* 19.3, published in fall 2007.

References

Baca, Damián, and Victor Villanueva, eds. 2010. *Rhetorics of the Americas: 3114 BCE to 2012 College English*. New York: Palgrave MacMillan.

Bruce, Heather E., Anna E. Baldwin, and Christabel Umphrey. 2008. *Sherman Alexie in the Classroom: "This is not a silent movie. Our voices will save our lives."* NCTE High School Literature Series. Urbana, IL: NCTE.

Elder, Cristyn L., Alexandra Hidalgo, and Laurie A. Pinkert. 2011. "American Indian Caucus: 'We wanted to have an open and welcoming space': An Interview with Malea Powell." In *Listening to Our Elders: Working and Writing for Change*, edited by Samantha Blackmon, Cristina Kirklighter, and Steve Parks, 6–27. Logan: Utah State University of Press.

Grande, Sandy Marie Anglás. 2008. "American Indian Geographies of Identity and Power: At the Crossroads of Indígena and Mestizaje." In *The Critical Pedagogy Reader*, edited by Antonia Darder, Marta P. Baltodano, and Rodolfo D. Torres, 183–208. New York: Routledge.

King, Thomas. (2003) 2005. *The Truth about Stories*. Minneapolis: University of Minnesota Press.

Lyons, Scott Richard. 2000. "Rhetorical Sovereignty: What Do American Indians Want From Writing?" *College Composition and Communication* 51 (3): 447–68. http://dx.doi.org/10.2307/358744.

Powell, Malea. 2002. "Rhetorics of Survivance: How American Indians Use Writing." *College Composition and Communication* 53 (3): 396–434. http://dx.doi.org/10.2307/1512132.

Ridolfo, Jim, and Dànielle Nicole DeVoss. 2009. "Composing for Recomposition: Rhetorical Velocity and Delivery." *Kairos: A Journal of Rhetoric, Technology, and Pedagogy* 13 (2). http://www.technorhetoric.net/13.2/topoi/ridolfo_devoss/index.html.

Silko, Leslie Marmon. 1997. "Language and Literature from a Pueblo Indian Perspective." In *Yellow Woman and a Beauty of the Spirit: Essays on Native American Life Today*, 48–59. New York: Simon & Schuster.

Stromberg, Ernest, ed. 2006. *American Indian Rhetorics of Survivance: Word Medicine, Word Magic*. Pittsburgh, PA: University of Pittsburgh Press.

Susag, Dorthea M. 1998. *Roots and Branches: A Resource of Native American Literature*. Urbana, IL: NCTE.

Villanueva, Victor. 1999. "On the Rhetoric and Precedents of Racism." *College Composition and Communication* 50 (4): 645–61. http://dx.doi.org/10.2307/358485.

Vizenor, Gerald. 1999. *Manifest Manners: Narratives of Postindian Survivance*. Lincoln: University of Nebraska Press.

Womack, Craig. 1999. *Red on Red: Native American Literary Separatism*. Minneapolis: University of Minnesota Press.

1

SOVEREIGNTY, RHETORICAL SOVEREIGNTY, AND REPRESENTATION
Keywords for Teaching Indigenous Texts

Lisa King

Representations of "Indians" are ubiquitous; imagine all the images of "Indians" you've seen in your lifetime. They adorn romance novels and butter brands, carpet trucks and cigarette cartons; their names are brands of clothing, models and makes of cars, and also cities, rivers, and landmarks; they are Halloween costumes and Thanksgiving decorations. They are John Wayne's antithesis, the Lone Ranger's sidekick (or a museum piece, in the case of Johnny Depp), and the subject of many an artist's rendering now found on greeting cards, in popular clothing chains, or hanging in museums. But where do these images and concepts come from? Though many seem a regular part of everyday discourse, the fact of the matter is that the images and ideas depicting what is "Indian"—like other images and ideas—are constructions deeply embedded in our everyday world. However, the very fact that they are constructions does not often make it into discussion, and the historically unbalanced power relationships surrounding the history of these constructions is also not often acknowledged. The question of American Indian sovereignty, then, and its implications in rhetorical constructions, receive even less attention in mainstream discussion.

Within this context of ever-present but rarely examined representations of American Indians and indigenous peoples, in order to understand how indigenous rhetorics function in relationship to these representations and their consequences, students frequently need a grounding in the key ideas that ground indigenous rhetorics. Furthermore, though many well-meaning instructors are interested in teaching American Indian or indigenous texts as part of their rhetoric and composition classes, without knowing some of the key concepts that shape indigenous discourses, these instructors' efforts run the risk of

DOI: 10.7330/9780874219968.c001

misrepresenting indigenous texts or even marking them as simply one more "minority" discourse in a multicultural sampling.

Sovereignty is one of these concepts, without which an understanding of indigenous texts remains incomplete. While it is beyond the scope of this chapter to provide an exhaustive discussion of indigenous sovereignty or representation, for the sake of providing some background, I will sketch a brief history of the concept of sovereignty as it has a history in North America, link it to historical representations of American Indian peoples, and bring the discussion together with Scott Lyons's contemporary formulation of "rhetorical sovereignty" as a foundational pedagogical framework. By understanding what sovereignty means in a (broadly) American Indian context, what representations have been made of American Indians by Euro-American cultures, and Lyons's call to rhetorical sovereignty—"the inherent right of [indigenous] *peoples* to determine their own communicative needs and desires" (Lyons 2000, 449)—instructors and students can be better equipped to work through the rhetorical exigencies and ramifications of a given indigenous text. The rest of the chapter covers some pedagogical strategies for teaching the recognition of sovereignty to assist instructors in helping their students make links between the representations of indigenous peoples students may have already seen, understand why the those representations are significant as texts, and work through how those histories and representations may be addressed in indigenous texts. Specifically, I outline the use of an advertisement-analysis essay that targets representations of indigenous peoples or cultures as a way to think through the implications of sovereignty, representation, and rhetorical sovereignty as they manifest themselves in images made of indigenous peoples and cultures and images made by Native peoples.

SOVEREIGNTY

The histories and definitions of sovereignty are complex, and they cover a wide range of issues; in contemporary indigenous discourses, *sovereignty* has emerged as a term that Joanne Barker observes "[signifies] a multiplicity of legal and social rights to political, economic, and cultural self-determination" (Barker 2005, 1). Laden with connotations from multiple cultures and eras, *sovereignty* has a history that changes its meaning according to who deploys it (see also Sundy Watanabe's chapter in this volume). Vine Deloria Jr. traces the concept of sovereignty back to early Asian and European religious conceptions of the "divine right" of deities that could be passed on to rulers with absolute power (Barker

2005, 2). Within feudal Europe, sovereignty defined an individual ruler as "accountable to no one save himself or God" (Lyons 2000, 450), then as an extension, an "assertion of absolute political authority at home, one that could imply designs on territories abroad" (Fowler and Bunck quoted in Lyons 2000, 450). Sovereignty was also part of how the early Protestant and Catholic churches conceived of themselves and their power, often arguing with monarchs who claimed "divine right" over who had the legitimate right to speak and rule on behalf of God (Barker 2005, 2). Eventually structures of church and kingdom in Europe gave way to structures of nations, whose idea of sovereignty still carried with it the assertion of political authority, but this time based not on divine right but on citizen rights. *Nationhood* is a term with particular implications in the United States; Lyons observes that the young United States, founded as it was on Enlightenment principles of individualism, understood itself as a nation-state made up of individuals that came together to form a public that acted as a whole to run the nation-state insofar as reason dictated and private individual rights and powers were preserved. Also, in periods of colonization, as countries and colonies began to vie with one another for authority, territory, and independence, to be called *sovereign* was to be understood as on par with one's international peers, with and among other sovereigns. This notion of power was translated into legislative and political rights. Sovereignty, therefore, carried and carries Euro-American connotations of power, independence, and—perhaps most crucial—recognition by others as powerful and independent in a nation's exercising of its rights to self-determination.

However, these ideas of nation and sovereignty do not necessarily reflect Native conceptions. Deloria and Lytle argue that the primary term behind sovereignty, *nationhood*, "implies a process of decision making that is free and uninhibited within the community, a community in fact that is almost completely insulated from external factors as it considers its possible options" (Deloria and Lytle 1998, 13–14). For Native nations, this kind of a nation is defined by peoplehood, a concept that has its roots in the preservation and prospering of the community and binds its members together in cultural and often religious terms. Culture and religion are in turn derived by the people from the land they inhabit; thus, the people, the culture, and the land take their meanings from each other. Deloria and Lytle observe, "[It] is important to understand the primacy of land in the Indian psychological makeup, because, as land is alienated, all other forms of social cohesion also begin to erode, land having been the context in which the other forms have been created" (12). Scott Lyons seconds this definition of peoplehood, adding that as nation-peoples, the priority was not primarily private individual rights but the survival and continuity of the community, its culture, and its land. Decisions were made by council, as a group, not by a single individual ruler. The example Lyons cites is the Haudenosaunee, which was and is a united confederation of six different Native nation-peoples (the Mohawk, Onondaga, Oneida, Seneca, Cayuga, and Tuscarora) with the goal of mutual prosperity and peace. Their idea of sovereignty, in Lyons's words, is "the right of a people to exist and enter into agreements with other peoples for the sole purpose of promoting, not suppressing, local cultures and traditions, even while united by a common political project" (Lyons 2000, 456). Sovereignty, characterized this way, is based both on the "power to self-govern and the affirmation of peoplehood" (456).

The term *sovereignty* as it is applied today has an inheritance from European, Euro-American, and Native nations, and the deployment of *sovereignty* currently "mark[s] the complexities of global indigenous efforts to reverse ongoing experiences of colonialism as well as [signifies] local efforts at the reclamation of specific territories, resources, governments, and cultural practices" (Barker 2005, 1). Recent developments in these sovereign struggles that encompass land, culture, and identity include the purchase of sacred land (Pe' Sla) in South Dakota by an alliance of Sioux tribal nations (Schilling 2012; "Tribes Raise $9M to Buy Sacred South Dakota Land" 2012) and the Idle No More movement that brings together the struggle for indigenous and aboriginal sovereign rights and environmental activism and protection in Canada and throughout North America (Idle No More 2012). On a global scale, the United Nations Permanent Forum on Indigenous Issues has formally recognized the rights of indigenous peoples the world over with its 2007 adoption of the "Declaration on the Rights of Indigenous Peoples" (United Nations Permanent Forum on Indigenous Issues 2013), exhorting the world's nations to recognize "the urgent need to respect and promote the inherent rights of indigenous peoples which derive from their political, economic, and social structures and from their cultures, spiritual traditions, histories and philosophies, especially their rights to their lands, territories, and resources" (United Nations Declaration on the Rights of Indigenous Peoples 2008, 2).

However, *sovereignty* is also a term that has been overgeneralized to the point of losing its meaning, and Barker warns that one of the most important things to remember about sovereignty is that its meaning depends upon its context. Rather, sovereignty in all its connotations, denotations, and actual uses "is embedded within the specific social relations in which it is invoked and given meaning. How and when it emerges and functions are determined by the 'located' political agendas and cultural perspectives of those who rearticulate it into public debate or political document to do a specific work of opposition, invitation, or accommodation" (Barker 2005, 21). Every new site, new context, new speaker, and new goal will require a shift in what sovereignty means, remaining rooted in its histories but also looking forward to preserve the integrity of indigenous nations and communities.

REPRESENTATION

Like the concept of sovereignty, the histories of both representations of indigenous peoples by non-Native communities and self-representations by indigenous peoples are overlapping, knotted, and interwoven. The general image problem for Native peoples as described in the introduction is pervasive and has its roots well documented with the first European contact. Roy Harvey Pearce's (1998) foundational study, *Savagism and Civilization*, outlines the Euro-American history of belief in the idea of the "savage" and "savagism," the particular rhetorical constructions that came out of contact with Native peoples and the historical acts that sprang from that belief and those constructions. His tripartite formation of "Idea, Symbol, and Image" traces the conceptualization of the general "savage" to American "Indian" as a formulation that grows out of, first, a need to find a solution to a perceived problem (the "Idea"), second, a need to discover or create a tangible medium to channel or represent the abstraction of the "Idea" (the "Symbol"), and finally, a need to create a more tangible still representation of the "Symbol" (the "Image") (Pearce 1998, xix). Regarding the "savage" and the "Indian," Pearce argues, "The Idea is that which Noah Webster and all those for whom he spoke called the savage and his savagism; the Symbol is the Indian; and the Images are those found in the social, historical, and imaginative writing of the period" (xix).

That definition of savage, as quoted from Noah Webster's *An American Dictionary of the English Language* in 1828, reads as follows: "Savage, n. A human being in his native state of rudeness, one who is untaught, uncivilized, or without cultivation of mind or manners" (Pearce 1998, epigraph). To be a "savage," then, is to live opposed to "civilization," and Pearce argues that the "theme" of savagism is "in effect a counter-theme to a larger one, civilization" (xix). "Indians" simply became the symbol for what civilization stood against, and the images created out of that symbolic Indian "savage" were the visual and rhetorical justification for Euro-American manifest destiny. Or, as Robert F. Berkhofer documents in his work, *The White Man's Indian,* that specifically American version of the savage, the "Indian," confirms that "although the social and cultural attributes of Native Americans influenced the conception of them by Whites, it is ultimately to the history of White values and ideas that we must turn for the basic conceptual categories, classificatory schema, explanatory frameworks, and moral criteria by which past and present Whites perceived, observed, evaluated, and interpreted Native Americans" (Berkhofer 1988, xvii). Therefore, it is possible to trace the shifting image of the Indian as one that reflects the changing history of Euro-American thought and self-image.

While I cannot cover five centuries of this image making in detail, I can highlight several examples students are likely well familiar with: the "Indian," the "savage," the "noble savage," and the "vanishing Indian." The most obvious is the term *Indian* itself: as the story goes, Christopher Columbus mistook the Caribbean island he landed on for India (because according to European geography of the time, anything east of the Indu river was "India") and so named the peoples he found there *Indios* (Berkhofer 1988, 5). The Spanish continued to use that designation for all the peoples of North and South America, and it is from *Indio* that the French receive the term *Indien,* the German, *Indianer,* and the English, *Indian* (Berkhofer 1988, 5). With the help of the printing press and the popularity of travel logs, Europe had soon invented the "Indian," a specifically American variety of "savage."

Berkhofer next demonstrates how the image of the Indian underwent a series of changes dependent on the reigning Euro-American ideological structure of a given time period. He maps out the Euro-American struggle to first classify Native Americans according to Christian cosmogony, the heart of which was to decide if the Indian were human and therefore educable and civilizable. With the Enlightenment, the reliance on biblical accounts decreased and, if the natural world were a system of causes and effects governed by laws a scientist could discover, then the existence and state of Native peoples could be explained by environmental causes (34–44).

Pearce and Berkhofer both observe the mid-nineteenth-century emergence of a history of humankind based on linear progress and evolution, which in turn created the image of the Indian as behind the evolutionary curve and as living artifact. The savage Indians, it was assumed, were throwbacks on an evolutionary scale of progress and civilization, and those who would not accept civilization were doomed. As part of a burgeoning scientific endeavor to study humankind, Berkhofer also shows a rising "scientifically" based racism coming out of the mid-nineteenth century that grounded itself in cranial and spinal studies, which were used to justify the cultural and racial superiority of white Euro-Americans over all others. Then, believing that Native peoples were on the verge of extinction, ethnographers, photographers, and artists rushed to Native communities to document the "vanishing Indian."

Pearce notes that pity often came with this belief—many in Euro-American society voiced it—and yet even that was filtered through a centuries-spanning romantic "primitivism" that begot an image of its own: the "noble savage" Pearce (1998) describes primitivist thought as "the belief that other, simpler societies were somehow happier than one's own," so primitivism became a mode of Euro-American social critique that desired "to recover that portion of the primitive self which civilization had corrupted and, in the process, to lay bare the faults of civilization" (136). Yet though noble savages had some natural virtues, they had no place in the larger American civilization because they were still savages.

By the early twentieth century, cultural anthropology developed as a counter to the tendencies described above, which in turn ushered in the new image of Indianness, the ethnographic "scientific Indian" of the 1950s (Berkhofer 1988, 56–66). Franz Boas and his students—among them Alfred Kroeber and Ruth Underhill—challenged the idea of "culture" as a signifier for "civilized," instead proposing a plural notion of "cultures" that rejected moral judgment on the subjects under study. However, many anthropologists tended to structure their ethnographies as recording cultures under erasure, not change, (therefore promoting a more modern version of the "vanishing Indian") and defined true "Indian" cultures as ahistorical entities that did not acknowledge the Native peoples of the present (64–65). Not until the 1970s, roughly correlating with the Red Power movement, would the image of "erasure" be challenged.[1]

Meanwhile, Euro-American images of Native peoples had become advertising, entertainment, and artwork staples and became entrenched outside of academia in popular culture. Building on Berkhofer's work, S. Elizabeth Bird points out that popular culture in all its manifestations continues to depict indigenous peoples as one-dimensional stereotypes based on the needs of white culture and not actual indigenous peoples, arguing that "to understand current imagery, it is essential to understand the history of its making" (Bird 1996, 7). Philip J. Deloria's (1998) work, *Playing Indian*, traces similar phenomena in the many ways the "Indian" became and remains an identity for the dominant culture. In the case of the United States, white culture puts on the "Indian" and shifts it according to the needs of the time and the white Americans invoking it: the Indian image becomes whatever the wearers in the Boston Tea Party (the original), nineteenth-century secret societies, writers of a uniquely "American" literature, the boy scouts, or New Agers need them to be. The creation of the "Indian" continues, even now.

And so it is that the "Indian" is most often a series of rhetorical constructions that suit the purposes of the people who create them. That is not to say that Native Americans haven't made various efforts to resist and redirect such portrayals—they have, and do—and scholar and writer Gerald Vizenor asserts that power to resist when he rejects the word *Indian,* favoring instead the concept of the "postindian," someone lives through survivance and trickster hermeneutics to win the rhetorical "cultural word wars" of "manifest manners." "Indian," he argues in concert with Pearce and Berkhofer, is a construction, and, more specifically, "the simulation of the *indian* is the absence of real natives—the contrivance of the other . . . *indians* are the actual absence—the simulations of the tragic primitive (Vizenor 1994, vii). The simulation of "*indian*" operates through and is fueled by the ongoing ideological framework he calls "manifest manners," defined as "the course of dominance, the racialist notions and misnomers sustained in archives and lexicons as 'authentic' representations of *indian* cultures. Manifest manners court the destinies of monotheism, cultural determinism, objectivism, and the structural conceits of savagism and civilization" (vii). The "postindian," then, is one who "ousts the inventions with humor, new stories, and the simulations of survivance" (Vizenor 1994, 5). Given there is no absolute, authentic "Indian" to return to, postindians do operate through simulations, but these are "the recreation of the real, not the absence of the real in the simulations of dominance" (5). As Kimberly Blaeser puts it, the key is that these postindian "recreations of the real" must "bear the 'simulations of survivance' to overcome the 'simulations of dominance'" (Blaeser 1996, 57); otherwise, these recreations may also fall into reproducing the *indian* image of manifest manners.

That *survivance,* the hallmark of the postindian, is a term Vizenor coins from *survival* and *resistance.* He defines it as the "active sense of presence, the continuance of native stories, not a mere reaction, or a survivable name. Native survivance stories are renunciations of dominance, tragedy, and victimry. Survivance means the right of succession or reversion of an estate, and in that sense, the estate of native survivancy" (Vizenor 1994, vii). In what he calls the "cultural word wars" of language and rhetoric, Blaeser observes in the connecting line of Vizenor's work that "[the] destiny of the American Indian rests with language. The Indian will survive or will 'vanish' through the merits of language: survive through tribal oral tradition, or be made to vanish through popular, scientific, literary, and political rhetoric" (Blaeser 1996, 39). Or, to put it in terms more familiar to contemporary rhetoricians, if we can establish that these constructions are Burkean terministic screens through which non-Native communities function, then "for many Native rhetoricians, the task [of rhetoric] has been to revise, replace, or tear down these screens" (Stromberg 2006, 5) for the sake of rhetorical and physical survivance.[2]

RHETORICAL SOVEREIGNTY

So it is that language and rhetoric are pivotal in discussions of Native images, and therefore they are pivotal in discussions of sovereignty. In other words, according to its context and the purpose to which it is put, sovereignty is highly rhetorical; as such, "rhetorical sovereignty," in Lyons's formulation, is yet another facet of the process of defining sovereignty, and it is in the realm of language and representation that he brings communicative action and interaction with colonial forces into focus. As an example, he cites the history of US legislative terminology, which reflects a particular image of Native peoples and illustrates the US government's historical exercise of rhetorical power. While initially treaties were made that named Native peoples as sovereign nations to be dealt with as equals, by the 1830s, US policy toward Native nations was altering in its rhetoric: the terminology changed from "nation" to "tribe," from "treaties" to "agreements," and Native peoples were characterized as "wards" instead of "sovereigns" (Lyons 2000, 453). Such nominal changes reflect a kind of "rhetorical imperialism" in the US legislation that worked to erode Native nation-peoples' rights and power in the name of a colonial nation-state. As Lyons observes, "He who sets the terms sets the limits" of discourse and law (452). It is for these reasons, among many, that Native peoples are working to reassert what sovereignty means, in language and representation just as much as legislation—for it is in the forge of language that such legislation is wrought. Lyons asserts, "Sovereignty is the guiding story in our pursuit of self-determination, the general strategy by which we aim to best recover our losses from the ravages of colonization: our lands, our cultures, our self-respect," and therefore, specifically, "*Rhetorical sovereignty* is the inherent right of *peoples* to determine their own communicative needs and desires in this pursuit, to decide for themselves the goals, modes, styles, and languages of public discourse" (Lyons 2000, 449).

In this way, through the language and rhetoric of representation, one can begin to see how language and image drive action and policy, and policy has material consequences for Native nations. Rhetorical sovereignty directly addresses the language, rhetoric, and representations concerning Native peoples and wishes to place more of the control over that language and rhetoric—and therefore control over the representation and the images derived from them, and therefore the policy and action derived from those—in Native nations' hands. To claim rhetorical sovereignty is to claim the right to determine communicative need and the right to participate in the process of public image making and meaning making. Some examples of contemporary rhetorical sovereignty include contemporary scholars and blogs, such as *Native Appropriations* (Keene 2013) and *Beyond Buckskin: About Native American Fashion* (Metcalfe 2013) and social media communities, such as F.A.I.R. Media (For Accurate Indigenous Representation) on Facebook, which address the ways in which indigenous cultures are appropriated for non-Native purposes and provide public Native-based critique of these representations (see also Angela Haas's chapter in this collection for more on the digital indigenous). Indigenous communities and allies continue to mobilize debate over and effect change in Native misrepresentations and appropriations in sports mascots—the highest profile case of late being the Washington Redskins and the January 2014 launch of the "Proud to Be" (National Congress of American Indians 2014) advertisement—and indigenous museums and allies work in places such as the National Museum of the American Indian to build better public representations of indigenous peoples. The claim to rhetorical sovereignty has in many ways been ever present, is strong today, and is growing.

CLASSROOM IMPLICATIONS: SOVEREIGNTY, RHETORICAL SOVEREIGNTY, AND REPRESENTATION

I take some time discussing sovereignty, representation, and rhetorical sovereignty in order to lay the groundwork for good classroom practice; that is, like any other rhetorical practices, without context, indigenous rhetorics cannot be made intelligible to their audiences—especially in a cross-cultural context. The crux for students in the writing classroom is this: for Native students, to understand that writing is an opportunity to explore and assert sovereignty and challenge misrepresentations; for non-Native students, to understand that the discourses surrounding

"Indian" images and rhetorics are not transparent and to begin interrogating how these images came to be. Together, students can learn to recognize rhetorical sovereignty and explore representations of Native nations and cultures—both images and texts *about* Native peoples and images *by* Native peoples—and the impact those representations have in multiple settings. Such an exploration is mutually beneficial in that the rhetorical constructions become recognized for what they are: constructed, not self-evidently truthful but context- and culture-bound, even as the writing students do is contextually and culturally delineated.

What I want to do in the remaining space here is suggest some ways this knowledge of rhetorical constructions of the "Indian" and the concept of rhetorical sovereignty can both fulfill the general goals of a writing/rhetoric course and address cross-cultural (mis)representations specific to American Indian and indigenous peoples. What I offer here are ideas for a revision of the stock advertising-analysis essay and a teaching unit based on a number of the sources above in order to accomplish the following:

1. Help students broadly recognize the situated nature of rhetorical representations and put them into context;

2. Foster critical thinking skills by asking students to build arguments based on links among the histories, contexts, and rhetorics they encounter;

3. Encourage critical inquiry into the potential rhetorical impact of representations, misrepresentations, and cross-cultural communication; and

4. Build an understanding of rhetorical sovereignty within the context of American Indian rhetorics, both broadly and locally.

Knowing that institutional and programmatic context also matters, as an example I will adapt the assignment and lesson plans to fit the University of Tennessee-Knoxville's English 102: Inquiry, Research, and Writing course, the second in the first-year composition sequence, while making further suggestions for how such analysis can also work as a case study in an upper-division civic rhetorics/persuasion course or cultural rhetorics course. Perhaps even more important, such teaching must be grounded in place and in the indigenous histories of that place; for me, though I am Delaware, this means beginning the discussion in terms of East Tennessee as traditional Cherokee homeland, Cherokee history, and local Native communities—in this case, the Eastern Band of Cherokee Indians.

As posted on the companion teaching resources website for this volume, the advertising-inquiry assignment is generally based on the concept of helping students analyze visual and textual rhetorics to understand persuasion as it happens in advertisements or images. This particular version of the assignment takes it one step further, and in keeping with the goals of UTK's English 102 course, requires that students build research skills in history and archives in order to make an argument about how a particular image or advertisement is rhetorically situated in time and place and what its rhetorical significance and effectiveness might be. As the second in the FYC program sequence, the English 102 class seeks to build on English 101 writing skills by working on research, specifically focusing on "strategies for formulating and investigating questions, locating and evaluating information, using varied sources and research methods, developing positions on intercultural and interdisciplinary issues from diverse texts (print, digital, and multimedia), and presenting research using appropriate rhetorical conventions" (University of Tennessee 2013). Furthermore, two of the required assignments—the historical-research assignment and the qualitative-research assignment—are particularly good matches for this kind of inquiry. While the qualitative-research assignment might focus more on contemporary perceptions of images or advertisements (doing observations, interviews, and surveys), due to the strongest affinity for the purposes outlined above, the historical-research assignment will serve as the frame here. The English 102 course may also have a designated thematic component, so a discussion of indigenous rhetorics and representations could fall under a rhetoric-and-culture, pop-culture, or place-based theme. In addition to the required readings on historical and archival research, the course readings for this unit would be based on selections from the bibliographic survey above, relying particularly on Pearce, Berkhofer, Bird, Lyons, Malea Powell (as I'll discuss below), and a selection of contemporary indigenous scholars and activists that feature local representatives as well.

The assignment particulars, as I have formulated them, require the students to find an advertisement, image, or series of advertisements/images that utilizes a particular representation of Native American ideas, individuals, or nations they find interesting or unique in some way. In conjunction with the readings I assign for the unit, students begin thinking through first what is actually present in the advertisement or image, the intended audience, the context, and the intended or hoped-for reaction by the creators, at least as far as the students can discern. Because the historical-research unit is articulated in part as "the study of beliefs and desires, practices and institutions, of human beings" (Benson 2012, 85), this is also part of the frame for helping students grasp what is going on in the advertisement or image and what this might mean in terms of the use of Native representation and rhetorical sovereignty and/or alliance. Students are asked to generate questions and seek answers by researching the product itself as well as the historical context in which it is placed and, as far as they can, the advertising techniques used in the ad. For example, if they are looking at an advertisement for a particular kind of clothing that uses a Native American nation's name, students might ask not only why this brand but also who produces the clothing (Native? Non-Native?), where the clothing is supposed to be worn, who is supposed to wear it, and what wearing this clothing is supposed to do or be with this name or logo. These questions may lead to larger questions concerning societal assumptions about what this image means to the community who produces it; how this image links to other historical ideas or stereotypes about "Indians"; how the use of the image is used to influence expectations for gender roles, or physical appearance, or the kinds of activities a person of a particular group is supposed to participate in; or ultimately what kind of identity someone, according to the advertisement or image, can or should adopt in a particular time and place. As an example, I have often taken my classes to the campus museum—McClung Museum of Natural History and Culture—and asked them to analyze the feature exhibit on local indigenous and Cherokee history, *Archaeology and the Native Peoples of Tennessee*. Who made this space? Who selected these images? How are we supposed to understand them? In what ways do they support or challenge our preconceptions of "Indians"?

For the first of the broad goals articulated above—helping students recognize the situated nature of rhetorical representations and put them into context—the advertising/image assignment prompt and, by default, working with the history of indigenous representation and how it occurs in the present, automatically link with the goals of a historical-research essay. By using Pearce, Berkhofer, and Bird as resources to establish how representations of indigenous peoples have been made by white or non-Native rhetors, students can begin to understand that the images of Indians they see every day can't be taken for granted and do not exist in a vacuum. In concert with the historicizing requirement for the course and assignment, students can begin learning about how rhetorical representations, both broadly and specifically of American Indian and indigenous peoples, are contextually and temporally grounded. For example, if a student wants to work with the November 2012 Victoria's Secret fashion show and model Karlie Kloss's "Indian" costume (see visuals at http://nativeappropriations.com/category/victorias-secret, the

November 9, 2012, entry), then the first thing the student would need to do is think through what the representation of a Plains-style headdress on a non-Native woman, "Navajo"-esque jewelry, and a fringed leopard-print bra and underwear are meant to signify, and for whom, in the context of a 2012 lingerie fashion show.

Connected to the first point, the second goal—fostering critical thinking skills by asking students to build arguments based on links among the histories, contexts, and rhetorics they encounter—the advertising/image assignment provides a forum for students to begin asking questions about the images and representations they encounter regularly. If these are constructions of indigenous peoples that were created for specific reasons in a certain time and place, how do the representations students have encountered resonate? If they are images by Native peoples, what does that mean? What are the representations' connection to these rhetorical histories? The advertising assignment thus provides a doorway into a discussion about a particular image or representation and a research agenda for the project: Where did the image come from? Has the brand or company always used it? What is the image's history? How does the company or brand justify it? How does the image link with the histories of rhetorical representation students have read? Who is (implicitly or explicitly) supposed to use the product? How does the viewer know? In the case of the Victoria's Secret costume, does the brand have a history of such representations? What was the context within this fashion show? How did the company and/or model justify the costume's use? And how does this particular representation or combination link historically with Euro-American perceptions of "Indians" and Native women?

Critical inquiry into the rhetorical impact of these images plays out of the second step into the third in a related series of questions: What is the intended rhetorical effect of the image? What are potential unintended effects, especially for the people depicted in the image? For whom do these effects matter the most? The least? Why does that matter? And why might these effects matter on this campus, on this land, in this place? This point in the assignment poses a particular challenge for many students who have not critically examined the images they take for granted, and perhaps even purchase, like, or identify with (especially in the case of sports mascots). As I have argued elsewhere specifically regarding Native-authored texts, the difficulty for the instructor and students together is to recognize rhetorical sovereignty and indigenous peoples' rights to rhetorical sovereignty—and that includes publicly critiquing representations and even requesting their removal—while at the same time understanding the need for rhetorical alliance (King 2012). Malea Powell's work on rhetorical alliance helps reinforce the understanding that the current moment is a physical and rhetorical inheritance we all share, and the question is not about who to blame but about how we reset the frameworks for discourse to understand what has been done and how we may change the shape of the future for our mutual survival, all communities together (Powell 2004). This, too, would be part of the background reading for the assignment to better facilitate discussion and analysis. In the case of the Victoria's Secret costume, the student would have to think through what the intended audiences and rhetorical goals for those audiences might have been and then also acknowledge the unintended consequences, ethical implications, and critical reactions from many indigenous viewers—especially given the level of sexual violence perpetrated against Native women at rates above all others. How does this construction of "Indian" find itself disconnected from indigenous realities, and what are the rhetorical consequences?

Finally, the ultimate goal of the advertising/image assignment, in many ways, is teaching not only historical analysis but also the recognition of rhetorical sovereignty. Based on Lyons's article, the final step in the assignment is to address the ways indigenous communities have weighed in, critiqued, altered, or reconfigured images and stereotypes. In what ways is the image the student has chosen related to the questions of rhetorical sovereignty, of indigenous communities' inherent rights to self-represent, to respond to cultural appropriation or misrepresentation? How might this image be a problem for indigenous communities? Can cross-cultural alliances be built with the image existing in use as it is? In terms of research, this is also a pertinent point at which students will need to work through conflict in their research in the sense that they must process multiple points of view on the subject and formulate their own syntheses. For the Victoria's Secret costume, the assignment's examination of rhetorical sovereignty is a way for students to process the importance of Native reactions to the image, not just as an "offended minority" that needs to "get over it" but as legitimate and complicated (and even conflicting) responses to the history of representation and misrepresentation of Native cultures and Native bodies as a form of rhetorical sovereignty. Furthermore, it is an opportunity to think through what positive action might be taken to build better understanding or ethical practices, if and when they are possible.

As a result of both the context of the course (inquiry and research, and specifically historical research) and the topic, students have the opportunity to go beyond potentially superficial analyses of rhetorical artifacts to get to those artifacts' potential significance for multiple audiences as those artifacts have developed in time and space.

As already noted, this assignment can also lend itself to qualitative research in order to help students understand contemporary perceptions of representations of indigenous peoples and what the actual impact of those images might be. Beyond the FYC sequence, this kind of assignment can also be tailored to upper-division courses. Within a civic/public rhetorics course, the discussion could turn to the ways representations of indigenous peoples are debated in the public—again, the persistent mascot debate, especially with high-profile cases such as the Washington Redskins, makes for timely discussion, as could museum representations of indigenous peoples or community issues related to local tribal or indigenous communities. Furthermore, in an upper-division cultural rhetorics class, this type of assignment lends itself well as a case study in how rhetoric is culturally constructed and the cultural impact particular rhetorics or discourses may have on the communities involved, particularly local Native communities.

CONCLUSION

Far from being an exclusive or partisan perspective that has no place in the writing classroom, a discussion of indigenous rhetorics alongside a research project can offer a valuable opportunity for Native and non-Native students to investigate the persistent phenomenon of "Indian" representation. As demonstrated above, such teaching and student work can take place in a variety of settings, from FYC to upper-division coursework, as they are situated in indigenous histories and the place the classroom rests upon. But at the same time, sovereignty and its rhetorical manifestations, in all its broad coverage and local specificity, is one of the key concepts to understanding the dynamics of representations of indigenous peoples, representations by indigenous peoples, and the tensions between them as they emerge in everyday discourse. Addressing sovereignty, rhetorical sovereignty, and representation together provides an essential framework for beginning to understand how those tensions function, and how students, willingly or not, are often a part of them. Without that frame, the conversation on indigenous representations remains one-sided, compromises the depth and ethics of student research, and implicitly denies the acts of survivance Native peoples present and have been presenting all along. Introducing that frame and that conversation into the classroom, however, continues the stories of indigenous survivance and the dialogue between communities in a more productive way.

Notes

1. Also worth noting is a victim myth parallel to the cultural-erasure image, explored by Fergus M. Bordewich in *Killing the White Man's Indian*; playing on Berkhofer's (1988) title, Bordewich uses a journalistic approach to portray Native peoples of the 1990s as they are and how the popular image of Indians-as-victims he observes is mistaken.

2. Scholarship that examines how these understandings of sovereignty, culture, and identity within Native communities are playing out is also important, especially in terms of the dynamics of reclaiming cultural, intellectual, and political sovereignty from colonial ideologies. For some recent work, see Scott Lyons's (2010) *X-Marks: Native Signatures of Assent* (2010) and Joanne Barker's (2011) *Native Acts: Law, Recognition, and Cultural Authenticity*.

References

Barker, Joanne. 2005. "For Whom Sovereignty Matters." In *Sovereignty Matters: Locations of Contestations and Possibility in Indigenous Struggles for Self-Determination*, edited by Joanne Barker, 1–32. Lincoln: University of Nebraska Press.

Barker, Joanne. 2011. *Native Acts: Law, Recognition, and Cultural Authenticity*. Durham, NC: Duke University Press.

Benson, Kirsten, ed. 2012. *Rhetoric of Inquiry*. 3rd ed. New Haven, CT: Bedford/St. Martin.

Berkhofer, Robert F. Jr. (1969) 1988. *The White Man's Indian: Images of the American Indian from Columbus to the Present*. New York: Random House.

Bird, S. Elizabeth. 1996. *Dressing In Feathers: The Construction of the American Indian in American Popular Culture*. Boulder, CO: Westview Press.

Blaeser, Kimberly M. 1996. *Gerald Vizenor: Writing in the Oral Tradition*. Norman: University of Oklahoma Press.

Deloria, Philip J. 1998. *Playing Indian*. New Haven, CT: Yale University Press.

Deloria, Vine Jr., and Clifford M. Lytle. (1984) 1998. *The Nations Within: The Past and Future of American Indian Sovereignty*. Austin: University of Texas Press.

Idle No More. 2012. "Idle No More Home Page." http://idlenomore.ca/.

Keene, Adrienne. (2010) 2013. *Native Appropriations: Examining Representations of Indigenous Peoples*. http://nativeappropriations.com/.

King, Lisa. 2012. "Rhetorical Sovereignty and Rhetorical Alliance in the Writing Classroom: Using American Indian Texts." *Pedagogy* 12 (2): 209–33. http://dx.doi.org/10.1215/15314200-1503568.

Lyons, Scott Richard. 2000. "Rhetorical Sovereignty: What Do American Indians Want From Writing?" *College Composition and Communication* 51 (3): 447–68. http://dx.doi.org/10.2307/358744.

Lyons, Scott Richard. 2010. *X-Marks: Native Signatures of Assent*. Minneapolis: University of Minnesota Press.

Metcalfe, Jessica. (2009) 2013. "Beyond Buckskin: About Native American Fashion." http://beyondbuckskin.blogspot.com/.

National Congress of American Indians. 2014. "Proud to Be," YouTube Video, 2:00, National Congress of American Indians, January 27. https://www.youtube.com/watch?v=mR-tbOxlhvE.

Pearce, Roy Harvey. (1953) 1998. *Savagism and Civilization: A Study of the Indian and the American Mind*. Berkeley: University of California Press.

Powell, Malea. 2004. "Down by the River, or How Susan La Flesche Picotte Can Teach Us about Alliance as a Practice of Survivance." *College English* 67 (1): 38–60. http://dx.doi.org/10.2307/4140724.

Schilling, Vincent. 2012. "Tribes Reach $9 Million Goal and Purchase Sacred Site of Pe' Sla." *Indian Country Today Media Network*. Nov. 30. http://indiancountrytodaymedia necitingtwork.com/article/tribes-reach-9-million-goal-and-purchase-sacred-site-pe-sla-146015.

Stromberg, Ernest. 2006. "Rhetoric and American Indians: An Introduction." In *American Indian Rhetorics of Survivance: Word Medicine, Word Magic*, edited by Ernest Stromberg, 1–12. Pittsburgh: University of Pittsburgh Press.

"Tribes Raise $9M to Buy Sacred South Dakota Land." 2012. *CBS News*. Nov. 30. http://www.cbsnews.com/8301-201_162-57556557/tribes-raise-$9m-to-buy-sacred-south-dakota-land/.

United Nations Declaration on the Rights of Indigenous Peoples. 2008. United Nations. http://www.un.org/esa/socdev/unpfii/documents/DRIPS_en.pdf.

United Nations Permanent Forum on Indigenous Issues. 2013. "Declaration on the Rights of Indigenous Peoples." http://undesadspd.org/IndigenousPeoples/DeclarationontheRightsofIndigenousPeoples.aspx.

University of Tennessee-Knoxville. Department of English. 2013. "FYC Course Descriptions." http://english.utk.edu/course-descriptions-for-first-year-composition/.

Vizenor, Gerald. 1994. *Manifest Manners: Narratives on Postindian Survivance*. Lincoln: University of Nebraska Press.

2

SOCIOACUPUNCTURE PEDAGOGY
Troubling Containment and Erasure in a Multimodal Composition Classroom

Sundy Watanabe

We no longer just write culture. We perform culture.
—Denzin and Lincoln 2011, x

[The story is] yours. Do with it what you will. Cry over it. Get angry.
Forget it. But don't say in the years to come that you would have lived
your life differently if only you had heard this story. You've heard it now.
—King 2003, 119

INTRODUCTION

Widely circulating public discourse that constructs literacy as the ability or inability to read and write makes for a divisive have-or-have-not situation by positing knowers against novices and privileged above marginalized. Literate activity, particularly in the composition classroom, has long relied on Greek rhetorical tradition "to create order, and to govern human action, and make it predictable, repeatable, whether this is internalized as a set of grammatical rules, or externalized as a script, a written procedure, a programme, a syllabus, etc." (Kress and van Leeuwen 2001, 10). Such ordering and governing practice often negatively affects American Indians,[1] and ample and justified concern exists about these divisive approaches to literate activity. As Mary Hermes suggests, the "greatest error in Indian education" (Hermes 2005, 48) has been viewing and practicing literate activity from a solely Euro-Western vantage point. Under this paradigm, lesson plans, subject areas, and course content attempt to act as "containers" (44) to either fix indigenous knowledge and lived experience as static and of the past—thereby erasing them as a contemporary reality—or establish them as stereotypes, as "simulations," to use Anishinabe scholar Gerald Vizenor's (1994) term.

DOI: 10.7330/9780874219968.c002

Most indigenous studies scholars agree that counteracting deficit and defeatist rhetoric involves confronting the "historical imbalances" caused by colonization (Marker 2004, 20), which have at best marginalized indigeneity and at worse erased it from academic contexts altogether. To counter containment, erasure, and simulation, Devon Mihesuah asks American Indians and their allies to more assertively bring Native scholars, theory, and terminology into the classroom, indigenizing the academy in ways powerful position holders might better accommodate (Mihesuah 2006; Mihesuah and Wilson 2004).[2] Similarly, Malea Powell calls for a fresh examination and nuanced interpretation of pedagogical practice, one that utilizes "a new language" and is performed at "intersecting sites of textual production," a pedagogy that allows "respectful and reciprocal relationships" (Powell 2004, 44, 41), but one that also resists an "easy and narrow reliance on . . . European American thinkers" (39–40).

This chapter answers these calls by reintroducing *socioacupuncture*, a term first used by Vizenor, as just such a pedagogy for composition studies (Vizenor and Lee 1999, 82). Metaphorically, the term calls to mind a kind of meta/physical intervention that occurs by pricking or needling the social consciousness. Socioacupuncture, in this vein, directs focus toward those nodes where positive movement is blocked and/or damaged. It works to shift or redirect maladjustments through releasing positive energy toward healing and change. In praxis,[3] socioacupuncture presents an opportunity to indigenize the composition classroom and, by extension, the academy. As pedagogy, it infuses indigenous concepts into curriculum design and delivery. It utilizes multimodal literate production to trouble control often wielded against those who wish to (or do) employ indigenous epistemologies to teach or learn composition. It works from an understanding that the cultural and racialized differences underscoring how and why we teach composition must not be diminished by either colorblind or monomodal approaches. It eschews attempts to subsume or domesticate literate action under conventionalized rubrics or monologic epistemologies, the constraints often used to govern literate activity and further marginalize indigeneity, sorting and shaping the next generation to fit status quo inequalities (see Shor 1997). It posits that pretending cultural and racialized differences do not exist is not helpful. Rather, in using socioacupuncture, a deliberate decision is made to confront and talk about differences directly and often—through visual, oral, gestural, architectural, and spatial modes—until doing so becomes as necessary for our experience "as breathing or eating" (Gonzales-Goenaga 2012).

Socioacupuncture pedagogy engages multiple modes and epistemologies,[4] focusing primarily on indigenous ones that are more concerned with literate activity as a holistic and concretely purposeful community endeavor, a tool of beneficial change (see Lyons 2010). Socioacupuncture pedagogy arises from the work of numerous years wherein I have learned to weave indigenous studies and new literacy studies methodological concepts together in composition, from basic to advanced courses. Of particular importance, given my positionality as a white instructor/researcher ally and given institutional majoritarian demographics where I teach, socioacupuncture initiates and advances what I will hereafter call *the 4Rs of interpersonal and intercultural exchange*: respect, reciprocity, responsibility, and relationship as outlined and explained by Barnhardt and Kawagley (2005) as well as Verna J. Kirkness and Ray Barnhardt (Kirkness and Barnhardt 2001).[5] While it might at times sting or prick the social consciousness—on the part of teachers as much as students—socioacupuncture pedagogy is "less an interrogation and more a meeting together and a labor together" (King 2012, 214).

In the following sections, I sketch out points pertinent to sufficiently understand socioacupuncture pedagogy. I illustrate relevant indigenous concepts of sovereignty, survivance, rhetorical sovereignty, and transmotion by storying them with material from research data. I also describe the connection between these concepts and multimodality as enacted in two composition courses. I take seriously Devon Mihesuah's (2006) admonition that "we only use terms if we know what those terms mean and use them only if we are truly doing that sort of work" (135). The experiences I story, then, arise from two data sets.[6] The first comes from critical, ethnographically oriented research conducted over four years with a group of Native students studying at a large research institution in the western United States. The second comes from an upper-division composition course taught at a land-grant institution where I was teacher of record. In these projects, I worked with both Native and non-Native students to recenter indigenous voices, stances, and commitments while accommodating Euro-Western academic conventions. Through conceptualizing and making connections in this chapter, I hope to convey how one might utilize socioacupuncture as composition pedagogy and in the process encourage others who wish to make similar attempts. This is not to suggest mine are definitive examples. Any experiences gained or lessons learned are humbly offered as a possible way, not *the* way, with gratitude extended to all who have come before me and who have been gracious teachers and mentors.

STORYING SOVEREIGNTY, SURVIVANCE, RHETORICAL SOVEREIGNTY, AND TRANSMOTION

STORY
*

Let me begin with a story gathered from my time spent with Native students as their writing mentor. As Vizenor says, "You can't understand the world without telling a story. There isn't any center to the world but a story" (quoted in Coltelli 1990, 156). I was sitting in on a mandatory supplementary instruction class that had been created specifically for Native students who were studying for a written exam to be taken that evening. I was sensitive about tensions between faculty desires for students to successfully take the exam and the control being exerted on their studying, the demand for buy-in regarding an extra hour of instruction a week on top of their already packed-to-the-brim schedules. I watched students and faculty members try to negotiate these tensions but felt them escalate little by little as these faculty members' efforts were met with resistance. During the session, one of the students, Connie,[7] seemed especially frustrated. She turned to the lead instructor and asked with a forced smile, "Can we just go study by ourselves?" The instructor replied that they were "only asking for one hour" of her time to "help the group effort," to which Connie replied, "Dana [a classmate] and I were quizzing each other at home. We were studying." With no response from the instructor, Connie sighed and settled into her chair.

Another instructor then initiated a question-and-answer pedagogy and asked Connie to define a concept related to material that might be on the test. Connie quickly and deliberately exhibited her knowledge, clarifying the question and giving not one but two possible answers. The instructor nodded and pushed further, asking about an additional concept in the context of a case study. Dana replied to this question, deftly referring to the case study to explain her answer. The instructor then turned to a third student, Anne, who was quietly studying some flash cards and pointedly asked, "Do you have any questions?" The student paused a moment and then calmly replied, "I'm not usually vocal. I learn from listening to discussion. If I have a question, I ask at another time." The lead instructor, who had been listening to the interactions from across the room, strode purposefully over to the student, forced eye contact, and insisted, "Well, this is that time!" The room, as you can imagine, suddenly became very quiet. I held my breath, waiting for Anne's reaction. As I waited, I thought, "I have just witnessed rhetorical sovereignty and, right on its heels, rhetorical imperialism.

RHETORICAL SOVEREIGNTY

Sovereignty

Before we can address rhetorical sovereignty and its inverse, it is important to understand the most important concept: sovereignty. In most public rhetoric, sovereignty is defined in individual terms rather than in terms of the group-based structure of tribal societies. It is a tool whereby individual rights are maintained, and it is considered to have "'instrumental' rather than 'intrinsic' value" (Coffey and Tsosie 2001, 197). It is a vague concept for most non-Natives, who often assume it has to do with ruling or ownership, connoting an enabling "freedom" extended by the US government to indigenous people after European conquest, when the US government made treaties[8] with groups already residing on the North American continent. Craig Womack (1999), however, points out that sovereignty is inherent in Native cultures. It is an intellectual concept and practice that predates European contact. Sovereignty thus refers to indigenous nations' already existing power or authority to exercise self-governance and independence as Native tribal units holding national sovereign status prior to and apart from US federal and state governmental organizations (Lomawaima 2000; Lomawaima and McCarty 2002). It implies indigenous peoples' self- and community determination and advocates at least some form of legally recognized nationhood[9] (Barker 2005; Biolsi 2005; Brayboy et al. 2012; Grande 2000; Shockey 2001; Wilkins and Lomawaima 2002).

Today, despite conquest and colonization, legally binding documents state that, in exchange for lands held "in trust," the US government is bound to provide for the health, the welfare, and—of special importance here—the education of tribal nations (Wilkins 2002; Wilkins and Lomawaima 2002). Providing effective education for, by, and about indigenous nations is thus a binding obligation, an ethical and legal rationale for indigenizing the academy. Because this presents some difficulty, Scott Lyons calls sovereignty "an ideal principle," suggesting that the ideal may not always be achieved but indicating that through at least attempting to achieve it, Native peoples can "see the paths to agency and power and community renewal" (Lyons 2000, 449). Sovereignty has as much to do with acknowledging a shared history and recentering indigeneity within US social and educational contexts as it does with current politics and legalities. According to Sandy Grande, it is "a restorative process" (Grande 2004, 57). Different ways of naming and addressing sovereignty merely exemplify the ways national and self- and community determination are at once politically and rhetorically constructed. Whether political or rhetorical, sovereignty is, as K. Tsianina Lomawaima asserts, "The bedrock upon which any and every discussion of Indian reality today must be built" (Lomawaima 2000, 3).

Attempts at sovereignty are undertaken with an accompanying sense of community responsibility and need (see Deloria 2001; Medicine 2001). Indigenous studies scholarship often refers to this community responsibility as self-determination (see Lipka 2002; Reyhner 1989), although it is understood in a communal sense where the People are considered as one. While acknowledging that not all agree on how the term is used or defined, I take *self-determination* to mean Native communities' abilities to choose, despite external power differentials, collective courses of action in their own best interests whether socially, politically, economically, or educationally and to operationalize those choices for highest benefit. My understanding of sovereignty and self- or community determination aligns with Lyons's (2000) concept of rhetorical sovereignty, which I will discuss in a later section and which is crucial to employing socioacupuncture pedagogy within contested cultural spaces like writing classrooms, where Native epistemologies are sometimes at political and cultural disadvantage.

The supplementary instruction session is one such contested cultural space having to do with classroom protocol and writing. In the example described, Anne acquiesced to the instructor's command ("Well, now is that time!") after a few seconds of silently considering her options. When she did begin to speak, we listened intently to what she had to say. She talked about her difficulty understanding what the instructor expected when she asked test questions, an issue that had obviously been bothering her. She began, "In class, [the instructor] throws in her opinion a lot. . . . As far as the case study, I was a little lost. There could be three choices and only two were right. [On the practice test,] I got it wrong. I get lost in the language. I know this is how research and books are written, but I want the clearest answer." She then began reading the case study out loud. It had to do with writing a student accommodation and "glossing" as a procedure to move deaf students toward reading. English print was involved.

Sitting beside Anne, a second instructor appeared to want to enter the discussion but was unsure whether it was expedient to do so, wondering whether it would interfere with or be viewed as countering the approach taken by the lead instructor. He entered the discussion nonverbally at first: raising his eyebrows, glancing at the other instructors, pursing his lips, and cocking his head. After an adequate pause, allowing the other instructors time to intervene if they chose (they did not), he

then suggested that case-study questions were, indeed, very complex—
maybe too nuanced for test situations—and that, yes, actually, more than
two answers could be construed as correct. The three instructors in the
room began to dialogue about possible right answers. They disagreed
on fine points but tried to come to agreement broadly. The students in
the room alternately watched and listened to the exchange between the
instructors and tried to study from their notes.

Dana then entered the exchange to offer an opinion about the via-
bility of case-study questions on an exam. She suggested that the course
instructor wanted students to recognize the issues involved but not
necessarily to know the "correct" answer. "I think," she said, turning to
Anne, "the instructor just wants us to be able to explain our reasoning."
One of the instructors acknowledged it was a good observation but said
the course instructor might also need students to "see it from a judge's
perspectives, not the teachers', because they might see things very differently. This is [after all] a law class." In the end, she, too, agreed that
the study guide for the exam—a bulleted list of items—was too general
to be very helpful.

Listening and watching the exchange, I was impressed by Connie,
Anne, and Dana's smart and strategic resistance to instructional authority. When called out, Connie aptly demonstrated knowledge. When
her request to engage the subject matter on her own terms was not
respected, Anne turned the spotlight to a questionable testing tactic.
Instead of attempting to smooth over the tension in the room, she
politely but pointedly confronted it. Dana supported Anne by attempting to clarify the issue and, perceptively, by following up with a valid
point about academic student/teacher discrepancy. If the instructor
hasn't made the intent or purpose of case-study questions clear, it would
be very easy for a student to become confused and sidetracked trying to
choose "correct" answers rather than looking for underlying issues and
defending choices based on knowledge of those issues.

As Anne's question demonstrated, many students are schooled to
look for "right" answers, the kind often governed by Euro-Western conventions. So what we see here are very complex interactions that could
be understood as student-initiated socioacupuncture. The exchange
certainly discomfited the instructors, releasing a tense energy into the
supplementary instruction session but resulting in, begrudging though
it may have been, an acknowledgment of Native academic intelligence.
Through this exchange, we can better understand survivance and rhetorical sovereignty.

Survivance

Connie exhibited survivance, which comprised both survival and resistance (Powell 2004; Vizenor 1994). She resisted the deficit implications implicit in mandatory additional instruction, and she survived that instruction by exhibiting knowledge in a way that was understandable and acceptable to her instructors. According to Vizenor (2008), survivance involves "narrative chance" and performs "new stories of tribal courage" (4). Confronting authoritative imbalances in this environment required courageous resistance for the purpose of survival. It required survivance. Acts of survivance work within the small fissures or cracks of historic and contemporary reality. For Native peoples, survivance indicates a quick responsivity, an ability to adapt to current circumstances in ways that ensure future possibilities. Vizenor and Lee (1999) conceptualize survivance as a "natural presence," like the wind or rivers or animals. It is ever present and variable, "always in motion" (38). Survivance implies a creative openness to change or at least the chance for change (Stromberg 2006), and it follows that indigenous rhetors must be cognizant of opportunity to act, to take advantage of chance occurrences.

[handwritten margin note: CREATIVE OPENNESS TO CHANGE]

Rhetorical Sovereignty

Indigenous rhetors must understand the underlying principles involved in rhetorical creation—here, speech, texts, and performance—to be able to invent response and make the more deliberate choice of rhetorical sovereignty. If survivance works with chance, rhetorical sovereignty involves considered action as a commitment to Native communities (Cushman 2008; 2011; Lyons 2000). Ann attempted rhetorical sovereignty by deliberately stating, "If I have questions, I ask at another time." Her action can be better understood in light of Lyons's definition: "The inherent right and ability of *peoples* to determine their own communicative needs and desires in pursuit [of sovereignty], to decide for themselves the goals, modes, styles, and languages of public discourse" (449–50). In this incident, however, instructors impinged upon Anne's deliberative action by exerting control based on authoritarian and Euro-Western epistemological norms: rhetorical imperialism.

Transmotion

Viewing the back-to-back combination of rhetorical sovereignty and rhetorical imperialism in this instance allows us to understand—however partially or incompletely—the historical component of "push back" in contemporary Native and non-Native interaction based upon a shared (and contentious) history. We see Native motion or *transmotion* (Vizenor 1998) in both survivance and rhetorical sovereignty. Transmotion indicates Native action that is always connected, linked to, or moving across some thing, other, or time (15; Vizenor 2009, 108, 162). When Native people story or interpret their contemporary acts of survivance and/ or rhetorical sovereignty, the stories become connected, linked to, or crossed with the folds of history. Native stories are the very "creases of transmotion" (Vizenor 1998, 15). Understanding transmotion as movement or action across time makes survivance and rhetorical sovereignty more visible. The key point, for instructional purposes, is action, doing as opposed to having or being, because motion or action across time brings more choice, more abundance, more possibilities.

Although the actions just described and explained occurred outside a composition classroom context, understanding them has direct application for the writing/composition classroom. As the scenario suggests, student enactments of indigenous concepts illustrate sophisticated literate action. Taken together, survivance and rhetorical sovereignty are performed to counter colonization, a history of "surveillance and [a] literature of dominance" (Vizenor 1998, 5). When we understand these terms as movements or actions, a sense of shared history (P. Deloria 1998) both political and rhetorical becomes more present and more possible. When imperialism, colonization, and/or simulation appear within classroom contexts, socioacupuncture can be employed to make their damaging presence more visible, more on the table, so to speak. Initially, addressing them might cause some discomfort in that those who resist can feel needled or stung. But this discomfort is to be expected. Socioacupuncture utilizes the cracks and creases of history toward transmotion and can eventually heal wounds between communities by releasing and redirecting energies toward those areas needing critical attention: sovereignty, survivance, and rhetorical sovereignty. One way to enact socioacupuncture toward transmotion is through multimodal products.

THE MULTIMODAL CONNECTION

Euro-Western conceptions of writing become problematic for indigenous populations because discriminations made in academic environments privilege or more highly value Euro-Western traditions concerning reading and writing. According to Kirkness and Barnhardt (2001), persons closely associated with Euro-Western universities understand entering the setting as a "coming to" some place or thing; it represents stepping out of the ordinary world in order to be embraced and assimilated in another rarified, elite, set-apart world. Here, academic practices are largely established and enacted from a written literacy standpoint. From a Native perspective, however, entering a university can be a "going to," with all the connotations of leave-taking. Anticipation is involved, yes, but also anxiety, mourning, and separation from the familiar. "Going to" the university can be aggravated from an indigenous viewpoint because assimilation is neither desirable nor the goal of education, and modes of representation either for self or community often lie outside the written literacy realm (4). Those students whose literate experiences fall outside conventionalized practice and who do not easily accommodate academic writing are often said to have failed in their "encounter[s] [with] the componentiality, specialization, systematicity, bureaucracy and literate forms characteristic of Western institutions and modern consciousness" (6). When students experience negative consequences because their literate demonstrations do not fit a Euro-Western form, for example, they are labeled as having failed. Not often does the academy label such an experience positively: as survivance or rhetorical sovereignty, a refusal by Native students to be governed or controlled. It certainly does not label the experience a failure of the *system*, a failure to recognize sovereignty or self- and community determination.

Universities teach composition courses as a way to socialize students into discursive academic norms. The classes are required and mandatory, and the implications are similar to the supplementary instruction sessions the Native students experienced. Such courses intend to provide instruction needed to successfully complete institutional coursework and eventually move into the workplace. The reasoning goes that if students can be taught to practice "metalanguage" that contributes to close analysis, they will be able to demonstrate literate competency and better succeed in their schooling and future career pursuits (Gee 2001, 135, 139). The theory purports to draw heavily on metalanguage, yet many actual courses appear to be designed without fully understanding James Paul Gee's argument regarding acquisition versus learning. Writing, Gee notes, is an acquired, not learned, discourse comprised of dominant cultural knowledge and the ability to bring that knowledge to conventional, monomodal form. As Lucia Thesen (2001) affirms, "The dynamics of access [inclusion/assimilation] and mechanisms of exclusion [discrimination]" are complicated and these dynamics have historically made minoritized students' success questionable (136), whether students are minoritized by race or by any other sociopolitical factor.

Euro-Western academic thinking has not typically encouraged alternative, participatory literate practice, especially indigenous intellectual practice that calls for collaborative, pragmatic (Medicine 2001), and "communitist" (Weaver 1997) modes of doing and being. Conversely, socioacupuncture pedagogy does encourage expanding academic canons and curricula in a radical rethinking of praxis to include just these modes. Indeed, as even a cursory glance at this book's index illustrates, multimodality is part and parcel of teaching indigenous rhetoric. If we understand that diverse perspectives are "inseparable from their distinctive modes of representation" (62), then we also understand the need to seek "radical alternatives" (50) and to use "difference intentionally" (42) as we approach any literate activity. Fortunately, contemporary technologies help us accommodate such praxis, one that incorporates "alternative images . . . and contradictory visions of outcomes" (Flower 2003, 56). Using multimodal literacies when engaging socioacupuncture pedagogy, then, is a way to "elicit real differences without polarizing people and to negotiate conflict without silencing it" (64). Hull and Nelson's (2005) term "braiding" (225) is useful here in that it connotes separate strands woven together simultaneously: collaborative, pragmatic, communitist—even beautiful—when it is done well.

SOCIOACUPUNCTURE IN MULTIMODAL COMPOSITION PRAXIS

Like most instructors, my approach to teaching draws upon my own scholarly interests and background. I long ago decided working from an indigenous viewpoint would be a valuable and informative practice. However, as mentioned earlier, the students at my institution and taking my courses are, by and large, white. They expect to participate in a typical composition course, which creates both a challenge and an ideal opportunity for socioacupuncture to guide course design and implementation, for putting Mihesuah's, Powell's, Gilmore and Smith's, and Lyons's radical approaches into praxis. The courses I discuss in this section—an upper-division Writing for the English Studies Major course and a basic Academic Writing and Thinking composition course—implemented socioacupuncture pedagogy.

The courses, as I taught them, interrogated intersections of language, writing, and culture in context, including notions of place and community. The primary text for the upper-division course was *The Truth about Stories* by Thomas King (2003). The course focused on close reading and analysis of the primary texts, which were also informed by secondary texts such as scholarly articles, films, newspaper columns, YouTube videos, and postings on social networking sites. Participatory activities, too, were part of the course, including mapping, storyboarding, group oral presentations, and collaborative Prezi and/or PowerPoint presentations. As students experienced each phase of the course, they were taught to pay attention to rhetorical moves made in these various texts as they developed their own academic composition styles. Students wrote reflective and interpretive essays. They also conducted critical, argumentative research, including ethnographic interviews, which challenged the rigidity of and enhanced their facility with discipline-specific conventions. Their final assignments were multimodal compositions and presentations.[10]

ACADEMIC WRITING FOR ENGLISH MAJORS 3090

If the Native students' survivance and rhetorical sovereignty discussed in the preceding section was student-initiated socioacupuncture, in the Writing for the English Studies Major course it was teacher initiated and began the first day as I introduced the course design and daily schedule. When questioned as to why all the texts were about "Indians," I explained that I, like other instructors holding PhDs, was drawing on my scholarly focus to construct the curriculum. I wanted them to understand indigenous intellectual thought as a natural and integral component of their education, exceptional only in the sense that it is extraordinarily rich. I explained that the secondary texts represented important and interesting contemporary theory by prominent scholars and writers who just happened to be American Indian: Blu, Burkhart, Cushman, Colonnese, Gubele, and others. I had designed the course so they could to connect with powerful examples of historic and contemporary American Indians storying their experiences, their place in the world.

Storying place became the theoretical and practical bridge to socioacupuncture pedagogy. I wanted telling stories to become inseparable from being, or the embodiment of the 4Rs in relation to our various communities. Marie Battiste tells us indigenous perspectives are inherently tied to the land (Battiste 2002, 13), and stories, when connected to specific geographic locations, are most "vibrantly felt . . . [and] vividly imagined" (Basso 1996, 145). As foundational knowledge for my instruction, I turned to Keith Basso's (1996) *Wisdom Sits in Places*, which introduced students to the way Western Apache epistemologies—stories as symbolic vehicles of knowledge and eventual wisdom—and places intertwine. In this way, place became a source of education with "transcultural qualities" (148) and was experienced as "a flash of recognition, a trace of memory" (106). As Basso says, "Relationships to places are lived most often in the company of other people, and it is on these communal occasions—when places are sensed *together*—that [N]ative views of the physical world become accessible to strangers" (109).

At the beginning of the semester, then, to establish a basis of interrelatedness, Native texts were juxtaposed beside non-Native texts. Vizenor's simulation theory and Sid Dobrin's ecocomposition theory, for example, were simultaneously read to acclimate students to Native and non-Native senses of representation, place, and land and to enhance the importance of tending to relationships both rhetorical and physical. Later, Burkhart's treatise on indigenous epistemologies introduced students to what and how Coyote teaches while an excerpt from Basso's ethnography, *Wisdom Sits in Places*, introduced them to the Western Apaches' ways of knowing through his non-Native anthropologist lens as a person who was granted the opportunity to conduct research on the Apaches' land. Students needed to be aware that, as Karen Blu (1996) taught, where people came from or where they "stayed at" "colored" their reading, composition, and presentation of texts. Finally, Powell's (2012) multimodal CCCC chair address, "Stories Take Place: A Performance in One Act," was placed beside Joseph Harris's *Rewriting* and Gerald Graff, Cathy Birkenstein, and Russell Durst's *They Say, I Say* to inform and challenge an often rigid "correctness" Euro-Western epistemologies and academic conventions represent. All these would become especially important during the time students were conducting their own research and creating their own analyses and interpretations.

I advised students in the beginning—and reminded them throughout the semester—that the course design and syllabus comprised a contract between us. Their ability to succeed in the course depended on mutual *respect*, just as succeeding in any communicative interaction or event would. I acknowledged that respecting persons and works deemed "Other" (including their spoken and written discourses) did not necessarily imply agreement or consent. It did, however, oblige us to take another's position seriously and to be *responsible* for our choices in language and action. It was necessary that we operate according to a *reciprocal* ethic of care and begin to understand our *relations* to one another, the texts, and the world around us. I reiterated it was my philosophy and practice to assist the class in functioning as a community of thinkers/creators who cared about the success of each member as well as the larger community surrounding them. I expected them to demonstrate that care as fully as possible by enacting the 4Rs: respect, reciprocity, responsibility, and relationship.

Changing understandings and approaches, however, as Lucille Watahomigie and Teresa McCarty assert, required a good amount of reedu-
cation in the form of "reverse brainwashing"[11] to experience how worth-
while the whole "counteracting contradictory stances" (Watahomigie
and McCarty 1994, 38) was in a writing class. An early assignment, an
interpretive essay, asked students to focus on a specific theme in the
text and make an argument based on evidence and interpretation. For
example, they might use King's creation stories to illustrate the way cos-
mologies structure his understanding of place. In the course, socioacupuncture pedagogy facilitated one student's shift from vigorous dis-
agreement with what she perceived as the thesis in King's (2003) text
to a more measured understanding of shared history and relational
responsibility in her final researched paper and multimodal presentation. She titled her interpretive essay "Christianity and Capitalism in *The
Truth about Stories*," saying she wanted to gain a better understanding
of King's assertion that "the truth about stories is that that's all we are"
(2). Instead, she was dismayed to find that King, as she said, "criticized
beliefs that I hold dear and suggested that American Indian beliefs are
more harmonious and communal than are those held by Christians
and Westerners." She came away from the text "feeling a need to
defend [her] Christian and Capitalist beliefs" and that "the greatest
purpose behind these essays was to pass judgment on Christianity and
Capitalism, and to claim that values held by American Indians are supe-
rior to Christian and Western cultural ideals." She concluded by stating
that King's work "lack[ed] an understanding of things that I strongly
believe and hold sacred; a God that I know to be loving and merciful,
and a nation that I love."

By the semester's end, the student's textual interpretation indicated her understanding had increased. She was able to explain how
King "infuse[d] the text with different representations" of American
Indians to reinforce the problem embodied in simulation or stereotype. She followed with "colonization of America" examples, both past
and present, including the miseducation of her own children because
of Thanksgiving school celebrations' employing stereotypical colonizing stories and "Indian" crafts. She largely blamed "popular culture
and art," though, for the problem, as "real depictions aren't generally
available in mainstream media." She concluded with a call for "activism
in not only Native artistic communities but in mainstream popular culture," an action needing "the support of all races."

Reading and viewing her compositions, I noted with approval a deli-
cate shift in perspective. However, as much as I appreciated this step in

the right direction, her conclusions also indicated movement "toward home" was yet necessary (Lyons 2010). In particular, there had to be more transmotion, more understanding of tribal sovereignty and community determination rather than an individualistic Euro-Western self-determination. Her statement "the presentation of Native peoples as individuals is what indigenous peoples want to achieve" unfortunately focused on individualistic traits as ideal. Furthermore, her sentiment "I hesitate to believe that Native artists and activists can attain such a lofty goal by themselves" indicated the need for a more nuanced understanding of alliance, one that did not arise from the superiority prevalent in "savior" complexes. Both assumptions minimized the power and ability, the rhetorical sovereignty, of indigenous persons and communities.

Socioacupuncture, however, meant confronting difference and the consequences of conquest. It meant working through indigenous texts and examples in such a way that Natives could no longer be simply "imagined" as stereotypes or "storied back to an absence . . . in history" (Vizenor and Lee 1999, 86). Rather, Native presence was brought to the fore as we looked at contemporary advertising and packaging, discussed un/offensive Halloween costumes, and took informal person-on-the-street surveys to gauge the distance between what we thought we already knew and what we still needed to know. Students were then more ready to listen to explanations of Silko's photography as representational art, photography that "encourages the storytelling that keeps the community alive—demonstrating American Indian people's ability to use Western form as part of their repertoires of representation to promote goals not sanctioned by European American society" (Katanski 2005, 24). Because they better understood Silko's art, they were more willing to applaud Native youths' attempts at disputing stereotypes in the video "More Than That" (see http://www.youtube.com/watch?v=FhribaNXr7A&sns=fb in response to ABC's documentary *Children of the Plains*). In addition, they were ready to conduct more in-depth research, beginning with more informed research questions, after seeing Native intellectuals in *Reel Injun* discuss media and cultural complicity in containing and erasing indigenous presence.

Another student's work indicated a similar effort at transmotion, as early on in the semester she shifted from a colonizing viewpoint to a rather sophisticated questioning that eventually resulted in an interesting final presentation wherein she troubled notions of accuracy in historical accounts of American Indian events. She recorded that initially, after "years of western model education," her understanding of American Indian history was "vague" and she held the misconception that oral and unrecorded histories were "unreliable" "stories." She "viewed the 'accurate' historical accounts of Indian peoples mainly through works of Anglo-Saxon historians" and was taught "American Indians had oral traditions [but] that these traditions included mostly myths and little actual (and no accurate) conveyance of their history." Then she noted:

> I suddenly found myself questioning the accuracy of a history documented by outsiders, foreigners and in the case of Native American peoples, recorded by the subjugators of Native lands and people. The governments involved certainly had reasons for wanting American Indian history to be recorded in a certain way. Christian missionaries, explorers, and even hunters had different reasons for the way they recorded the history they were witnesses to. In light of this observation, my personal inquiry became: Is there a way to know Native American Indian history that is accurate? Or is this history only viewable from perspectives that are written down, validated, investigated by the western scientific model, cleaned up up, cross-referenced, and researched until the stories make sense and conform to the western mind-set?

A third student used audio, visual, and performative elements to analyze three stories important to Euro-Western understanding—the curse of Canaan, the first Thanksgiving, and the portrayal of "the Indian" in film. The student's classmates acknowledged her reflective questioning as valuable and loudly applauded her final presentation's rhetorical quality. They came to understand at a deeper level that, as the presentation suggested, for every story that "heals or inspires and instigates change for the better," there are stories that hurt and destroy. "If a story is told incorrectly or misinterpreted," the student asked, "can it cause damage to those who hear the story?" Her answer and that of her classmates was "a resounding yes" because "like dropping a large rock into a pond," the force causes an outward ripple effect for generations. "If a story is retold again and again," she ultimately argued, "it is similar to pebbles being dropped over and over again into the pond until the entire body of water feels the movement. The story will continue to make waves as long as it is being told."

As these few examples illustrate, socioacupuncture pedagogy can facilitate a catalytic impulse that propels respect, reciprocity, responsibility, and relationship forward. Continuing the momentum, though, is tricky. It can be a one step forward two steps back/push pull/stop start. Nevertheless, it is do-able, especially when multimodalities are a present and highly valued aspect of composition requirements. The generative idea behind multimodality is not that authority figures design courses around multimodal content but that students have opportunities to compose multimodal products. Multimodality does not just involve textual or visual analysis/critique, then; rather, it calls for alternative products, ones that allow students to demonstrate control over content in ways (modes) they themselves determine, according to criteria valued by their peers. The students' written queries and arguments gained additional force when presented in the visual, nonlinear, and broad view afforded by multimodal compositions and presentations.

Due to space and time constraints, the conversations I have brought to this chapter largely omit addressing Walter Ong's (2001) outline of Euro-Western epistemological literacy, yet parts are key to why this conversation about multimodal literacy is so critical to socioacupuncture pedagogy. According to Ong, philosophically analytic thought is "possible only because of the effects that *writing* [has] on mental processes" (22; emphasis added). It is perceived as unavailable to those who used and still embrace multimodal, specifically oral, traditions. He says, "[These] thought processes and modes of expression were disruptive of the cool, analytic processes generated by writing" (22). When such ideas underpin how we enact composition, they cannot help but skew how Non-Western knowledge constructions are viewed and, consequently, justify attempts to govern them. Different communities, we know, utilize different rhetorical traditions, which results in different rhetorics and/ or different stories. As a student in the class stated, "I cannot ignore our successful American Indian genocide. Not in a literal [contemporary] slaughter kind of way but in an ideological kind of way. The American Indian has been covered [contained] and lost [erased] within the expectations of Western philosophy." And this by the same student: "The American Indian has been lost not by extortion, religion, and diseases but lost, however, in translation."

CONCLUSION

Socioacupuncture pedagogy highlights indigenous peoples' abilities to act for themselves, bypassing traditional praxis for creating and composing knowledge. It exemplifies a deliberate process of critical resistance to colonizing practices. Let me give just two examples beyond my own. At a national conference, seven educators, diverse in disciplinary focus and life background, collaborated to write and perform a readers' theater production for the purpose of confronting tensions American Indians encounter in postsecondary education (White et al. 2002). In a participatory action-research project on health and wellness, Native instructors and students used digital video to develop their identities as knowledgeable leaders and researchers within and without their home communities as they planned, interviewed, wrote, created, and archived film projects (Riecken et al. 2006).

Examples such as these are not typically, however, at a composition teacher's fingertips. To counter containment and erasure, we must think more carefully about the challenge of indigenizing a higher educational system that continues to "perpetuate . . . practices that historically have produced abysmal results" (Kirkness and Barnhardt 2001, 2). Those who work with language and communicative practices for a livelihood, especially, have a responsibility to translate (as the student said) our shared stories more emphatically and accurately. I am not suggesting it is easily done. It can be downright uncomfortable. James Cox (2006) reminds us that stories define "the basic structures and values of a community, and when two communities or nations come into conflict, so do their storytelling traditions" (62). Some stories are used to control or dominate; some are used to exert community sovereignty and indigenize the academy (see Powell 2012). But I reiterate. It is do-able. Socioacupuncture pedagogy can help. When students encounter deficit or simulation, they can also have survivance and rhetorical sovereignty in their memory banks. They can name the experiences of Anne, Connie, Dana, and many others who are now represented in the canon and curriculum. Students (and instructors) cannot say they would have reacted differently if they had only known. They know now.

Notes

1.   While noting the debates surrounding naming terminology concerning First Nations people of North America—that is, some may take exception to the terms used here or use others—I have chosen to use *American Indian, Native,* and *indigenous,* following current indigenous studies scholarship. These terms are used interchangeably, with *indigenous* specifically referring to North American Indian populations in this context.

2.   See Gilmore, Smith, and Kairaiuak (1997) for an example of how difficult (non) accommodation can be for Native students.

3.   I define praxis in this context as action "relating theory to practice in a specific context that challenges limiting situations" (Shor 1996, 3). It can also be defined as "critical reflection" upon such action (Moraes 1996, 111). Praxis, as it relates to socioacupuncture pedagogy, means making what we study "relevant to and reflective of actual populations on this land" (Lyons 2000, 465).

4.   In this document, I rely on key indigenous studies scholars' definitions and explications of epistemologies. These scholars assert that, in indigenous thought, axiologies (ways of valuing) and ontologies (ways of being) are not separable from epistemologies (ways of knowing) and that Native people utilize this understanding to meet the daily challenges of life in their communities (Brayboy and Maughan 2009; Gegeo and Watson-Gegeo 2001; Maughan 2008; Meyer 2003; Nicholls 2009).

5. Other indigenous scholars have also included relevance and reverence in the Rs. See Ball (2010), Brayboy et al. (2011), Fixico (2003), Kimmerer (2002), Romero (1994), and World Parliament of Indigenous Peoples (2011).
6. Research from the first two data sets is IRB approved. The third arises from classroom experience.
7. All names have been changed to protect identities.
8. The earliest of these treaties occurred between 1722 and 1805, and the last occurred in 1868. See http://earlytreaties.unl.edu and also http://www.firstpeople.us /FP-Html-Treaties/Treaties.html.
9. Nationhood is a modern, Western construct that existed in Europe and arose in North America as a result of war and conquest (1812, Civil War, World War I, World War II).
10. Full course-design materials are located on the accompanying website.
11. See Grande (2004) and Smith (1999) on decolonization.

References

Ball, Jessica. 2010. "Enacting Indigenous Research Ethics through Community-University Partnerships." Childhood Development Intercultural Partnerships. http://www.ecdip .org/ethics/.

Barker, Joanne. 2005. *Sovereignty Matters: Locations of Contestation and Possibility in Indigenous Struggles for Self-Determination.* Lincoln: University of Nebraska Press.

Barnhardt, Ray, and Angayuqaq, Oscar Kawagley. 2005. "Indigenous Knowledge Systems and Alaska Native Ways of Knowing." *Anthropology & Education Quarterly* 36 (1): 8–23. http://dx.doi.org/10.1525/aeq.2005.36.1.008.

Basso, Keith. H. 1996. "Wisdom Sits in Places." In *Wisdom Sits in Places: Landscape and Language among the Western Apache,* 105–149. Albuquerque: University of New Mexico Press.

Battiste, Marie. 2002. *Indigenous Knowledge and Pedagogy in First Nations Education: A Literature Review with Recommendations.* Ottawa, ON: National Working Group on Education and the Minister of Indian Affairs. PDF e-book.

Biolsi, Thomas. 2005. "Imagined Geographies: Sovereignty, Indigenous Space, and American Indian Struggle." *American Ethnologist* 32 (2): 239–59. http://dx.doi.org /10.1525/ae.2005.32.2.239.

Blu, Karen I. 1996. "'Where Do You Stay at?' Home Place and Community among the Lumbee." In *Senses of Place,* edited by Steven Feld and Keith H. Basso, 197–227. Santa Fe, NM: School of American Research Press.

Brayboy, Bryan McKinley Jones, Heather R. Gough Beth Leonard, Roy F. Roehl II, and Jessica A. Solyom. 2011. "Reclaiming Scholarship: Critical Indigenous Research Methodologies." In *Qualitative Inquiry,* edited by Stephen D. Lapan, Mary Lynn T. Quartoli, and Frances J. Riemer. San Francisco: Jossey-Bass.

Brayboy, Bryan McKinley Jones, et al., eds. 2012. *Postsecondary Education for American Indian and Alaska Natives: Higher Education for Nation-Building and Self-Determination.* ASHE Higher Education Report vol. 37, no. 5. Hoboken, NJ: Jossey-Bass.

Brayboy, Bryan McKinley Jones, and Emma Maughan. 2009. "Indigenous Knowledges and the Story of the Bean." *Harvard Educational Review* 79(1): 1–21.

Coffey, Wallace, and Rebecca Tsosie. 2001. "Rethinking the Tribal Sovereignty Doctrine: Cultural Sovereignty and the Collective Future of Indian Nations." *Stanford Law & Policy Review* 12 (2): 191–210.

Coltelli, Laura. 1990. *Winged Words: American Indian Writers Speak.* Lincoln: University of Nebraska Press.

Cox, James H. 2006. *Muting White Noise: Native American and European American Novel Traditions.* Norman: University of Oklahoma Press.

Cushman, Ellen. 2008. "Toward a Rhetoric of Self-Representation: Identity Politics in Indian Country and Rhetoric and Composition." *College Composition and Communication* 60 (2): 321–65.

Cushman, Ellen. 2011. *The Cherokee Syllabary: Writing the People's Perseverance.* American Indian Literature and Critical Studies Series, vol. 56. Norman: University of Oklahoma Press.

Deloria, Philip. 1998. *Playing Indian.* New Haven, CT: Yale Historical Publications.

Deloria, Vine Jr. 2001. "Knowing and Understanding." In *Power and Place,* edited by Vine Deloria Jr., and Daniel Wildcat, 41–46. Golden, CO: Fulcrum Resources.

Denzin, Norman K., and Yvonna S. Lincoln, eds. 2011. *The SAGE Handbook of Qualitative Research.* 4th ed. Thousand Oaks, CA: SAGE.

Fixico, Donald. 2003. *The American Indian Mind in a Linear World.* New York: Routledge.

Flower, Linda. 2003. "Talking Across Difference: Intercultural Rhetoric and the Search for Situated Knowledge." *College Composition and Communication* 55 (1): 38–68. http://dx.doi.org/10.2307/3594199.

Gee, James P. 2001. "Literacy, Discourse, and Linguistics: Introduction and What Is Literacy?" In *Literacy–A Critical Sourcebook,* edited by E. Cushman, E. R. Kintgen, B. M. Kroll, and M. Rose, 525–44. Boston: Bedford/St. Martin's.

Gegeo, David, and Karen Watson-Gegeo. 2001. "'How We Know': Kwara'ae Rural Villagers Doing Indigenous Epistemology." *Contemporary Pacific* 13 (1): 55–88. http://dx.doi.org/10.1353/cp.2001.0004.

Gilmore, Perry, and David M. Smith. 2005. "Seizing Academic Power: Indigenous Subaltern Voices, Metaliteracy, and Counternarratives in Higher Education." In *Language, Literacy, and Power in Schooling,* edited by Teresa McCarty, 67–88. Mahwah, NJ: Erlbaum.

Gilmore, Perry, David M. Smith, and Apaquar Larry Kairaiuak. 1997. "Resisting Diversity: An Alaskan Case of Institutional Struggle." In *Off White: Readings on Race, Power, and Society,* edited by Michelle Fine, Lois Weis, Linda C. Powell, and L. Mun Wong, 90–99. New York: Routledge.

Gonzales-Goenaga, Félix. 2012. "We Are Racially Mixed and Beautiful People of Color, and Yes, We are Americans." *FGG Interpreting Services* (blog), January 24. http://www .felixgonzalez-goenaga.com/1/post/2012/01/we-are-racially-mixed-and-beautiful -people-of-color-and-yes-we-are-americans.html.

Grande, Sandy. 2000. "American Indian Identity and Intellectualism: The Quest for a New Red Pedagogy." *Qualitative Studies in Education* 13 (4): 343–359. http://dx.doi.org/10 .1080/095183900413296.

Grande, Sandy. 2004. *Red Pedagogy: Native American Social and Political Thought.* Lanham, MD: Rowman & Littlefield.

Hermes, Mary. 2005. "'Ma'iingan Is Just a Misspelling of the Word Wolf': A Case for Teaching Culture through Language." *Anthropology & Education Quarterly* 36 (1): 43–56. http://dx.doi.org/10.1525/aeq.2005.36.1.043.

Hull, Glynda, and Mark Nelson. 2005. "Locating the Semiotic Power of Multimodality." *Written Communication* 22 (2): 224–61. http://dx.doi.org/10.1177/0741088304274170.

Katanski, Amelia. 2005. *Learning to Write "Indian": The Boarding School Experience and American Indian Literature.* Norman: University of Oklahoma Press.

Kimmerer, Robin W. 2002. "Weaving Traditional Ecological Knowledge into Biological Education: A Call to Action." *Bioscience* 52 (5): 432–38. http://dx.doi.org/10.1641 /0006-3568(2002)052[0432:WTEKIB]2.0.CO;2.

King, Lisa. 2012. "Rhetorical Sovereignty and Rhetorical Alliance in the Writing Classroom." *Pedagogy* 12 (2): 209–33. http://dx.doi.org/10.1215/15314200-1503568.

King, Thomas. 2003. *The Truth about Stories: A Native Narrative.* Minneapolis: University of Minnesota Press.

Kirkness, Verna J., and Ray Barnhardt. 2001. "First Nations and Higher Education: The four R's–Respect, Relevance, Reciprocity, Responsibility." In *Knowledge Across Cultures: A Contribution to Dialogue Among Civilizations*, edited by Ruth Hayoe, and Julia Pan. http://www.ankn.uaf.edu/IEW/winhec/FourRs2ndEd.html.

Kress, Gunther, and Theo van Leeuwen. 2001. *Multimodal Discourse: The Modes and Media of Contemporary Communication*. New York: Oxford University Press.

Lipka, Jerry. 2002. Schooling for Self-Determination: Research in the Effects of Including Native Language and Culture in the Schools. ERIC Document No. ED459989.

Lomawaima, K. Tsianina. 2000. "Tribal Sovereigns: Reframing Research in American Indian Education." *Harvard Educational Review* 70 (1): 1–21.

Lomawaima, K. Tsianina, and Teresa L. McCarty. 2002. "When Tribal Sovereignty Challenges Democracy: American Indian Education and the Democratic Ideal." *American Educational Research Journal* 39 (2): 279–305. http://dx.doi.org/10.3102/00028312039002279.

Lyons, Scott Richard. 2000. "Rhetorical Sovereignty: What Do American Indians Want from Writing?" *College Composition and Communication* 51 (3): 447–68. http://dx.doi.org/10.2307/358744.

Lyons, Scott Richard. 2010. *X-marks: Native Signatures of Assent*. Minneapolis: University of Minnesota Press.

Marker, Michael. 2004. "Theories and Disciplines as Sites of Struggle: The Reproduction of Colonial Dominance through the Controlling of Knowledge in the Academy." *Canadian Journal of Native Education* 28 (1–2): 102–10.

Maughan, Ella. 2008. *American Indian Rhetorical Sovereignty under Disciplinary and Institutional Constraints*. PhD diss., University of Utah, Salt Lake City.

Medicine, Beatrice. 2001. ""My Elders Tell Me." In *Learning to Be an Anthropologist and Remaining Native*, edited by Beatrice Medicine and Sue-Ellen Jacobs, 73–82. Chicago: University of Illinois Press.

Meyer, Manulani. 2003. *Ho'oulu: Our Time of Becoming: Hawaiian Epistemology and Early Writings*. Honolulu: Ai Pohaku.

Mihesuah, Devon. 2006. "'Indigenizing the Academy': Keynote Talk at the Sixth Annual American Indian Studies Consortium Conference, Arizona State University, February 10–11, 2005." *Wicazo Sa Review* 21 (1): 127–38.

Mihesuah, Devon A., and Angela Cavender Wilson. 2004. *Indigenizing the Academy: Transforming Scholarship and Empowering Communities*. Lincoln: University of Nebraska Press.

Moraes, Marcia. 1996. *Bilingual Education: A Dialogue with the Bakhtin Circle*. Albany: State University of New York Press.

Nicholls, Ruth. 2009. "Research and Indigenous Participation: Critical Reflexive Methods." *International Journal of Social Research Methodology* 12 (2): 117–26. http://dx.doi.org/10.1080/13645570902727698.

Ong, Walter. 2001. "Writing Is a Technology That Restructures Thought." In *Literacy: A Critical Sourcebook*, edited by Ellen Cushman, Eugene R. Kintgen, Barry Kroll, and Mike Rose, 19–31. Boston: Bedford/St. Martin's.

Powell, Malea. 2004. "Down by the River, or How Susan La Flesche Piccotte Can Teach Us about Alliance as a Practice of Survivance." *College English* 67 (1): 38–60. http://dx.doi.org/10.2307/4140724.

Powell, Malea. 2012. "2012 CCCC Chair's Address: Stories Take Place: A Performance in One Act." *College Composition and Communication* 64 (2): 383–406.

Reyhner, John. 1989. "Changes in American Indian Education: A Historical Retrospective for Educators in the United States." ERIC Document No. ED314228. http://www.ericdigests.org/pre-9213/indian.htm..

Riecken, Ted, Frank Conibear, Corrine Michel, John Lyall, Tish Scott, Michele Tanaka, Suzanne Stewart, Janet Riecken, and Teresa Strong-Wilson. 2006. "Resistance through

Re-presenting Culture: Aboriginal Student Filmmakers and a Participatory Action Research Project on Health and Wellness." *Canadian Journal of Education* 29 (1): 265–86. http://dx.doi.org/10.2307/20054156.

Romero, Mary E. 1994. "Identifying Giftedness among Keresasn Pueblo Indians, the Keres Study." *Journal of American Indian Education* 34 (1): 35–58.

Shockey, Frank. 2001. "'Invidious' American Indian Tribal Sovereignty: Morton v. Mancari Contra Adarand Constructors Inc., v. Pena, Rice v. Cayetano, and Other Recent Cases." *American Indian Literature Review* (25): 275–313.

Shor, Ira. 1996. *When Students Have Power: Negotiating Authority in a Critical Pedagogy.* Chicago: University of Chicago Press.

Shor, Ira. 1997. "Our Apartheid: Writing Instruction and Inequality." *Journal of Basic Writing* 16 (1): 91–104.

Smith, Linda Tuhiwai. 1999. *Decolonizing Methodologies: Research and Indigenous Peoples.* New York: Zed Books.

Stromberg, Ernest. 2006. "Rhetoric and American Indians: An Introduction." In *American Indian Rhetorics of Survivance: Word Medicine, Word Magic,* edited by Ernest Stromberg, 1–12. Pittsburgh, PA: University of Pittsburgh Press.

Thesen, Lucia. 2001. "Modes, Literacies and Power: A University Case Study." *Language and Education* 15 (2–3): 132–45. http://dx.doi.org/10.1080/09500780108666806.

Vizenor, Gerald. 1994. *Manifest Manners—Narratives on Postindian Survivance.* Lincoln: University of Nebraska Press.

Vizenor, Gerald. 1998. *Fugitive Poses: Native American Indian Scenes of Absence and Presence.* Lincoln: University of Nebraska Press.

Vizenor, Gerald, ed. 2008. *Survivance: Narratives of Native Presence.* Lincoln: University of Nebraska Press.

Vizenor, Gerald. 2009. *Native Liberty: Natural Reason and Cultural Survivance.* Lincoln: University of Nebraska Press.

Vizenor, Gerald, and A. Robert Lee. 1999. *Postindian Conversations.* Lincoln: University of Nebraska Press.

Watahomigie, Lucille, and Teresa McCarty. 1994. "Bilingual/Bicultural Education at Peach Springs: A Hualapai Way of Schooling." *Peabody Journal of Education* 69 (2): 26–42. http://dx.doi.org/10.1080/01619569409538763.

Weaver, Jace. 1997. *That the People Might Live: Native American Literatures and Native American Community.* New York: Oxford University Press.

White, Carolyne, Joe Martin, Pat Hays, Guy Senese, Jean Ann Foley, Diane Nuvayouma, and Elaine Riley-Taylor. 2002. "Confronting Tensions in Collaborative Postsecondary Indigenous Education Programs: A Reader's Theater Presentation." Performance Session presented at the meeting of the American Educational Research Association, New Orleans, LA, April 1–5.

Wilkins, David E. 2002. "Indian Peoples Are Nations, Not Minorities." In *American Indian Politics and the American Political System,* 41–62. Oxford: Rowman & Littlefield.

Wilkins, David E., and K. Tsianina Lomawaima. 2002. "'With Greatest Respect and Fidelity': The Trust Doctrine." In *Uneven ground: American Indian Sovereignty and Federal Law,* 64–97. Norman: University of Oklahoma Press.

Womack, Craig S. 1999. *Red on Red—Native American Literary Separatism.* Minneapolis: University of Minnesota Press.

World Parliament of Indigenous People's Facebook Page. 2011, March 21. http://www.facebook.com/notes/world-parliament-of-indigenous-peoples/statement-of-first-round-table/134598073272674.

3

DECOLONIAL SKILLSHARES
Indigenous Rhetorics as Radical Practice

Qwo-Li Driskill

Learning happens through our bodies, through embodied practice, through doing.
Acts of survivance are tangible, embodied, and material acts that continue our lifeways as indigenous people. Decolonization is learned
through embodied practices that restore cultural memory to our bodies
and communities. Colonization and genocide in the Americas and elsewhere depend on the destruction of cultural memory through attacks
on indigenous rhetorical practices. To counter these attacks, indigenous
people in the United States and Canada are in the process of reassert-
ing the importance of indigenous traditions, languages, and knowledges
through community-based events such as language-immersion classes,
arts courses, and indigenous garden projects as a part of decolonizing
our lives and land bases and asserting what Robert Warrior (1995) calls
"intellectual sovereignty" and Scott Richard Lyons calls "rhetorical sovereignty" (Lyons 2000). Our work as teachers and scholars of indigenous
rhetorics can contribute to decolonization through teaching our rhetorical practices within a radical decolonial framework that contributes
to survivance as "an active sense of presence over absence, deracination,
and oblivion; survivance is the continuance of stories, not a mere reaction, however pertinent" (Vizenor 2008, 1).

Scholars such as Janice Gould, Malea Powell, and Victor Villanueva
have long pointed out that rhetoric and writing classrooms—and universities more broadly—are often complicit in colonization. As Janice
Gould makes explicit, "It is obvious that there is not a university in this
country that is not built on what was once native land. We should reflect
on this over and over, and understand this fact as one fundamental point
about the relationship of Indians to academia" (Gould 1992, 81–82).
Through a focus on rhetorical theories and compositional practices
rooted in an Enlightenment concept of the Greco-Roman tradition, the

DOI: 10.7330/9780874219968.c003

discipline participates in not only a physical occupation of indigenous lands but also in intellectual colonialism. In order to counteract this, indigenous and allied scholars from numerous disciplines have called for decolonization of our scholarship, theories, and practices. In her 2012 Conference on College Composition and Communication chair's address, Powell explains:

> When I'm talking about the decolonizing of our discipline, our scholarship, and our teaching, I *am* talking about the actual students in our classrooms—their bodies, how their bodies are marked and mobilized in dominant culture, their language and how their language is represented in dominant culture, their lives and how their lives are denigrated as not quite good enough without the fix of Western literacy instruction, how so many of us believe they should be "saved" from their lowly, savage lives. (Powell 2012, 401)

In order to counter colonial practices, my rhetoric classroom recenters rhetoric on indigenous practices in the Americas. As part of this recentering, students are asked to not only learn *about* indigenous rhetorics but to learn indigenous rhetorics through linguistic, embodied, and material practices. Drawing on the idea of the skillshare from popular education movements and indigenous craft circles and language groups, I use the idea of decolonial skillshares as a guiding pedagogy in my classroom.

DECOLONIAL SKILLSHARES

I created the term *decolonial skillshares* to refer to indigenous rhetorics, pedagogies, and radical practices that ask us to continue our rhetorical (visual, material, performative, linguistic, etc.) traditions as indigenous people, to transform cultural memories for both indigenous and nonindigenous people, and to create spaces for all of us to learn and teach embodied rhetorical practices as a tactic of decolonization. While decolonial skillshares necessarily prioritize colonized peoples—indigenous people and other people of color—they are also underpinned by two concepts from indigenous diplomatic relationships with nonindigenous people represented in wampum records and treaty agreements: the Two Row Wampum and the concept of Linking Arms Together. The Two Row Wampum treaty belt, or the *Gus-Wen-Tah*, is one of the oldest peace treaties between indigenous people and colonists. Robert A. Williams provides the following description:

> The *Gus-Wen-Tah* is comprised of a bed of white wampum shell beads symbolizing the sacredness and purity of the treaty agreement between

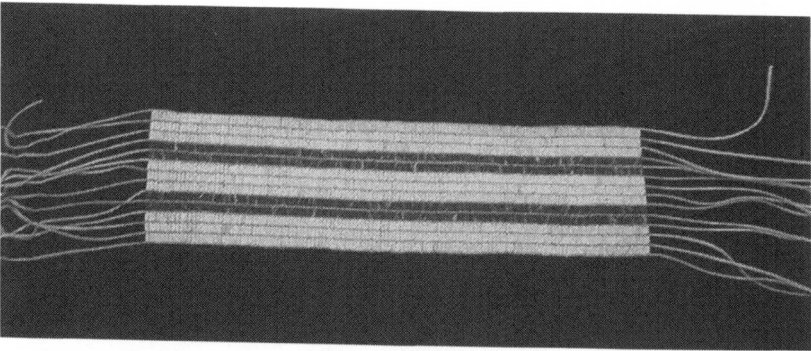

Figure 3.1. Author. Gus-Wen-Tah replica.

the two sides. Two parallel rows of purple wampum beads that extend down the length of the belt represent the separate paths traveled by the two sides on the same river. Each side travels in its own vessel: the Indians in a birch-bark canoe, representing their laws, customs, and ways. In presenting the *Gus-Wen-Tah* to solemnize their treaties with Western colonial powers, the Iroquois explained the basic underlying vision of law and peace between different peoples as follows: we shall each travel the river together, side by side, but in our own boat. Neither of us will steer the other's vessel. (Williams 1999, 4)

As Malea Powell explains in "Down by the River," the concept of "Linking Arms Together" is part of the "tropology of reciprocal relations" and comes "from diplomatic discourses that were rooted in indigenous insistence on shared relations and shared responsibilities between partners" (Powell 2004, 42).[1] She continues, "If we are to be allies, we must share some understanding of one another's beliefs. We don't have to *believe* one another's beliefs, but we do have to acknowledge their importance, understand them as real, and respect/honor them in our dealings with each other" (42). Linking Arms Together is not only a verbal tropology but also a visual tropology woven into wampum belts in which two or more figures are depicted holding hands or with interlocking arms, as seen in the William Penn treaty belt between Penn and the Lenape Nation, the 1762 Treaty of Niagara Covenant chain belt, and the 1794 Canandaigua treaty belt.

Together, the Two Row Wampum and Linking Arms Together underpin decolonial skillshares in the rhetoric and writing classroom. Decolonial skillshares argue that indigenous rhetorics are separate and independent from non-Native rhetorics and also argue that part of decolonization is for both Native and non-Native people to engage with Native rhetorical practices as part of Linking Arms Together to "share

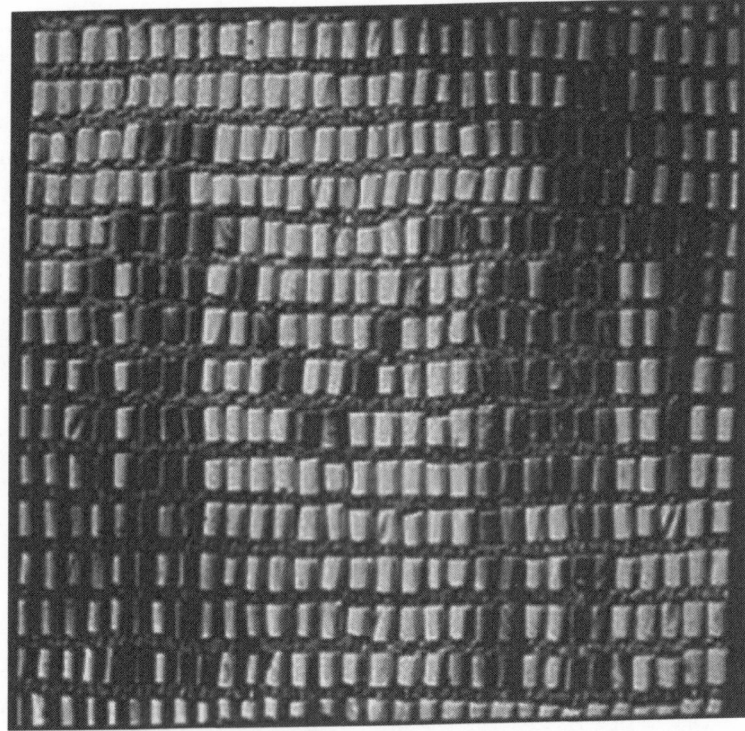

Figure 3.2. Detail of William Penn treaty belt.

some understanding of one another's beliefs," and particularly for both Native and non-Native people to understand Native rhetorical practices.

The concept of a decolonial skillshare comes from my experiences as a grassroots activist in primarily queer and trans communities of color on the West Coast. For over a decade, my activist work has focused on popular education and arts that can work to heal historical trauma and build communities of responsibility and resistance. In order to provide a context for a decolonial skillshare, I want to briefly talk about the experiences that gave rise to the idea.

Skillshare, while undoubtedly having countless origins, is a concept I locate within punk and anarchist communities seeking to disrupt authoritative and capitalist powers though sharing specific do-it-yourself skills that aid in building cooperative, egalitarian economic and social structures. Building egalitarian social structures while disrupting hegemonic powers is a value I share with punk and anarchist communities. However, within the United States and Canada, punk and anarchist activism tends to be dominated by white people (often men) from

Figure 3.3. Canandaigua Treaty belt.

middle-class backgrounds who, rather than disrupt hegemonic powers, actually reinforce them through oppressive organizing.[2] The skillshares I'm familiar with often have a narrow analysis of oppression and power that tends to ignore colonization, racism, sexism, ableism, and queer/ transphobia. The skills shared at such workshops tend to follow pat themes of interest to particular activist communities, such as bicycle repair.[3] While I have no problem with the foci of these workshops— learning to repair a bicycle is certainly an important skill for anyone who rides them—I worry that skillshares tend to ignore the skills Native people and other people of color see as necessary to the continuance of our communities. The concept of a decolonial skillshare deliberately subverts and critiques claims to radicalism that—in actuality—reinforce white colonial powers.

The idea for a decolonial skillshare comes directly from my own frustrating, disheartening experience with a white-dominated trans community on Vancouver Island, BC. Such an experience is one familiar to many activists of color, one that reflects larger patterns of racism and colonialism throughout the United States and Canada. In February 2004, a call for workshops and artists was distributed for an event on Vancouver Island called *The Trans Mission Festival.* The original call read:

> Have you ever been part of a trans community event? Ever wanted to do comics, make film, write, produce art or lead a discussion, workshop or

activity? The first annual Trans Mission Festival is looking for trans-direct-
ed talent, creativity and enthusiasm! The Festival will take place in May
2004 in Victoria, BC and will include art, workshops, a sex party, sports/
fun activities, and a BBQ, among other things! (Donovan 2004, 3)

I responded to the call saying I would be interested in conducting a
workshop and reading poetry, and my proposal was met enthusiastically:
"At this point, we're building the schedule, so we're very open to a variety of formats. Your website looks great—it looks like a lot of what you
do would fit in really well" (Donovan 2004, 3).

When I proposed a workshop specifically for indigenous two-spirit
and trans people, however, the organizers began backpedaling on their
initial enthusiasm. I was told by one of the festival organizers, "I'm wondering if we would have enough First Nations people attending for your
workshop to take off—how many people would you like to see to make it
a success in your mind" (Donovan 2004, 4)? I responded to this question
with an open letter of concern and critique about the place of antiracist
organizing at the Trans Mission Festival. "What does it mean," I asked,
"that an event for Trans folks is expecting there to be a small turn out
of First Nations folks or other folks of color? What does it mean to be
creating a non-Native/non-folk of color Trans movement" (Donovan
2004, 5)?

The response from the organizers of the conference was—to say the
least—defensive, and the focus of the festival began to shift. An orga-
nizer responded to my concerns by writing, "One of the things that we
might be shifting towards slightly is focusing the workshops on 'hands
on' or 'do-it-yourself' kinds of things, and especially around art and
creativity, as that was one of the key things about the festival. Most people were pretty clear that we want a 'festival' atmosphere rather than a
'workshop' one" (Donovan 2004, 7).

Two-spirit Mi'kmaw artist and activist Louis Esmé Cruz likewise wrote
an open letter to the organizers of the Trans Mission Festival about
concerns over racism in regards to my request to have an indigenous-
focused workshop. Cruz was told, "The main reason why I had raised
concerns with Qwo-Li about hir workshop proposal was because the
idea itself was excellent, but it didn't fit within the format of the festival
(which is 'hands on,' skills-based, and celebratory)" (Donovan 2004, 9).

Now deeply upset by the shifting terms of the festival's goals, I wrote
yet another open letter to the organizers that included the seeds of the
idea of a decolonial skillshare: "If your intent for workshops was a skills-
share, as is now reflected on your website, it should have been made
clear in your initial call. (And, on that note, I would argue that there

are few skills more important to First Nations people and other people of color than to find ways to survive the continuing destruction of our peoples and the continuing occupations of our homelands)" (Donovan 2004, 12). Needless to say, the festival did not include my workshop or any other workshops or events with a focus on colonization or race. While the challenges to the Trans Mission Festival continued after these dialogues, what is most important for my purposes here is to contextualize my personal and community experiences with skillshares and outline one of the genealogies of a decolonial skillshare.

The other genealogy for a decolonial skillshare comes from craft circles that take place in Native communities. As in many other communities, craft circles in Native communities are places where people can come together and talk while working on specific art projects. My experiences in Native craft circles have shown me that they are places to learn specific indigenous arts. Edge beading, weaving Cherokee double-woven baskets, and weaving wampum are all skills I learned in craft circle settings.[4] And, through craft circles, I have been able to pass on these skills to other Native people.

The skillshare and the craft circle came together for me in a context of decolonial activism after I was invited to submit a workshop proposal to the 2006 Homo A Gogo, a biannual queer music and arts festival. Informed by my PhD coursework, the rhetorical work on memory being done by Haas, Villanueva, and Powell, and by my own poetic and activist work on memory and historical trauma, I designed a workshop entitled "Memory as Resistance: A Decolonial Skillshare":

> Colonization and genocide in the Americas and elsewhere depends on the destruction of cultural memory. Knowledges and lifeways of people of color/mixed-race people are routinely appropriated, erased, or interrupted by systems of colonization and white supremacy. How can and do we relearn and/or continue our artistic (visual, material, performative, etc.) traditions as Queer and Trans folks of color/mixed-race people? How do we restore, continue, and transform the embodied practices that create cultural memory? How can engagement with our traditional/community-specific arts aid in healing historical trauma? How can we work to pass cultural memory on to others? Using interactive theater, traditional, and contemporary arts, this workshop will examine our cultural memories and practices as Queer/Trans people of color/mixed-race/non-white people. (Homo A Gogo 2008)

A decolonial skillshare creates spaces for Native people to both learn and teach specific embodied *practices* as a specific *tactic* in processes of decolonization. I see the decolonial skillshare as a process of collaborative labor that answers community needs. Further, the decolonial skillshare has a focus on both activist and pedagogical concerns of Native people. Like other skillshares, it focuses on teaching and disseminating specific embodied practices. And like Native craft circles, the decolonial skillshare focuses on embodied practices that continue cultural memories. Decolonial skillshares have intentional and specific goals to heal historical trauma, resist colonization, and continue our traditions.

Decolonial skillshares work to ensure that the information and knowledge making generated though scholarship do not remain within the academy or only disseminated through academic discourse. It calls for knowledge to not only be built reciprocally but to also be shared with indigenous communities both inside and outside of academia. Decolonial skillshares have a specific focus on practice. The research that emerges from our work should help generate and continue embodied practices that aid in larger struggles for decolonization. Likewise, decolonial skillshares are not limited to academic pedagogy; they include grassroots pedagogy and community settings. For example, Cruz has employed the decolonial skillshare as a model in the 2spirit Skillshare Toronto (2010), a collective of two-spirit artists and activists working for decolonization.[5] The teaching of indigenous rhetorics and practices must hold decolonization and indigenous cultural continuance for indigenous peoples as its ultimate goal. The purpose of a decolonial skillshare is not only to disseminate scholarly or theoretical work but also to learn and share specific *embodied* practices.

It's important to note here that while I have always taught in predominately white institutions, I have yet to teach a course that didn't have indigenous students. In conversations with other teachers, however, I find that there is often a predetermined assumption about Native *absence* in the classroom and that "terministic screens" regarding race in the United States "unsee," to use Powell's (1999) term, indigenous presence in the classroom. Native students are often mis-seen as white, Black, Latin@, or Asian. These identities may also be a part of their experiences, but often it is the imposition of a teacher's racialized assumptions—which all of us in a white supremacist culture have—that erase indigenous identities.[6] My pedagogy, however, asks students to talk about their own experiences, to think critically about how their own histories and bodies are caught up in complex systems of power. These conversations (and, no doubt, my presence as a Native teacher), particularly around Native identity and settler colonialism, often lead students to discuss being Native. For example, in a Modern Rhetorical Theory course I taught at Texas A&M University, a central text was *Borderlands/*

La Frontera: The New Mestiza by Gloria Anzaldúa (2012). During the discussion of this text and Anzaldúa's occasional use of Nahuatl, one of my students discussed her own relationship to Nahuatl and a family of Nahua immigrants from Mexico and how she and her cousins had created an exchange of language instruction in which she taught her relatives English as they taught her Nahuatl. When teachers assume Native absence, they are, inevitably, erasing the identities and experiences of Native students in their classrooms.

What follows are three examples of decolonial skillshares that I use in the classroom and that teachers of indigenous rhetorics can use as a models in their own classroom practice.

Decolonial Skillshare #1: Indigenous Languages

Language revitalization and continuance is one of the central struggles of Native people in the United States and Canada. After a systematic effort by colonial governments and churches to end our languages—particularly through the boarding school and residential schools in the United States and Canada—Native people are working to ensure our languages continue.

To contribute to these efforts, the Modern Language Association Committee on the Literatures of People of Color in the United States and Canada (CLPCUSC) produced two major documents in support of Native American and indigenous languages: Statement on Native American Languages in the College and University Curriculum and Statement on Indigenous Languages of the World in the College and University Curriculum. The Statement on Native American Languages in the College and University Curriculum makes the following recommendations:

1. To grant credit for the study of Native American languages when undertaken to fulfill undergraduate and graduate requirements in foreign languages.

2. To include, where appropriate, Native American languages in the curriculum in the same manner as foreign languages and to grant proficiency in Native American languages the same full academic credit as proficiency in foreign languages. Institutions of higher education are particularly encouraged to teach the languages of Native American nations in their regions, whenever possible.

3. To encourage research to create and update dictionaries, grammars, orthographies, curricula, and other materials to support the teaching of Native American languages. The preparation of these materials is

especially important for languages for which they have never been developed. (MLA Committee on the Literatures of People of Color in the United States and Canada 2005, 227)

Similarly, the Statement on Indigenous Languages of the World in the College and University Curriculum asserts:

Preserving and revitalizing Indigenous languages must be central to that objective. Therefore, the Modern Language Association recommends that institutions should, whenever possible, support the study of and research in Indigenous languages and literatures worldwide and devise means for native speakers of Indigenous languages to fulfill foreign language requirements with their Indigenous languages. (MLA Committee on the Literatures of People of Color in the United States and Canada 2007)

Both statements were endorsed in 2008 by the CCCC's Language Policy Committee (Glenn 2009). Together, these endorsements bolster the National Council of Teachers of English/CCCC's Students' Right to their Own Language (SRTOL) as a resolution and commitment by the field of rhetoric and composition that includes not only "dialects" outside of the "standard American dialect" but also languages other than English (Students' Right to their Own Language). SRTOL reads:

We affirm the students' right to their own patterns and varieties of language—the dialects of their nurture or whatever dialects in which they find their own identity and style. Language scholars long ago denied that the myth of a standard American dialect has any validity. The claim that any one dialect is unacceptable amounts to an attempt of one social group to exert its dominance over another. Such a claim leads to false advice for speakers and writers, and immoral advice for humans. A nation proud of its diverse heritage and its cultural and racial variety will preserve its heritage of dialects. We affirm strongly that teachers must have the experiences and training that will enable them to respect diversity and uphold the right of students to their own language. (Conference on College Composition and Communication n.d., 1)

SRTOL is often understood as focusing on speakers of marginalized Englishes, but SRTOL—particularly in tandem with the Language Policy Committee's endorsement of the MLA statements mentioned above— should also be understood as a statement that supports the rights of indigenous people to speak and learn their heritage languages in the classroom. For those of us teaching indigenous rhetorics, these statements both support and encourage us to use and teach indigenous languages in our courses.

While indigenous rhetors have resisted colonization through dominant languages for hundreds of years, indigenous rhetorics remain largely ignored in the dominant discipline and are too often analyzed exclusively through (Anglo-Americanized) Greco-Roman terms and concepts. Consequently, it is important for those teaching indigenous rhetorics to resist "inclusion" of those rhetorics in a "multicultural" canon and instead recenter our modes of analysis to prioritize indigenous lifeways, languages, and practices.

As a Cherokee and as a teacher of indigenous rhetorics, I have taken the stance that students should have some kind of exposure to indigenous languages in the classroom. Indigenous languages not only carry cultural memory, because language is so central to rhetoric, they also change the way we think about rhetoric and how rhetoric works. I have used Cherokee language as part of two courses I developed while I was faculty in the Department of English at Texas A&M University: a graduate-level course, Native American Rhetorics and Literatures, and an undergraduate course, Native American Rhetorics and Literatures.

I am a Cherokee language learner and mostly speak the Giduwa dialect as spoken in North Carolina.[7] I learned Cherokee from Bo Taylor at the Museum of the Cherokee Indian during Cherokee language immersion classes. I started teaching Cherokee, in part, as a way of continuing to practice and learn Cherokee as someone living outside of Cherokee linguistic areas. I began by creating an informal language group of interested graduate students at Texas A&M that met once a week to learn Cherokee. In *How to Keep Your Language Alive*, Leanne Hinton (2002) argues that language learners "should take on just one responsibility beyond learning the language: *teach whatever you learn to someone else!*" (2002, xvii). Darrell Kipp (2002), a Blackfeet language educator, admonishes language learners not to wait until they know the language well before trying to teach it; if you learned two words today, he says, knock on your neighbor's door and say, "Turn off the TV! Get the kids! I have two new words" (xvii).[8]

Taylor uses total physical response (TPR) and immersion techniques to teach Cherokee, and I have incorporated these techniques into the classroom. I teach Cherokee for the first ten to twenty minutes of each class. Immersion means that, for the period in which I teach Cherokee, I use exclusively or almost exclusively Cherokee, and communicate meanings to students through demonstration, action, and pantomime. For example, to learn the Cherokee word for green (*atse*), I hold up various green things and point to green things in the classroom, repeating the word several times until students understand my meaning. TPR involves asking students to physically interact, through both speaking and moving, with the language. For example, to teach the command "sing," *tinogi*, I sing, say *tinogi* several times, direct students to repeat me, and then ask students to sing when I say *tinogi*. While I don't expect that in a term students will become language speakers in this context, they do have to engage an indigenous language. I don't grade students on their language proficiency. Instead, I frame language instruction as a vital part of indigenous rhetorics that students of Native rhetorics should be exposed to. I have found, however, that at the end of the semester students are able to form basic sentences and speak basic greetings and that they have a strong beginning vocabulary. Just as important for my purposes, they often leave class with an interest in Cherokee and other Native languages and are excited that they were able to learn Cherokee in class. I include the following statement in the syllabus in order to contextualize the Cherokee language lessons we'll be participating in class:

Giduwa Cherokee (ᏌᏍᎦ ᏣᏫᎩ) Language

As part of our daily classroom activities, I will be teaching you basic words and phrases in the Giduwa dialect of the Cherokee language. The purpose of this is two-fold: (1) To provide an introduction to an Indigenous language in order to develop a more complex analysis of issues in Native rhetorics and literatures and (2) To introduce you to some of the language immersion techniques currently being employed by Native people in order to continue Native languages. You won't be graded on this—the point is to participate and learn what you can.

Because the position of indigenous languages in the United States and Canada is precarious due to genocidal and assimilationist policies of colonial governments, teaching indigenous languages—even if minimally—is a deeply radical act. Estimates made in 2005 by the Cherokee Preservation Foundation, for instance, found that there were only 460 Giduwa Cherokee language speakers and that 72 percent of those speakers were over the age of fifty (Cherokee Preservation Foundation 2013).

While I think everyone living on indigenous land—that is, everyone—has an ethical and political responsibility to learn indigenous languages, I also know that for monolingual language speakers in the United States, learning languages—particularly less commonly taught languages—can be an intimidating prospect. While I think learning a new language is a particular anxiety of dominant Anglo-American monolinguals—and I hope to persuade monolingual speakers to examine where such anxiety comes from—the truth is that, even while language revitalization efforts are reversing language dormancy and language shift in ways that are deeply hopeful, indigenous languages in the United States remain at risk and there is an urgency about teaching indigenous languages that means we—frankly—don't have time. You don't need to be a fluent speaker of a language to teach a language—as Hinton and Kipp urge above, you can teach a language as you learn it. The following steps can be taken to incorporate indigenous languages into the classroom:

1. If you don't already have a familiarity with an indigenous language, find online resources for the languages indigenous to the land you teach on. While not all languages have online resources, many do. You can learn simple phrases and words and teach them in your classroom as you learn.

2. Many universities teach indigenous languages. Seek out language teachers at your institution. Invite them to class to give a language lesson.

3. One of the amazing privileges of being affiliated with universities is that internal and external funding is available for scholars to pursue a number of projects. Apply for grants to learn languages. Encourage graduate and undergraduate students to apply for funding to study indigenous languages.

Decolonial Skillshare #2: Wampum Rhetorics

Wampum records are traditionally a central mode of transmitting information, agreements, and histories for Native people east of the Mississippi River. I learned to weave wampum with Malea Powell through our teacher and friend Robin McBride Scott at a summer workshop through the National Center for Great Lakes Native American Culture. After learning this technique, I taught other Eastern native people I knew who wanted to learn this skill as part of decolonial practice.

One of the verbal critiques I have received from non-Native scholars in the field about decolonial approaches and critiques of rhetoric is that indigenous people have used, and continue to use, European rhetorical forms and modes, so to understand indigenous rhetorical tactics one must understand European forms of rhetoric. I don't disagree with this assertion. However, I also know that, in the words of Joy Harjo, "There is no such thing as a one-way land bridge" (Harjo 2001, 38). Critiques of decolonial approaches to the study of rhetoric operate from a warrant in their argument that because indigenous people have used nonindigenous forms of rhetoric, indigenous rhetorical forms aren't broadly useful outside indigenous contexts.

This thinking is rooted in the idea that European and Euro-American discourses and rhetorics are uninfluenced by indigenous rhetorics, erasing hundreds of years of reality in which Europeans were minor intrusions into indigenous political systems and land bases and, in fact, in which Europeans *by necessity* adopted indigenous languages and indigenous rhetorical forms. One cannot understand legal discourse in

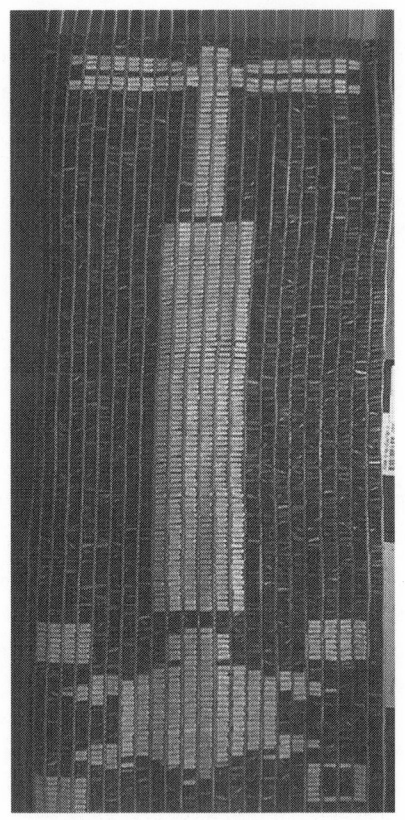

Figure 3.4. Author. Dissertation belt.

the United States and Canada if one doesn't understand that indigenous rhetorical practices are inseparable from the existence of US and Canadian legal systems.[9] Wampum records are complex rhetorical makings that not only involve their material production but are also dependent on community memory. As Angela Haas explains, "Wampum embodies memory, as it extends human memories of inherited knowledges via interconnected, nonlinear designs with associative message storage and retrieval methods" (Haas 2007, 80–81).

I first incorporated wampum weaving and recitations into my graduate course Native American Rhetorics and Literatures at Texas A&M University. Students are asked to engage wampum as an indigenous rhetorical form by reading work by Angela Haas (2007), Tehanetorens (1999), Paul Wallace (1994), and Robert A. Williams (1999). In class, I teach students to weave wampum. In order to prepare students for this project, I ask them to read broadly about wampum traditions and rhetorics, particularly the work of Haas and Williams. Real wampum beads are quite expensive—they run anywhere from $5.00 to $10.00 a bead. Instead, I ask students to contribute a few dollars so I can purchase replica wampum beads in bulk, artificial sinew, and spools of leather lace. I tell students how to make small beading looms consisting of three small pieces of wood and two nails to secure the leather. I include this statement in the syllabus:

Other Materials

Imitation wampum beads, needles, imitation sinew, leather laces, wampum frames. (Students are encouraged to pool their resources for these materials.) The best imitation wampum beads are available at http://home.cshore.com/waaban/wampum.html. Imitation sinew and leather laces are available at: http://www.crazycrow.com. (Wampum frames are simple to make, but will require small pieces of wood, nails, a hammer, and some elbow grease).

For the final phase of this project, students are asked to deliver a formal wampum recitation that keeps within wampum records as a visual, material, performative, and community rhetoric. During the wampum recitations for the graduate course, students speak of family memories, love, cultural practices, and personal difficulties and challenges. Many of us—including myself—are often in tears listening to the stories the wampum records hold.[10] Through this project, we all participate in an indigenous rhetorical practice that not only teaches us, in a purely intellectual sense, about the rhetorical power of wampum records but also teaches us the power of wampum rhetorics through the embodied practice of weaving the record and performing the recitation of the record with the community.

After developing this assignment for the graduate course Native Rhetorics and Literatures, I assigned this wampum project to my students in an undergraduate Native Rhetorics and Literatures course. Many of the students took this project very seriously, created brilliant wampum records, and told stories were all deeply engaged in.

Decolonial Skillshare #3: Weaving Baskets

I was taught to weave Cherokee double-wall baskets during trips to Oklahoma and was later taught to weave Cherokee double-woven baskets by Robin McBride Scott. Double-wall baskets, also called *root-runner baskets,* are a style of baskets popular among Oklahoma Cherokees because they're often made from the roots of plants like brush bark and honeysuckle. They're also often made from commercial materials. Double-wall baskets have both an inner and an outer wall, which are connected together by the ribs of the basket. Double-woven baskets are one of our oldest forms of basket. Traditionally made from rivercane, the weaving of double-woven baskets involves weaving the inside of the basket and then turning the walls of the basket back down against itself, weaving the splints into an outer wall.

I originally learned to weave double-wall baskets during a trip to Oklahoma with a small group of other Cherokees, including Angela Haas, in order to meet our online Cherokee language teachers. During this trip, we were taught to weave Cherokee double-wall baskets by Anna Huckabee, a Cherokee national treasure. I was terrible at it and became frustrated fairly quickly, so I retreated into a finger-weaving project I was working on. Later in the day I was spending time with another Cherokee friend of mine, Beloved/Tsigeyu Sharp, trying again to start weaving a basket. "I just can't *get* this," I told her.

"When I start a basket, I don't use that extra weaver," she told me. "I was taught to just use an odd number of reeds." She unweaved my basket and helped me start over. "Over two, under two. Hold it *this* way. Make sure that everything is even when you start. Pull the reeds out like spokes. Otherwise, they'll be uneven later." There was something about sitting with my friend—perhaps because I wasn't intimidated by her— that shifted the way I was thinking about weaving the basket. My body literally had to learn how to make the movements to weave the basket. I had to learn how to hold my hands, how to hold my body, how to hold the basket reed, and suddenly something "clicked." And it wasn't verbal—it was kinesthetic.

During this same trip, I was shown by our Cherokee language teachers how to identify sassafras and how to pick off a small twig and chew on it as part of a prayer, and I attended a stomp dance for the first time. These were pivotal moments for me in my own decolonial practice. They weren't something you could learn in a book—they were embodied learning through *doing*, through *practice*. And, as I told my friend Tsigeyu during that trip, something inside me was healed. It wasn't magical; it was a different feeling in my body. It felt as if at least three generations of colonial trauma started to melt away.

If part of a learning experience is kinesthetic or somatic, another part of a learning experience is reflection on what and how we learned. And one of the things I learned about learning during these experiences was that I must *do* something over and over again until my muscles actually begin to learn it.

Basket weaving is a decolonial, embodied practice that can be used as a way of reflecting on learning, so basket weaving has become a way I have taught graduate students to learn about learning, to teach and to become reflective about the experiences students might be having in their classrooms.

I first taught students to weave Cherokee double-wall baskets in an academic context when I was invited by Malea Powell to teach students in her Material Rhetorics course how to weave.[11] What was exciting to me about this process was reflecting on how different pedagogy is when dealing with material, observing how students began helping one another, and listening to students reflect on their own learning process as they wove baskets.

I transferred this lesson into the graduate course Native American Rhetorics and Literatures, framing it within the context of pedagogy and tying it to a course assignment in which students were required to create a teaching philosophy. Weaving baskets, in countless ways, is nothing like writing a paper. And it's this radical departure that makes this practice so useful for rhetoric and writing, literature, and other fields in which alphabetic writing has become an almost singular and privileged mode of production. Certainly this activity held special meaning for Cherokee and other indigenous students in the class, but what was particularly useful in this context was that many students had no idea how to weave a basket, had difficulty handling the materials, and had to learn to reorient their bodies in order to weave. I'm reminded of Powell's memory of learning beadwork from a Miami elder:

> I squint and struggle until she lays her hands on top of mine and rearranges the way that I am holding everything—the beaded thread and needle, the buckram circle, my head and shoulders. She tells me, "Honey, don't work so hard—it should feel just right when you do it, just like this, comfortable but controlled—you don't want your hands to cramp up. Everybody's different, y'know, but you want to be comfortable while you're beading—I can show you what I know, and then you'll learn to feel it and really get it down (Powell 2004, 43).

When you teach basket weaving, and other material making, you must often actually reposition people's hands and bodies. And, for graduate students, this activity forced them to think about their own students in their writing classrooms who may feel very intimidated or uncomfortable with the writing process. We tend to take for granted that writing as a form of discourse. Putting ourselves in learning situations that feel unfamiliar helps us, as teachers, develop empathy for our students.

Figure 3.5. Photograph by Malea Powell. Qwo-Li Driskill facilitating a basket weaving workshop in Powell's Material Rhetorics course at Michigan State University, 2008.

CONCLUSION

One of the different qualities of skillshares, as opposed to many other learning activities I've used, is that *students actually talk to each other.* Students who have picked up the skill more quickly help other students. Students look to their peers for help. And while weaving, people talk to each other. Not necessarily about weaving. Or pedagogy. But they talk to each other about their lives, and their fingers weave over and under the ribs of a story they're creating with their hands.

Decolonial skillshares can help reroot scholarly and pedagogical practices in the traditions of the Americas in order to interrupt ongoing colonization. It is our responsibility as both Native and non-Native scholars and educators living on occupied land to disrupt colonial projects through our work. It is our responsibility to provide spaces in our classrooms for students to engage indigenous practices, to use the classroom as a decolonial skillshare in order to intervene in systems of oppression both inside and outside of academia. It is our responsibility to put into practice activist scholarship that aids in decolonization and radical social change.

So, in a graduate course in Native rhetorics, on learning that my students were not receiving critical and reflective pedagogical training in their other classes, I taught students to weave double-wall baskets. One of the many useful things about this activity is that—and this is no surprise in an English department—my students feel comfortable in their writing and in theorizing about literature. Their own students, however, don't necessarily have those particular literacies, so to ask teachers to engage in an activity they're *not* familiar or comfortable with creates a situation in which they can learn about learning. And, you can't teach basket weaving from a lecture—you must *do* it. And you must learn through observation and practice. And, while basket weaving is materially very unlike writing, there's a way in which *learning about learning* enables my students to rethink their pedagogies in their classrooms.

One of the aspects of learning outside of the classroom that I've seen through indigenous craft circles is that the physical relationship with the materials being used, and the engagement with our bodies in a particular kind of learning, actually opens up conversation in ways starkly different, and I think more pedagogically effective, than many of the ways we learn in formal classroom settings. So, for instance, while learning to weave baskets, or weave wampum records, or through edge beading, there are numerous levels of learning taking place at once:

1. There is the physical learning of *making*. Learning to weave a basket, learning to speak a language.

2. There is a simultaneous learning that takes place through story. Talking about learning, talking about daily life, exchanging stories, building community.

3. There is a layer of learning about making through asking questions, being shown what you're doing, through getting feedback on your work. Collaborative learning.

4. There is learning through your teacher. Learning from those who have learning.

5. And then, ideally in a decolonial approach, there is the learning you have through teaching. Teaching others what you know through embodied practice. For instance, as a language learner, teaching Cherokee has been one of the best ways to learn Cherokee.

As my students wove their baskets, they talked with each other. They talked about their lives, they helped one another with their baskets, they created a learning space that was much more organic to the way we learn as human beings than the kinds of formalized structures that often exist in mainstream higher education models.

Decolonization commits itself in solidarity by acknowledging and engaging with both the commonalities and the differences in experiences of oppression and struggles for change. For those of us who are part of oppressed communities, it is our bodies—first and foremost—that disrupt and disturb oppressive systems because, as Audre Lorde (1992) reminds us, "we were never meant to survive" (32). Theories of oppression and liberation emerge from the lived experiences of oppressed people. I want our practices and continuing scholarship and teaching to treasure these lives—my life, the lives of those I fiercely love—to understand the material conditions of oppressed peoples and to commit to social transformation. It is our responsibility as both Native and non- Native people living on occupied land to disrupt colonial projects through our work. Such acts of resistance and alliance contribute to our survivance as Native people and can transform our current story of colonization into a future decolonized reality.

Notes

1. See also Williams (1999).
2. Similarly, scholarship such as Geoffrey Sirc's (2002) *English Composition as a Happening*, while very valuable in some ways, often removes a critical understanding of race and power from the "happenings" he argues for as a model for pedagogical practice. Sirc's scholarship and theories could be complicated and bolstered by Robin D.G. Kelley's (2002) *Freedom Dreams: The Black Radical Imagination*.
3. I am picking on bicycle repair here because it is such a common trope with skillshares. It cannot go without saying here that Métis artist, scholar, and activist Dylan Miner uses bicycles as part of his own art and activism. See Ball (2013).
4. GV to my teachers Aidan Dunn Robin McBride Scott, Malea Powell, Kimberli Lee, Tsi-ge'yu Sharp, and George Wiske for teaching me beadwork, rivercane weaving, double-wall basket weaving, wampum weaving, and finger weaving.
5. The Two-Spirit Skillshare describes itself as follows:
    The Two-Spirit Skillshare is a project of Tities Wîcinímintôwak/Bluejays Dancing Together Arts Collective. The Skillshare brings together Indigenous people to create work and exchange knowledge that speaks to being Native to Turtle Island. This work helps us to connect to ourselves as Two-Spirit people while allowing for these self-labels to be engaged through a creative process. We are artists, musicians, performers, writers, educators, community workers and activists. We are all-encompassing of Indigenous expressions of our genders and sexualities (2spirit Skillshare Toronto 2010).
6. It is not only Native identities and experiences that are erased through the racialized readings of people's bodies; the erasure of Native identities through these readings carries particular genocidal implications within an historical and contemporary context in which discourses of blood and phenotype remain fixed within the colonial imagination. These discourses exist to ensure that indigenous people are never "enough" to lay claim to land, sovereignty, and lifeways.
7. The Overhill dialect is spoken in Snowbird, North Carolina, as well as throughout Cherokee communities in Oklahoma. It is usually called the *Oklahoma dialect.*
8. It is important to note that not all indigenous communities want their languages taught outside of their own community spaces. Further, some indigenous commu-

nities have specific cultural protocols that must be adhered to in order to teach a language. Teachers have a responsibility to the community whose language they're teaching to find out the current cultural and political contexts of language teaching before incorporating indigenous languages into the classroom.

9.   See Williams 1999.
10. This, in fact, is often a part of particular wampum traditions through condolence ceremonies.
11. Powell's scholarship focuses on American Indian material rhetorics. She argues, "We need to theorize, and that theory can't engage in textual fetishism—neither by relying on alphabetic print texts nor by textualizing non-alphabetic objects. We need, in fact, to move our conversations and our practices toward 'things,' to a wider understandings of how all made things are rhetorical, and of how cultures make, and are made by, the rhetoricity of things" (Agnew et al. 2011, 123).

References

Agnew, Lois, Laurie Gries, Zosha Stuckey, Vicki Tolar Burton, Jay Dolmage, Jessica Enoch, Ronald L. Jackson II, LuMing Mao, Malea Powell, Arthur E. Walzer, et al. 2011. "Octolog III: The Politics of Historiography in 2010." *Rhetoric Review* 30 (2): 109–34. http://dx.doi.org/10.1080/07350198.2011.551497.

Anzaldúa, Gloria. 2012. *Borderlands/La Frontera: The New Mestiza.* 4th ed. San Francisco: Aunt Lute Books.

Ball, David P. 2013. "Dylan Miner: An Anti-Authoritarian Artist on Bikes Beyond Borders." *Indian Country Today Media Network.com,* February 8. http://indiancountry todaymedianetwork.com/gallery/photo/dylan-miner-anti-authoritarian-artist-bikes -beyond-borders-148074.

Cherokee Preservation Foundation. 2013. "Cherokee Language Revitalization." Cherokee Preservation Foundation. http://cherokeepreservation.org/what-we-do /cultural-preservation/cherokee-language/.

Conference on College Composition and Communication. n.d. Students' Right to Their Own Language. http://www.ncte.org/library/NCTEFiles/Groups/CCCC/New SRTOL.pdf.

Donovan, Colin Kennedy, ed. 2004. *Racism at the TransMission Festival.* http://www .wearetheones.info/transmission.pdf.

Glenn, Cheryl. 2009. "2008 CCCC Chair's Letter." *College Composition and Communication* 60 (3): W63–73.

Gould, Janice. 1992. "The Problem of Being 'Indian': One Mixed-Blood's Dilemma." In *De/Colonizing the Subject: The Politics of Gender in Women's Autobiography,* edited by Sidonie Smith and Julia Watson, 81–87. Minneapolis: University of Minnesota Press.

Haas, Angela M. 2007. "Wampum as Hypertext: An American Indian Intellectual Tradition of Multimedia Theory and Practice." *Studies in American Indian Literatures* 19 (4): 77–100. http://dx.doi.org/10.1353/ail.2008.0005.

Harjo, Joy. 2001. *A Map to the Next World: Poems and Tales.* New York: W. W. Norton.

Hinton, Leanne. 2002. *How to Keep Your Language Alive: A Commonsense Approach to One-on-One Language Learning.* Berkeley: Heyday Books.

Homo A Gogo. 2008. "Workshops." May 15. *Homo A Gogo* http://www.homoagogo.com /2006/info/index.html.

Kelley, Robin D.G. 2002. *Freedom Dreams: The Black Radical Imagination.* Boston: Beacon.

Kipp, Darrell. 2002. Introduction to *How to Keep Your Language Alive: A Commonsense Approach to One-on-One Language Learning,* edited by Leanne Hinton, xiii–xviii. Berkeley: Heyday Books.

Lorde, Audre. 1992. *The Black Unicorn: Poems.* New York: W. W. Norton.

Lyons, Scott Richard. 2000. "Rhetorical Sovereignty: What Do American Indians Want from Writing?" *College Composition and Communication* 51 (3): 447–58.

MLA Committee on the Literatures of People of Color in the United States and Canada. 2005. Statement on Indigenous Languages of the World in the College and University Curriculum. Modern Language Association. http://www.mla.org/state ment_on_indigenous.

MLA Committee on the Literatures of People of Color in the United States and Canada. 2007. Statement on Indigenous Languages of the World in the College and University Curriculum. February 23–24. http://www.mla.org/statement_on_indigenous.

Powell, Malea D. 1999. "Blood and Scholarship: One Mixed-Blood's Story." In *Race, Rhetoric and Composition,* edited by Keith Gilyard, 1–16. New Hampshire: Boynton/ Cook.

Powell, Malea D. 2004. "Down by the River, or How Susan La Flesche Picotte Can Teach Us about Alliance as a Practice of Survivance." *College English* 67 (1): 38–60. http:// dx.doi.org/10.2307/4140724.

Powell, Malea D. 2012. "2012 CCC Chair's Address: Stories Take Place: A Performance in One Act." *College Composition and Communication* 64 (2): 383–406.

Sirc, Geoffrey. 2002. *English Composition as a Happening.* Logan: Utah State University Press.

Tehanetorens (Ray Fadden). 1999. *Wampum Belts of the Iroquois.* Summertown, TN: Book Publishing Company.

2Spirit Skillshare Toronto. 2010. http://2spiritskillshare.tumblr.com.

Vizenor, Gerald, ed. 2008. *Survivance: Narratives of Native Presence.* Lincoln: University of Nebraska.

Wallace, Paul. 1994. *White Roots of Peace: The Iroquois Book of Life.* Santa Fe: Clear Light.

Warrior, Robert. 1995. *Tribal Secrets: Recovering American Indian Intellectual Traditions.* Minneapolis: University of Minnesota.

Williams, Robert A. Jr. 1999. *Linking Arms Together: American Indian Treaty Visions of Law and Peace, 1600–1800.* New York: Routledge.

4

PERFORMING NAHUA RHETORICS FOR CIVIC ENGAGEMENT

Gabriela Raquel Ríos

I was in Kingsville, Texas, sitting with about four other master's students at the Texas A&M University-Kingsville (TAMUK) campus when I first discussed David Bartholomae's (1985) "Inventing the University." I hated it.[1] What concerned me about the article was the implicit assumption that the "university" is self-contained and that while students are essentially *forced* to "invent" the university, they are in practice only performing an act of mimesis: "What our beginning students need to learn is to *extend themselves* into the commonplaces, sets, phrases, rituals, gestures, habits of mind, tricks of persuasion, obligatory conclusions, and necessary connections that determine the 'what might be said' and constitute knowledge within the various branches of our academic community" (461). It concerned me even more to learn that this text was considered foundational to the field of rhetoric and composition, which I was just about to enter.

In order for you to get a better sense of the reasons it concerns me, you probably need to learn a little bit more about me. You probably need to know that I am a Chicana who grew up in Kingsville, Texas, "born and raised" in a city I have heard some refer to as "one big ghetto with a few rich ranchers holding it together." You also probably need to know I am what academics call *a first-gen student*, the first student in my immediate family to earn a college degree. And, you definitely need to know that my father used to drive my siblings and me up to the TAMUK campus every once in a while, past all the caliche roads that made up the driveways in my neighborhood, past three welfare housing projects—two of which are located across the street from the back of the TAMUK campus, right before the turn leading to University Boulevard, where the streets are paved and there is always construction going on. Social progress and upward mobility, I was also told, stem from universities like

DOI: 10.7330/9780874219968.c004

these. For this reason, my father would drive us all the way into the university campus, showing us the various buildings, encouraging us to one day graduate from the university he only briefly attended.

So, there I was, sitting in a classroom on that very campus where I had recently earned a bachelor's degree. For the first time, I was learning about how my professors saw me—how professors generally see students—and it didn't quite make sense to me at the time why a university, a space that, in my own experience, prided itself on being representative of diversity and community, would be founded on and complicit with the idea of hegemony implicit in Bartholomae's pedagogy.

It's important to note that for Bartholomae, inventing the university as a discursive gesture is not necessarily one that manifests as the physical space of the university. Nevertheless, as I have often struggled to "inhabit" the university (to appropriate its discourses), I have often found that the discourses we inhabit manifest materially as the literal spaces of the universities we inhabit. That single essay has haunted me ever since I first read it because I am reminded of it every time I struggle to rewrite my thoughts into "academese" (or at least into "proper English"), every time I step back to revise my behavior to meet academic expectations, and every time I see landscapers—often (im)migrant workers—working to tame and reshape the land the university is built on. And I am increasingly reminded of it as I read scholarship on spatial praxis (SP).

According to its department website, the School of Geography, Environment, and Earth Sciences at Victoria University of Wellington in New Zealand incorporates cultural geography, critical theory, postmodernism, cultural studies, and "Indigenous action-oriented approaches" into its study of the relationship between the social and the spatial. Rhetoric and composition has recently taken up this attention to spatial praxis as a means of understanding how knowledge is practiced and composed with regard to space and materiality. In what is being called the *material* or *corporeal turn* in our discipline, scholars have been building a body of work focused on the body—embodiment, to be more precise.

The move to the body, this particular work suggests, asks academics to consider the social production of space alongside the embodiment of social space. Disability rhetorics scholar Jay Dolmage (2012) has written and done research on spatial metaphors and disability in a manner that makes more explicit the physical manifestation of ableist discourses linked to the university. In a keynote address given at TAMUK, "Steep Steps, Retrofit and Universal Design: Spaces, Economies, and

Pedagogies of Disability in Higher Education," he argued that the steep-steps metaphor common to educators is at once figurative and literal. He began by describing the Jack K. Williams Administration Building on the TAMUK campus, which, like a Greek temple, was designed with iconic marble columns and a huge set of stairs leading to the entrance. The Williams building is positioned at the center of campus, with a long green and gray carpet leading up to the steps guarding its entrance. "You couldn't find a better example of the 'steep steps' to academia if you tried," he argued. Traditionally, these steps have been used to exclude particular kinds of bodies quite literally, but they have also been used as metaphors in much the same way: "The 'self' or 'selves' that have been projected upon the space of the university are not just able-bodied and 'normal,' but exceptional, *elite*. The university is the place for the very *able*" (4–5).

What's more, the move to the material and to spatial praxis also necessitates a move to service learning and civic engagement. The online rhetoric and composition journal *Kairos*'s call for its summer 2012 publication, for example, quotes Edward Soja speaking about scholarly approaches to the study of thirdspace, cautioning us to remember that we "must be additionally guided by some form of potentially emancipatory *praxis*, the translation of knowledge into action in a conscious—and consciously spatial—effort to improve the world in some significant way."

For example, in her influential book *Geographies of Writing*, Nedra Reynolds (2007) argues, "Material conceptions of space begin with the assertion so familiar in cultural and postmodern theories that space is socially constructed—and that identities are constructed as bodies move through the sociospatial world" (43). For Reynolds and many others, this movement begins with difference, particularly the "geography that difference makes" as bodies move through "the sociospatial world" (16). As such, a key figure in Reynolds's text is border theorist Gloria Anzaldúa (1987). According to Reynolds, Anzaldúa's work offers a tension between the borderlands as a metaphor and the borderlands as material spaces from which marginalized folks come to know that "freedom of movement is often necessary for survival" (36). However, as Terese Monberg (2008) points out, "Service learning's predominant assumption that 'change' only happens when we move across borders precludes the possibility that change can happen by moving recursively over time within the same space or dwelling" (27).

In addition, Reynolds has misread Anzaldúa's (1987) articulation of the borderland as a spatial metaphor. Rather than being "places where the silenced might be heard," the borderland is "una herida abierta where the Third World grates against the first and bleeds. And before a scab forms it hemorrhages again, the lifeblood of two worlds merging to form a third country, a border culture" (25). Anzaldúa means this quite literally. The borderlands *as physical spaces* bleed. Borderlands are not spaces of possibility inherently, nor are they spaces that function in the same way for *everyone* who inhabits them.[2] Borderland culture emerges out of particular embodied relationships to particular histories of particular land bases. What's more, though in English the concept of a borderland as embodied must be articulated through some kind of metaphor,

Anzaldúa resists the way in which these metaphors and discourses are taken up as immaterial in a strange binary opposition between "metaphor and materiality":

> I ponder the ways metaphor and symbol concretize the spirit and etherealize the body. The Writing is my whole life, it is my obsession. This vampire which is my talent does not suffer other suitors. Daily I court it, offer my neck to its teeth. This is the sacrifice that the act of creation requires, a blood sacrifice. For only through the body, through the pulling of flesh, can the human soul be transformed. And for images, words, stories to have this transformative power, they must arise from the human body— flesh and bone—and from the Earth's body—stone, sky, liquid, soil. This work, these images, piercing tongue or ear lobes with cactus needle, are my offerings, are my Aztecan blood sacrifices. (Anzaldúa 1987, 97)

For Anzaldúa the metaphor and the discursive are always-already material, *and* they are afforded material effect (particularly for Chican@s or Mexican-Americans). What's more, while, according to Reynolds, ecocomposition has focused on the relationships between writers and the "natural world" as isolated from the social realm, and geographies of writing concentrate on the "social" world as isolated from the "natural world," Anzaldúa was already challenging that bifurcation when she wrote *Borderlands* so many years ago.

The (mis)appropriation—whether explicit or implicit—of indigenous (embodied) knowledge in spatial praxis studies writ large calls for indigenous rhetorical sovereignty.

IN IXTLI IN YOLLOTL, SPATIAL PRAXIS, AND SOVEREIGNTY

The notion of sovereignty for indigenous peoples has been contested and reconfigured within a variety of discourses/practices, which manifest both outside and inside the academy. For Example, Robert Odawi Porter (2005) noted that indigenous sovereignty has been difficult to define on a global level because of the diverse situations in which indigenous people find themselves with respect to geographic location. Nevertheless, as Porter suggests, sovereignty for indigenous folks essentially means that indigenous peoples have the freedom to determine their past, present, and future. As an academic point of inquiry, sovereignty is sometimes construed as an "intellectual" enterprise, that is, "Indigenous intellectual sovereignty" (Turner 2006; Warrior 1995). Within my own position as a scholar of both indigenous studies and rhetoric and composition studies, Scott Lyons's work on rhetorical sovereignty becomes pivotal for understanding not only how indigenous notions of sovereignty emerge but also how the "inherent right and ability of peoples to determine their own communicative needs and desires in [the pursuit of self-determination], to decide for themselves the goals, modes, styles, and languages of public discourse" challenges rhetoric and composition to rethink how and what we teach as writing (Lyons 2000, 449).

I would like to extend Lyons's argument to say that I think rhetorical sovereignty asks us as scholars, and particularly scholars in the field of rhetoric and composition, to also radically rethink what we teach as rhetoric. In fact, Lyons's insistence that scholars understand rhetoric as praxis, along with his claim that indigenous rhetorical sovereignty is always linked to land and peoples, places his work in conversation with current work done on spatial praxis, including work that intersects with Anzaldúa's border theory. Here is where I would like to propose another kind of "move," one that centers indigeneity with respect to theoretical contributions on spatial praxis and civic engagement as an act of sovereignty.

I want to make this move for several reasons, one of which is that indigeneity is implicated in discussions about spatial praxis, primarily because of the influence the study of geography has on SP. Earlier I mentioned that scholarship on SP is influenced by "indigenous action-oriented approaches" to the study of the relationship between space and metaphor and materiality. However, the discussions about SP still come from a Western separation of humans and nature, from Western *relations* to specific spaces, and from Western notions of embodiment, civics, and citizenship. In addition, though Anzaldúa's work is central to discussions of SP in rhetoric and composition, the indigenous influence on her theory is hardly interrogated in current use or conversation. In short, a glaring gap in the scholarship stems from a larger problem of "unseeing" that Malea Powell has argued allows the discipline of rhetoric and composition studies in particular to "unsee" the "foundation of blood and bodies upon which it constitutes itself," which, in turn, "perpetuates the myth of the empty continent" (Powell 1999, 11). Ultimately, this scholarship keeps folks of color, and particularly indigenous folks and indigenous scholars, at the border or margins of scholarship. If we take indigenous scholarship seriously in a discussion of spatial praxis, however, it will question that very foundation, and it will make visible the blood and bodies that constitute what we mean by "civic" engagement, what theories we use to enact it, and how we define space. As an act of sovereignty, I want to reclaim this land that "was Indian always/and is/ and will be again" by centering discussion about the social relations of space and social justice on a philosophy and way of being indigenous to the continent: *in ixtli in yollotl* (Anzaldúa 1987, 113).

So, here is one of my contributions to SP scholarship, pedagogy, and practice. This is also a practice for me on a personal level. This is me practicing myself into history and into this very moment through rhetorics of survivance.[3]

There was once a famous Nahua thinker. His name was Nezahualcoyotl. He is considered the first Nahua philosopher because of his written work in the *Cantares Mexicanos* (Bierhorst 1985). However, Nezhualcoyotl documented what Mexicas[4] and other Nahuatl speakers had been practicing for years before the Spanish conquered Anahuac.[5] The concept of *in ixtli in yollotl* is something he learned while part of the Calmecac, which was a collective of people who gathered together to learn and pass on inherited wisdom.

In ixtli in yollotl is something that teachers or sages help the people to build. It translates literally as "a face a heart." *In ixtli in yollotl* is also an example of what Angel Maria Garibay (1978) calls a *difrasismo*. In his book *Llave Del Nahuatl*, he claims that the term *difrasismo* refers to the process by which two or more words are used together to signify a single meaning.[6] An English language example might be the phrase *bread and butter*, three words used together in a single phrase that signifies money or livelihood. Difrasismos are overwhelmingly common in Nahuatl language, in the songs/poems that constitute our knowledge or philosophies and in our rhetorics. Another common difrasismo associated with knowledge is *in xochitl in cuicatl*, or "the flower/the song." Together, the words *in xochitl in cuicatl* signify the arts. But, *in xochitl in cuicatl* is also a foundational philosophy for Nahua speakers. While many scholars study difrasismos in written texts, my friend, Manuel, who is a Native Nahua speaker and a linguist, has told me you can hear difrasismos. In fact, his thesis project was focused the use of difrasismos in "modern" Nahuatl spoken in his hometown in Tepecxitla, Vera Cruz. What this suggests to me is that difrasismos come together through practice. They are not necessarily set in stone. In other words, while *in xochitl in cuicatl* is a commonly used and recognized difrasismo, others can be and are (re)made. Some even go out of mode. For example, my Nahuatl tutor and friend (also from Tepecxitla), Eduardo, recognizes *in ixtli in yollotl* as a concept that "works" and is "very beautiful," but he had never heard of it before I brought it to his attention.

I want to refer back to a claim I made in the introduction regarding the use of indigenous rhetorics in the field of rhetoric and writing. A central concern for me as an indigenous (Chicana) scholar has been the problematic ways many Chican@s and others have taken in advancing a Nahua form of indigenous rhetoric because we have done so using primarily a Western frame of reference and because we exercise a Mestizaje hegemony over other indigenous peoples in Cemanahuac (Latin America) when articulating a Chican@ or Mestizaje rhetorical tradition.

In rhetoric and composition, we talk about how Nahua's "appealed" to certain colonial figures during the first waves of colonialism in Cemanahuac, or about how certain "tropes" can be analyzed in precolonial stories that have been written down in the *Cantares Mexicanos* or elsewhere. For example, in his article "On Rhetoric and the Precedents of Racism," Victor Villanueva (1999) argues that the Mexica used *in xochitl in cuicatl* to appeal to the Spanish because it was already an established mode of rhetorical inquiry and appeal that was based on five parts that were all parts of Greco-Roman rhetorical appeal: proemium, narratio, dispositio, refutatio, conclusio (646–47). Loosely translated, those concepts refer to an introduction, a narrative, a claim and counterclaim, and then a conclusion. While Villanueva's focus on Nahua rhetoric is poignant, I believe his articulation of Greco-Roman rhetorical appeals in relation to *in xochitl in cuicatl* potentially undermines the potential of Nahua forms of rhetoric. In addition, Villanueva is using this Western framework to discuss a moment of *in xochitl in cuicatl* in which Mexica people are arguing about the marked *difference* between their traditions and the traditions of the Spanish invaders:

> You have said that we do not know the lord-of-the-intimate-which surrounds-us, the one from whom the-heavens-and-the-earth come. You have said that our gods were not true gods. We respond that we are perturbed and hurt by what you say, because our progenitors never spoke this way. (quoted in Villanueva 1999, 646)

In xochitl in cuicatl is a mode of knowledge making (rhetoric) that is *different* from the Greco-Roman rhetorical appeal: *in xochitl in cuicatl* is performed and does not necessarily begin with any concrete matter at hand (dispositio). It is a way of building relationship with the earth in order to gain more self-knowledge, and it is performed through song and dance.

Difrasismos offer a way to think about knowledge and argument in terms of relationality, specifically the kind of relationality that emerges from a Nahuatl cosmology. The rhetorical value of difrasismos comes out of a relationship to materiality and embodiment enacted through performance. In other words, if we are to learn about *in xochitl in cuicatl* in a rhetoric and composition classroom, such an approach simultaneously posits the limits of writing as a mode of inquiry and suggests that students need to *perform* some form of art as a way of better understanding their relationship to the land they currently inhabit. It also suggests they will learn something about the world and society more generally through doing so, but it does not necessarily suggest *what* the students will or should learn. The only given in this process is that language practices are linked to knowledge about Nature and that we come to *in xochitl in cuicatl* with the understanding that we are related to all the living things that surround us. But, it also suggests that forms of art like songs are alive and are "active sites," as Kimberli Lee (2007) has argued regarding American Indian song making.

Similarly, as a difrasismo, *in ixtli in yollotl* applies to insight and to what it means to be a human being. In other words, Mexicas build in *ixtli in yollotl* as a process of becoming human. Yolanda Leyva (2003) has argued that it is the process by which we as a people build "humanizing love" for one another (15). I want to highlight two things here: (1) insight or knowledge is not only gained through the body, but the body is also constituted upon on this knowledge, and (2) building knowledge is always already a community-centered practice for Nahuas.

In ixtli in yollotl is a *practice*. While traditional rhetorical inquiry might have me look at texts like the *Cantares Mexicanos* in order to further develop what we might call a *Nahua rhetoric*, I want instead to talk about how my students and I attempt to practice *in ixtli in yollotl* in the classroom. *In ixtli in yollotl* (and all difrasismos) enact a kind of relationality I wish to practice with regard to how indigeneity is taken up in the academy. Knowledge is formed vis-á-vis *relationships*. In the remaining sections of this essay, I will talk about my experiences teaching *in ixtli yollotl* (what *in ixtli in yollotl* asks of me as a teacher) in the first-year writing (FYW) course Difficult Dialogues and Social Justice and about (to a lesser degree) my students' experiences in trying to practice *in ixtli in yollotl* through dialoguing about social justice.

PERFORMING *IN IXTLI IN YOLLOTL* IN THE FYW CLASSROOM: DIFFICULT DIALOGUES

I first began using *in ixtli in yollotl* as a rhetorical mode of inquiry in the classroom at Texas A&M University (TAMU), College Station. Though I attended a satellite school of the A&M system, my experience as both a student and teacher at TAMU was drastically different from my experience learning and teaching at TAMUK. Nevertheless, a lot of the institutional processes remained the same.

My students and I discussed issues regarding civic engagement: social justice, structural oppression, and difficult dialogues. At A&M, those of us teaching this special section of first-year writing were doing so with a grant from the Ford Foundation's Difficult Dialogues Initiative. We were encouraged to frame our courses around the notion of "civil" dialogues because "calling it difficult dialogues [would] make students feel like this is hard" and also because students should learn to understand difference though the practice of civility. Instead, with the support of my mentor, I stuck with the title Difficult Dialogues because we believed students needed to understand that having these discussions *is* difficult. In addition, civility has often been the mechanism by which social *in*justice has formed. Instead, I asked students to confront their own cultural logics with respect to difference. I asked them to think about and interrogate notions of civility and social justice with respect to how difference is constructed and how it might not be constructed.

The Western assumption, however, that space is a social realm disconnected from "nature" or the environment dematerializes space and presumes a dichotomy between humans and land/nature. The move that needs to happen, here, then, would be a potentially dangerous one if taken up in a reductive manner: indigenous notions of space do not place humans at the center of activity but instead place Nature there. In terms of spatial praxis, this means we must struggle to (re)consider the separation between metaphor and materiality with respect to space in a literal fashion. I chose to contain our discussions about space around experience and affect: we began with a question for inquiry based on a tentative premise that ideologies construct space even while space also influences the creation of ideologies by shifting the foundation (literally) of the spatial setting of our discussion from the United States to Anahuac.

In making this shift, I asked students to read about Nahua philosophy in Leyva's article and also in Miguel Leon-Portilla's (1990) *Aztec Thought and Culture*. Students were challenged to consider that, in the words of cartographer Mark Warhus (1997), there could "another America" existing within the space of the one constructed as the United States. This was not an exercise in going back in time so much as it was an exercise in understanding spatial praxis as constellated more generally. The concept of *in ixtli in yollotl* is still very much alive on this continent, and I am not the only indigenous scholar to use it (inside or outside of a classroom).

In the following sections, I mostly want to talk through some of the things I think are important for a teacher to consider when teaching *in ixtli in yollotl*, especially since this is the primary concept the *tlamantine*, or "wise people/teachers," were responsible for teaching students. In doing so, I'll share some poignant classroom moments, and I'll end with what I would do differently (or what I might consider to be "ideal" classroom situations for *in ixtli in yollotl*).

The Nahuatl word for teaching, *temachtiani*, means "one who makes others know something, to know what is on the earth" (Leon-Portilla 1990, 125). Teachers were responsible for playing five major roles: *teixtlamachtiani, teixcuitiana, tetezcahuani, tlayolpachivitia,* and *netlacaneco.* Ultimately, the teacher's role was to help people foster the attributes of these roles as phases of *in ixtli in yollotl*—developing a (wise) face/heart. *In ixtli in yollotl* is both what it means to acquire knowledge and what it means to be human. Human beings, according to the Nahua *tlamantine*, are responsible for formulating *in ixtli in yollotl*—for learning about the world around them in order to become fully human. *In ixtli in yollotl* also asks us to understand ourselves as relatives.

Teixtlamachtiani, which means "the one who gives knowledge, especially traditional knowledge to the faces of others," is a word that links the eyes with the face (Leyva 2003, 103). In Nahua culture, the face (or the countenance) of a person represents their humanity. Teachers were responsible for *teixcuitiana*, or "causing others to take face" by *tetezcahuani*, "putting a mirror in front of the faces of others" (Leon-Portilla 1990, 126). In doing so, teachers can *tlayolpachivitia*, "make others' hearts strong," and encourage *netlacaneco*, "humanizing love for all people and tempering relationships between people" (Leyva 2003, 103).

In Nahua culture, teachers are not responsible for lecturing or "dispensing" knowledge to students so much as they are responsible for guiding students in acquiring knowledge for themselves. As Leyva points out, "Most Indigenous learning was experimental and occurred in the course of 'doing work.' When the time came to learn specifics, general rules were given and a context was set up. However, each person chose the way and how much he or she would learn based on his or her own way of learning and doing" (97). In my own teaching experiences, enacting this framework has been difficult, not only because of the strict kinds of guidelines stipulated by university standards but also because students are not accustomed to learning in this fashion in Western institutions. In fact, learning in this way seems counterintuitive to most students I have taught, who typically see teachers who don't have a heavy hand in their learning process as "not doing anything." Additionally, enacting an indigenous pedagogy is difficult in a *writing* classroom because it also asks students to see writing as a politicized act that has as much potential for bad as it does for good. What's more, because writing classrooms are also rhetoric classrooms, an indigenous pedagogy asks students to decentralize writing as the primary mode of epistemic engagement. Indigenous peoples have historically used music, dance, theater, and other types of nontextual practices to make meaning, and we still do. Therefore, my students and I also aimed to compose nonalphabetic projects alongside writing projects.

Not all students were receptive to the aims of the course. In addition, it was not always easy for me to guide students in seeing themselves beyond their own terministic screens. Here is one scene of a classroom moment. In this scene, we had just finished discussing Eli Clare's (1999) "Freaks and Queers." In this piece, Clare offers a history of the words *freak* and *queer*. He talks about how these words have been used to exploit people of color, gender nonconforming people, peoples with disabilities, and people who simply did and do not fit the mold of normalcy advanced by dominant culture. But, he also talks about how people have used their "freak" status to resist oppression and exploit that same fear of and wonder about disabled folks by getting paid to perform in freak shows. The students used the moment to talk about how peoples with disabilities are treated in the workforce today. One student wouldn't have it.

Student 1: You see, now, this is ridiculous. I go over to the Taco Bell, and I see this little guy with some kind of disability, and he is an inspiration to me, and he should be to all of us! He makes no excuses for anything. And, I don't understand how one minute these people are crying about their disability and they want special treatment, but then the next they get all offended if you act like you notice they are different. The fact of the matter is that they should be grateful that they even have a job.

Student 2: Well, yea, but this one woman who worked over at the McDonald's—that is kind of messed up that the manager made her work the back just because she has a scar on her face.

Student 3: Weeeeelll, I mean can we really assume that he made her work the back just because she had this scar? And, should she really feel entitled to sue McDonald's? I mean, this is the problem with society today—entitlement.

Student 1: Exactly! Like I say, she should be lucky she even has a job. If her boss wants her to . . . I dunno, do jumping jacks . . . then by golly she should just do it. People have got all sorts of entitled feelings these days. Not to mention all the excuses they want to make. You know what, if you got a splotch on your face, then that's because god made you that way and how dare you try and complain about that!?

Eventually, that discussion became pretty heated, mostly fueled by student 1's insensitive comments about how lazy or entitled peoples with disabilities are. This conversation continued into the next class meeting, which involved a discussion about how Mexican migrant workers were being pathologized as migrants in terms of their "hyperabilities" as farm workers and their potential threat to the health and safety of US citizens.

Student 1 (same student): Ma'am, this may surprise you, but I am of the opinion that we should grant these Mexicans amnesty, and every farm owner I know is on my side. I agree with the people who this author apparently disagrees with. We need the Mexican workers, mam.

[he looks very directly at me at this point and tips his hat before continuing]

These Mexicans are good little workers, no doubt. Fact is, white folks just can't work as hard. I wish the Mexican-Americans could remember their roots instead of always making excuses for why they can't be civilized like the rest of us.

After this class, which he was *characteristically* twenty-four minutes late for, he came up to me ask for an extension on the paper due that day.

Student: Oh, you just don't even begin to understand the ordeals I've had to face. My girlfriend broke up with me, and I have two tests this week alone, and I am the new leader of my Bible Club . . ."

This was the third time this student has asked for an extension. I had tried subtle approaches to get him to see that what he was arguing in class might reflect more on his own behavior than on the people we were discussing. I saw this an opportunity to take a more direct approach for practicing *tetezcahuani,* for putting a mirror to his face:

Me: You know, those sound an awful lot like excuses to me.

[He stares at me in bewilderment]

Student: Are you kidding me?? I don't think you understand how busy I am.

Me: I'm a graduate student—I think I understand.

Student: [*chuckles*] No, ma'am, with all due respect . . . I was dumped. I had a *calculus* test this week *and* a . . .

Me: [*cutting him off*] I'm sorry. I have had all of five hours of sleep this week—this *entire* week. One of your classmates lost a relative this week, too, and they still got their paper in. These things happen to everyone—that doesn't mean that you get a free ride. It sounds an awful lot to me like you feel more entitled than the rest of us.

Student: [*looking utterly shocked*] I don't believe you are gonna understand me, ma'am.

That student never did see what I was trying to show him—or perhaps I didn't see what he was trying show me—but I also know the work teachers did in the Calmecacs was never intended to be complete in one sitting or even in one year. I also know that according to Nahua teaching philosophy, teachers are supposed to learn from their students just as much they learn from us. These lessons are ongoing.

But I recall this scene because it was a moment for me when I realized that what *tetezcahuani* required of me was *less* of me. Furthermore, *tetezcahuani* cannot be separated from *teixcuitiana* or any of the other attributes a teacher must *practice* in terms of helping all of us develop *in ixtli in yollotl*. I thought of my Nahuatl tutor, Eduardo, who often initially frustrated me because I felt as if he gave so little to our sessions. Eventually, I realized that while I thought he gave very little, he often followed my cues and gave me work to do based on what I wanted to do. Every lesson he asked, "What do you want to do today?" He never had a lesson plan that he handed to me or that we discussed in advance; we simply walked the streets of Zacatecas, working around whatever activity I wanted to do that day. I realized I had to let go and allow this student to explore what social justice might look like on his own terms. In the end, he chose to do a final project based on his new leadership role as a Christian leader in his "cell group." He wrote a sermon of sorts that was much more compassionate and kind than anything I had ever heard him argue in class. Does this mean he changed his mind? I'm not sure. I'm also not sure that using *in ixtli in yollotl* asks for that—what it does ask is that a teacher provide guidance and resources a student can use as they embark on their own journey, setting *their own* limits for what and how much they will learn with the only stipulation being that they understand knowledge is community based and embodied. (Social) justice is not blind or objective but is instead based on compassion.

In the end, using *in ixtli in yollotl* as a pedagogical framework helped me to be more generous with students who made comments that—to be blunt—pissed me off and hurt me. It helped me to realize that part of making others' hearts strong means making my own heart strong enough to recognize when students are giving as much as they possibly can give, even though it isn't what I am expecting or wanting. It also helped me to recognize my own misgivings and racist, ableist, and so forth, attitudes toward student behavior. But, in using *in xitli in yollotl* as a mode of inquiry in class, students were also able to advance a way of thinking that *they* argued was fundamentally opposed to traditional forms of rhetoric based on pure debate.

In ixtli in yollotl, students argued, forced them to think about each issue we raised in terms of humanizing love for society in a way that did not allow for blame to be placed on any individual. Though some students believed that in *ixtli in yollotl* was idealistic, they were intrigued and even perplexed by the idea that entire groups of people based their lives and forms of knowledge on this philosophy. What I am suggesting, then, is that using traditional forms of rhetorical inquiry, such as tropes, enthymemes, and even appeals can extend a form of analysis not concerned with making connections for civic engagement. Traditional rhetorical approaches for inquiry, in fact, often work to promote the "American" ideal of freedom that is counter to the aims of social justice or civic engagement. Interestingly, some students found *in ixtli in yollotl* to be oppressive because it forced people to monitor their behavior for the betterment of other people. In another class, a student who was a philosophy minor raised this concern regarding slavery: "Slavery was never really wrong—we just voted against it at a certain point, but there really wasn't anything inherently bad about it. We could easily have it back if we were all to agree on it." I asked this student what kinds of philosophical frameworks she was using to make this claim. She said she was borrowing from Machiavelli and Hobbes but that she was ultimately speaking from universal principles. I then challenged the idea that her thinking could be universalized, citing *in ixtli in yollotl* as a philosophical framework for understanding slavery. She was skeptical, to say the least: "I think that sounds like a communist attempt to control people. Slavery wasn't a bad thing, and it wasn't something based on hate or inhumanity. Lots of slave owners loved their slaves. But, I think freedom is a better framework for understanding slavery because it was wrong that we were not allowing people to be free when American culture is all about freedom." Another student then raised a question:

> If we use freedom as a framework, then couldn't you argue that not allowing people to enslave other people takes away from their freedoms? It makes more sense to me to use this concept of *in ixtli in yollotl* for social justice because at least it makes us really think about whether or not an argument someone is making is based on love. When we talked about the rhetorical

triangle and all that, we never really went anywhere with it other than to point out how people were trying to persuade us one way or another.

Implicit in that argument is also the idea that traditional rhetorical analyses are good for understanding the assumptions of a particular claim while *in ixtli yollotl* could add a different perspective that questions the extent to which our underlying assumptions are predicated upon relationality. In other words, *in ixtli in yollotl* asks us to think of ourselves as relatives. Or, as one student put it, "Before this class, I would always think about gay rights as issues, and I guess I was a little a homophobic, and I probably still am, I won't deny that. But I always thought I could separate that from the issue or argument at hand. But, *in ixtli in yollotl*—I mean thinking about this *as* a condition of the argument—made me realize that gay people are just human after all." In other words—*in ixtli in yollotl* calls the notion of objectivity into question, and it forces students to think of "issues" as embodied.

Generally, students found that traditional forms of rhetorics are more pragmatic and promote *political* change effectively; however, *in ixtli in yollotl* challenged their very notions of what justice is, and they found it to be more effective for enacting *social* change. But, as I have shown in this essay, our relations, our kin, include Nature and the rest of the cosmos. Civic engagement, then, must also include engaging with and learning from Nature, not as a thing disconnected from humans but as an origin for knowledge and for becoming fully human.

PERFORMING NAHUA RHETORICS IN RETROSPECT

As I have continued to rethink how this kind of course could work in a rhetoric and civic engagement classroom (or any classroom committed to dialogue on social justice or difficult dialoguing), I have shifted my approach to *teixcuitiana* and *tetezcahuani* (causing another to take face and holding a mirror to a student's face, respectively). I have found it more fruitful to have students interrogate power as it manifests in their everyday practices, giving rise to and being influenced by the discourse spaces they inhabit.

Currently, I am teaching and working in Orlando, Florida. Florida is home to many of the nation's migrant farmworkers, many of whom work the landscape of the local universities and community colleges here in the Sunshine State. A civic engagement course I am currently developing will (with the help of a grant) be held primarily in a local community garden owned by the Youth and Young Adult Network of the National Farm Worker Ministry (YAYA-Nwfm). Students will learn what I call *land-based literacies*, which include both the types of *skilled* labor farm-workers use every day as well the Nahua rhetorical theories that emerge from this land base. In this way, I hope students will learn to recognize and dismantle the structures that uphold the university's privileged status rather than simply "re"inventing them.

Notes
1. While I do not mean to disrespect Bartholomae or his work, this chapter's focus on spatial praxis requires me to engage the visceral, embodied discourses that emerge from the space/s I inhabit/ed.
2. Here, I make a distinction between Anzaldúa's primary and secondary audiences. While folks whose bodies are not marked by the Mexico-United States border can certainly relate to a lot of what Anzaldúa says, it would be irresponsible to assume that these folks can take up the concept of borderlands and borderland culture as part and parcel of how they negotiate their own identities.
3. Rhetorics of survivance is a concept Malea Powell has built alongside Gerald Vizenor's concept of survivance, which is a neologism constructed to capture the act of resisting and surviving at once. Rhetorics of survivance are tactics by which Native peoples make space for themselves by undermining and "tricking" dominant narratives.
4. *Mexica* is the term Nahuatl speakers from "Mesoamerica" use/d as an identity marker, though a more commonly known term is *Aztec*. I privilege the term used by the Nahuatl speakers themselves.
5. I use the Nahuatl name to refer to the land currently being called *Latin America*.
6. Though difrasismos are commonly recognized as being constructed of only two elements, there are some difrasismos that contain more than two root words.

References
Anzaldúa, Gloria. 1987. *Borderlands, La Frontera: The New Mestiza.* San Francisco: Aunt Lute Books.
Bartholomae, David. 1985. "Inventing the University." In *When a Writer Can't Write: Studies in Writer's Block and Other Composing-Process Problems,* edited by Mike Rose, 134–65. New York: Guilford.
Bierhorst, John. 1985. *Cantares Mexicanos: Songs of the Aztecs.* Stanford, CA: Stanford University Press.
Clare, Eli. 1999. *Exile and Pride: Disability, Queerness, and Liberation.* Cambridge: South End Press.
Dolmage, Jay. 2012. "Steep Steps, Retrofit and Universal Design: Spaces, Economies, and Pedagogies of Disability in Higher Education." Keynote address at Retrofitting English Studies: When Diversity Becomes an Afterthought Graduate Student Conference, Southwestern University English Department and English Graduate Student Association, College Station, TX, April 14.
Garibay, Angel Maria. 1978. *Llave del Nahuatl: Coleción de trozos clásicos, con gramática y vocabulario para utilidad de los principiantes.* Mexico City: Porrua.
Lee, Kimberli. 2007. "Heartspeak from the Spirit: Songs of John Trudell, Keith Secola, and Robbie Robertson." *SAIL* 19 (3): 89–114.
Leon-Portilla, Miguel. 1990. *Aztec Thought and Culture: A Study of the Ancient Nahuatl Mind.* Norman: University of Oklahoma Press.

Leyva, Yolanda. 2003. "*In Ixtli In Yollotl/*a Face a Heart: Listening to the Ancestors." *SAIL* 15 (3–4): 96–127.

Lyons, Scott. 2000. "Rhetorical Sovereignty: What Do American Indians Want from Writing?" *College Composition and Communication* 51 (3): 447–68.

Monberg, Terese. 2008. "Writing Home or Writing *As* the Community: Towards a Theory of Recursive Spatial Movement for Students of Color in Service-Learning Courses." *Reflections: A Journal of Public Rhetoric, Civic Writing, and Service Learning* 8 (3): 21–51.

Porter, Robert Odawi. 2005. *Sovereignty, Colonialism, and Indigenous Nations: A Reader.* Durham, NC: Carolina Academic Press.

Powell, Malea. 1999. "Blood and Scholarship: One Mixed-Blood's Story." In *Race, Rhetoric and Composition,* edited by Keith Gilyard, 1–16. Portsmouth, NH: Boynton/Cook-Heinemann.

Reynolds, Nedra. 2007. *Geographies of Writing: Inhabiting Places and Encountering Difference.* Carbondale: Southern Illinois University Press.

Turner, Dale Antony. 2006. *This is Not a Peace Pipe: Towards a Critical Indigenous Philosophy.* Toronto: University of Toronto Press.

Villanueva, Victor. 1999. "On Rhetoric and the Precedents of Racism." *College Composition and Communication* 50 (4): 645–61.

Warhus, Mark. 1997. *Another America: Native American Maps and the History of Our Land.* New York: St. Martin's.

Warrior, Robert. 1995. *Tribal Secrets: Recovering American Indian Intellectual Traditions.* Minneapolis: University of Minnesota Press.

5

UNLEARNING THE PICTURES IN OUR HEADS

Teaching the Cherokee Phoenix, Boudinot, and Cherokee History

Rose Gubele

Like eagle that Sunday morning
Over Salt River.[1] Circled in blue sky
In wind, swept our hearts clean
With sacred wings.
We see you, see ourselves and know
That we must take the utmost care
And kindness in all things.

—Joy Harjo 1990, 65

Driving through rural northwestern Missouri, I saw a large bird, its dark shape blurred by heat and road haze, sitting in the country road ahead of me. At first I assumed it was a raven, but as I approached, I realized it was far too large. As I came closer, I saw the bird's large round eyes, deep black-brown plumage, and golden talons. I put on the breaks as I realized I was looking at an eagle.[2] The bird lifted its head to look at me as I sat open mouthed, staring. I had seen pictures of eagles in books and images of them on nature shows, but I had never seen one in real life. Through the fog of awe, I realized the eagle had been eating road kill.[3] I was stunned despite the fact that I knew eagles ate carrion. Here was a bird that represented so much—ᎤᏬᎭᎵ (*wohali*), sacred bird to Cherokees, and a national symbol to the United States.[4] I could not imagine a creature so precious doing something that seemed so "profane."

The eagle turned and flew across the road, then up into the hazy sky, leaving me with much to ponder. After he[5] left, I wondered why I had been so shocked to see an eagle eating road kill. I realized I had fallen into the trap of romanticizing the birds. I had also forgotten the

DOI: 10.7330/9780874219968.c005

important truth that Harjo describes in "Eagle Poem," that we are all "born, and die soon within a/True circle of motion," a cycle of life and death that is sacred (Harjo 1990, 65). I saw ᏌᏈᏛ, and I saw myself; I realized that idealizing eagles had caused me to not see them as they really are. This saddened me because I understand how impossible it is to live up to a romanticized image.

So many people unintentionally do the same thing when they think of Native Americans. They romanticize us—we are the "noble savage," a representation of an idealized past. People who do this are not intentionally racist; in fact, they may be striving to achieve cross-cultural understanding. But when people don't see Indians as we really are, when they compare us to a media-perpetuated romantic image, it causes them to erase our existence and blind themselves to our realities. I find that, in my classrooms, the best way to dislodge idealized images of Indians is to show students "real" Indians, Indians who surprise them because they contradict stereotypical images with which students are familiar.

ᎠᎵᏍᎪᏗᏎ[6]

> *Our foremost plight is our transparency. People can tell just by looking at us what we want, what should be done to help us, how we feel, and what a 'real' Indian is really like. (Deloria 1969, 1)*

Since the time Standing Rock Lakota scholar Vine Deloria wrote *Custer Died for Your Sins*, many things have changed. Yet the above quote still holds resonance. The noble and ignoble savage[7] dichotomy still remains, and we are still made transparent because stereotypes cause people to make assumptions about us. But confronting stereotypes concerning Native Americans in the classroom is a difficult task for a variety of reasons. If students learn to recognize their own thinking as stereotypical, that realization creates a guilt reaction. Many people equate stereotypes with racism, and few people want to be perceived as racist.[8] So, in the classroom, I usually begin by explaining the history of the term *stereotype*.

The word *stereotypes* originally was used in the printing industry; the first modern usage of *stereotypes* was coined by Walter Lippmann, who used Plato's *Allegory of the Cave* to illustrate the distortion that can come from stereotypical images. Lippmann saw stereotypes as the "pictures in our heads" that we use out of necessity, noting that "there is economy in this. For the attempt to see all things freshly and in detail, rather than as types and generalities, is exhausting, and among busy affairs practically out of the question" (Lippmann 1922, 88). No one human being can possibly know everything about everyone, so stereotypes are the way our minds struggle to understand people and things we don't know personally. Thus stereotyping is a natural human activity. However, it is also harmful. Any stereotype, whether it is a positive one or negative one, presents a skewed image of reality.

Since Lippmann's time, the increase in technology has expanded our ability to communicate with each other. This expansion has created a greater potential for cross-cultural understanding but also the potential to widely disseminate stereotypes. The media images make it virtually impossible to completely evade stereotypes as well, so I tell students and others[9] they should not feel bad about their own stereotypical views. No one is immune to stereotypical thinking. Stereotypes can only be dislodged by reality, and if non-Native students have had little exposure to American Indians, they are bound to resort to stereotypes.

But dismantling stereotypes isn't always as simple as presenting students with "real" images of American Indians. Stereotypes are deeply ingrained in the modern psyche, and people believe them; they are easy as well, so many people are reluctant to forsake them. Moreover, many stereotypes are based, in part, on reality. Whenever students see Native people doing things that fit common stereotypes, the images in their minds are reinforced. Even the most respectful representations can reinforce stereotypes when they present students a one-sided view that distorts their image of contemporary Native people. So, the key is balance; students must be exposed to a variety of texts by Native people, but each text must be presented in context. So, the history surrounding Native texts, relevant cultural information, and discussions of sovereignty must accompany any classroom examination of an American Indian text.

ᏏᏯᏫᏂᏯᏂ[10]

> There is no neutral story, but instead many stories weighted with the implications of their time and place, the influences of the individual speaker-writer and listener-reader, and the way that race and culture are constructed and inscribed by all. The narratives we keep and tell shape our discursive practice, with material consequences. (King 2012, 211)

In classes, teaching students about stereotypes is linked to the process of teaching them critical skills they need to survive in the academy and beyond. I strive to help students achieve a critical consciousness, or using Paulo Freire's term, *conscientização*, "learning to perceive social, political, and economic contradictions, and to take action against the oppressive elements of reality" (Freire 1970, 19). This consciousness is achieved when a teacher uses dialogue that enables students to reach "a perception of their previous perception" (108). In order to do this, I begin by talking to my students and asking them questions. I listen to my students and let them listen to each other, and I do this without judgment. I find out what they think of American Indians, what they assume to be true, what they have learned, and where they have gained their knowledge. I don't correct them. In fact, I affirm their knowledge to a limited extent by acknowledging that the images are out there, so their assumptions are understandable.

I then begin a dialog. I tell my students that my perception of American Indians is different from theirs. I'm very careful to not qualify my perception as more accurate or "better" in any way, just as different. I speak from my own experiences of Native Americans I know, and we talk about the differences. The dialog is a crucial part of the process. I usually present a poem by an American Indian writer during this process as well. In the past, I've used "I Walk in the History of My People," by Chrystos.[11] I find this poem to be an excellent segue into a discussion of the relevance of history. In the poem, Chrystos carries her history with her, and though the wounds from the history are extremely painful, she is "still walking" (Chrystos 1988, 7). This poem is especially useful because it helps students become aware that our histories are filled with unspeakable trauma, and it does so without presenting Native Americans as victims. Even more important, the poem talks about the way our histories stay with us. Students have trouble understanding this idea at first, but I promise to show them more to support this notion.

I then move into a discussion of history in preparation for the introduction of a Cherokee text. As I prepare them, I talk generally about how we are all shaped by our histories. In the case of American Indians, our histories have shaped popular stereotypes. But contrary to the warlike stereotypical Indian of the American imagination, most tribes did whatever was necessary to survive during colonial times. Noted historian Ed Castillo argues that there were three main types of resistance to colonialism: "fight, flight, and accommodation" (Castillo 1991, 15), so it makes sense that written rhetorics would follow a similar pattern. But as Steve Brandon (2003) argues, "An American Indian literary canon seems to be emerging that strongly favors the literature of protest over the literature of accommodation, and this canon glosses over the many traditionalist/progressive struggles that have helped define Native identities" (161). It is for this reason that I introduce students to excerpts from the *Cherokee Phoenix*, a bilingual newspaper published by the Cherokee Nation before the Trail of Tears. The *Phoenix* was created, in part, to foster rhetorics opposing removal, so it is filled with protest rhetorics. However, the paper is also a part of an accommodationist strategy that was adopted by a segment of the Cherokee Nation. In addition, the editor of the *Phoenix*, Elias Boudinot, is a deeply controversial figure in history because he changed his stance and adopted a proremoval rhetoric, signed the Treaty of New Echota, which brought about the Trail of Tears, then was assassinated by members of his tribe for his crimes.

I provide students with excerpts from the *Cherokee Phoenix*, but before they read the texts, I give a lecture on Cherokee history before the Trail of Tears. I don't lecture students often, and when I do I always make my slides available outside of the classroom (my university uses Blackboard, and so I usually post them there). I also have a very open lecture style; I invite students to interrupt me and ask questions. In the following section I provide a brief overview of the historical context I provide for my students.

ᎠᏗᎡᏍᏗ[12]

In the early 1800s, through wars and treaties, the Cherokee lands had been reduced to about two hundred miles of territory, most of which were within the state of Georgia (Conley 2005). In the years between initial, prolonged contact with the British, the Cherokees, under pressure from the United States, had relinquished more than half of their original lands (Hudson 2006). But despite all the changes the Cherokees had undergone, and all the land cessions they had endured, the newly formed state of Georgia posed an ever-increasing threat.

Georgia possessed a colonial contract that entitled it to the land that now makes up Mississippi and Alabama. In 1802, the Georgia Compact was instituted. This resulted in negotiations between Georgia and the federal government; Georgia relinquished the claims to the lands in Mississippi and Alabama and fixed Georgia's state boundaries. As a part of the transaction, the federal government gave Georgia a cash settlement of over a million dollars, assumed some of its financial responsibilities, and promised to peacefully and quickly secure Cherokee lands that fell within Georgia's borders (Perdue 2005).

Conflict arose because the United States government claimed that it recognized Indian sovereignty although the contract it made with Georgia demonstrated that it didn't, in practice, honor Indian sovereignty. The US government continued to want peaceful negotiations with the Cherokees, so it devised a lottery to entice the Cherokees to sell their land, but many refused. Despite intertribal differences, there was one factor that most Cherokees agreed upon; they would not relinquish their homelands (Perdue 2005).

Georgia then began to apply pressure upon the US government in an effort to force compliance with its agreement to Indian removal. By the 1820s, many Cherokee leaders had conformed to European notions of civilization, though most Cherokee peoples remained traditional in their personal identities. The state of Georgia was against the civilizing policies of the US government, but many Cherokee leaders were literate in English, and Georgia found that this literacy made control of the Cherokee peoples difficult (Perdue 2005).

When the Cherokee Nation ratified its constitution in 1827, Georgia was outraged. The governor of the state saw the constitution as an affront because Cherokee homelands were defined within the constitution, and these lands fell within the boundaries of Georgia. The lands identified as Cherokee included the Tennessee River, which Georgians saw as important to their developing economy. In addition, the Cherokee Nation was declared sovereign in the constitution, a fact that clearly indicated that the Cherokees had no intention of either moving or submitting to Georgia's laws (Perdue 2005). At the same time the Cherokee constitution was ratified, a tribal newspaper was in the planning stages; this paper became the Cherokee Nation's battleground.

GWY ᏚᏓ ᎠᎤᎧᎩ [13]

As the struggles with Georgia were in process, leaders of the Cherokee Nation were making plans to use written rhetoric to resist removal. In 1825, the Cherokee Nation set aside funds for the publication of a national newspaper. Elias Boudinot[14] was selected to raise funds for the newspaper, and he began to tour the country, speaking to groups of Europeans about the progress Cherokees had made and how "civilized" they had become. Boudinot was later selected to edit the *Phoenix* (Littlefield and Parins 1984). Boudinot was a wise choice for editor. He had been educated at the Cornwall mission school, where he had learned Classical rhetoric. Boudinot was a product of historical factors, including the changes brought about by mission schools that had led to a political division in the Cherokee Nation (Brandon 2003). Mixed-blood Cherokees who favored assimilation, spoke English, and considered themselves "progressives" made up a fraction of the population,[15] while the majority of Cherokees were less likely to speak English and considered themselves "traditionalists." As a member of the middle-class elite, Boudinot had been exposed to European culture. He was a mixed-blood himself, though only about one-eighth white, and he identified as Cherokee.[16] Even so, his close association with Europeans made it possible for him to comprehend both cultural perspectives. Boudinot's comprehension of European audiences enabled him to apply appropriate rhetorics in an effort to sway them (Brandon 2003).

The revenue from Boudinot's lectures, combined with funds from the Cherokee Nation and funds from the American Board of Foreign Missions, was used to purchase equipment for the newspaper. Non-Native missionary and ally of the Cherokee Nation, Samuel Worcester, was called upon to assist Boudinot with the paper (Littlefield and Parins 1984). John Wheeler and Isaac Harris were hired as printers, and John Candy, a mixed-blood, served as Wheeler's apprentice. Wheeler and Harris were white, and neither could speak Cherokee. Still, the goal of the paper was to feature articles in both English and the Cherokee syllabary. Boudinot and Worcester handled most of the work with the syllabary while the printers struggled to learn Cherokee (Mooney 1992).

The *Phoenix* was four pages long and featured five columns on each page. In size, it measured twenty-one inches in length and fourteen inches in width (Awtrey 1941). It was a weekly paper and was initially available on Thursdays. However, on May 6, 1828, the paper's weekly publication date moved to Wednesdays due to difficulties with the postal service (Boudinot 1828).

The masthead for the newspaper was strikingly beautiful and featured an emblem with a phoenix rising from flames and the word *protection* stylistically positioned between the tips of the bird's wings (see figs. 5.1 and 5.2). Cherokee syllabary characters on either side of the emblem spelled out the phrase ᏣᎳᎩ ᏗᏗᎤᎭᎥᎿᎦ, which means *Tsalagi Asdeliski*, "Cherokee Phoenix," or, literally, "Cherokee, the resurrected one" (Mooney 1992). The *Phoenix* title came from a fundraising speech that Elias Boudinot had delivered to a European audience; in the speech Boudinot said, "The Indian must rise like the Phoenix after having wallowed for ages in ignorance and barbarity" (Boudinot 1996, 78–79).

The first issue of the *Phoenix* was published on Thursday, February 21, 1828 (see fig. 5.3). In that issue, Boudinot promised that the newspaper would contribute to the Cherokee Nation's attempt at civilization. He stated:

> We would now commit our feeble efforts to the good will and indulgence of the public, praying that God will attend them with his blessings, and

Figure 5.1. Original masthead for the Cherokee Phoenix, which was used from the first issue on February 21, 1828, throughout the first year of publication.

Figure 5.2. Detail of the central phoenix emblem on the masthead.

hoping for that happy period, when all the Indian tribes of America shall arise, Phoenix-like, from their ashes, and when the terms "Indian depredations," "war whoop," "scalping-knife," and the like, shall become obsolete, and forever be buried deep under ground.[17] (Boudinot 1828b, 3)

In the second issue, Boudinot also included a prospectus for the newspaper that provided further detail concerning the purpose of the *Phoenix*. The prospectus stated that the newspaper would publish

1. The laws and public documents of the Nation.

2. Account of the manners and customs of the Cherokees, and their progress in Education, Religion and the arts of civilized life; with such notices of other Indian tribes as our limited means of information will allow.

3. The principal interesting news of the day.

4. Miscellaneous articles, calculated to promote Literature, Civilization, and Religion among the Cherokees. (Boudinot 1828a, 3)

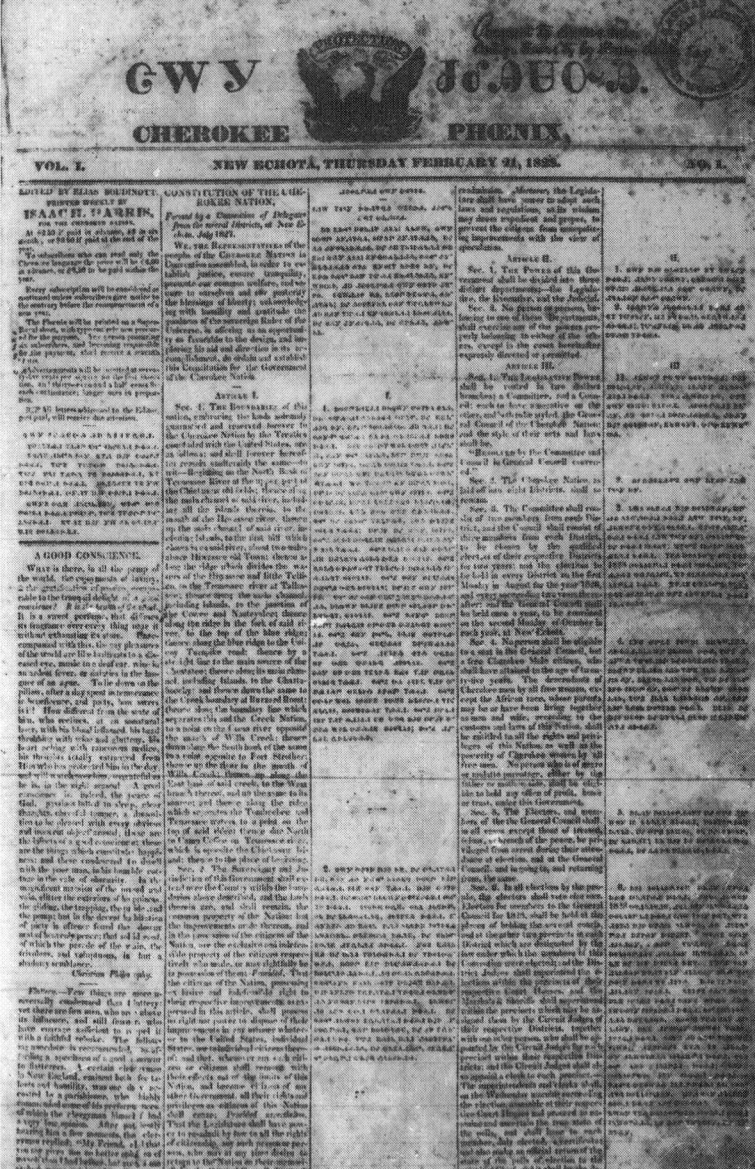

Figure 5.3. First page of the first issue of the Cherokee Phoenix, published in New Echota on Thursday, February 21, 1828.

Boudinot actively attempted to fulfill his promise, publishing the constitution and laws of the Nation, national news, poetry, explanations of the Cherokee syllabary, and translations of Bible verses and hymns.

While the first issue featured an equal amount of Cherokee and English, the Cherokee portions soon shrank considerably. The process of setting Cherokee text in the *Phoenix* was arduous because of the printers' lack of fluency in the language, so in the second issue, Boudinot promised to include only Cherokee translations of shorter English articles below the English text (Boudinot 1828a; 1828b).

The paper's greatest threat came from the mounting tension between the Cherokee Nation and its neighbors. Both Tennessee and Georgia, especially the latter, wanted the Cherokees to move out of their state boundaries. Since the *Cherokee Phoenix* was a symbol of the growing nationalism of the Cherokees, it was viewed as a threat by advocates of removal. In addition, the *Phoenix* often published articles opposing removal, and the newspaper helped foster support from anti-removal whites. Perhaps because of the growing antagonism, the newspaper's name was changed to *Cherokee Phoenix and Indians' Advocate* on February 11, 1829 (Malone 1950). The new masthead omitted the phoenix emblem.

In 1829, when gold was discovered in Cherokee lands that fell within Georgia's borders, the already intense pressure on the Cherokee Nation from hostile Georgians increased dramatically. Cherokees had to face a swarm of gold miners entering their lands. To make matters worse, the state of Georgia did nothing to stop the miners. In fact, it encouraged their actions (Malone 1950). Throughout this crisis, the *Cherokee Phoenix* published articles in favor of sovereignty and articles that condemned Georgians, even going so far as the call them "savages" (Boudinot 1829c).

In response, Georgia enacted a special legislative session, concluding that in 1830, Georgia laws would supersede all Cherokee laws (Malone 1950). Andrew Jackson had become president in 1828. Jackson passed the Indian Removal Act in 1830 and was by all accounts opposed to tribal sovereignty. Compounding the existing pressure upon the Cherokee Nation was Andrew Jackson's withdrawal of the Nation's annual annuity, a sum owed to the Cherokees as part of previous land cession agreements. The withholding of these funds created a desperate climate, especially for the *Cherokee Phoenix* (Perdue 1996).

The Cherokee Nation fought the state of Georgia both in the courts and in the pages of the *Phoenix*. The articles in the *Phoenix* helped the Nation gain support from whites; as a result of the increased support, court cases were often flooded with petitions from white supporters and missionaries. Soon, Boudinot began receiving threats because Georgians were displeased with the "unsavory" articles that appeared about them in the *Phoenix* (Malone 1950).

In 1832, Boudinot returned from his fund-raising tour. Something had happened to change his view on relocation, though it isn't clear what caused this shift. Boudinot's disillusionment led to his signing a petition in July of 1832 favoring removal. Boudinot's reversal resulted in his removal as editor of the *Phoenix*. On September 8, 1832, Boudinot was replaced by Elijah Hicks, Principal Chief of the Cherokee Nation, John Ross's brother-in-law (Malone 1950).

Although Hicks was against removal, he lacked Boudinot's abilities, experience, and rhetorical skill. The paper began to decline after Boudinot left, and Hicks experienced extreme pressure as the situation began to worsen in Georgia. President Jackson had also approved a lottery, and as a result, sections of Cherokee lands were given to whites, who invaded Cherokee territory freely. Finally, on May 31 of 1834, the last issue of the *Phoenix* was published. In it, Hicks said the paper would cease publication temporarily due to lack of funds and the editor's ill health (Malone 1950). The hiatus lasted until after the Trail of Tears.

Ᏺ[18]

Many scholars view the *Phoenix* as a surrender in the sense that they see it as an example of cultural assimilation. Hugh R. Awtrey, for example, in blatantly racist language, calls the story of the *Phoenix* "the record of a people raised in a scant decade, by its own intellectual bootstraps, from unlettered savagery" (Awtrey 1941, 1). Theda Perdue, though she doesn't display the prejudice apparent in Awtrey's account, sees the *Phoenix* in similar terms. She argues that "for many native peoples, physical survival has seemed to dictate cultural destruction" (Perdue 1996, 3). Such views position Cherokees in the role of victims of a much larger force, a force they couldn't hope to resist. The *Phoenix* is then reduced to a well-crafted, but ultimately feeble and childlike, attempt at "playing" rhetorician.

However, I argue that the *Phoenix* is much more than that. The paper itself was indeed an act of accommodation, but the accommodation was limited. While Boudinot primarily used English to write his editorials, and the European printing press was used, the ideas he expressed were Cherokee. The Cherokee syllabary was also used, and this made the newspaper unique and "exotic" to Europeans. Boudinot used that exoticism to the Nation's advantage, spreading the word and gaining allies from outside the Cherokee Nation. The paper was a trickster-like way to use the oppressors' tools to combat the oppressors.

As many Native scholars have argued, American Indian writers use trickster tactics in their writing. Trickster discourse is a decolonizing strategy that works subversively. Malea Powell argues that trickster discourse contains the potential to "open space for counter-stories and resistance" (Powell 1999, 8). In order to understand trickster discourse, it is important to examine the ways in which trickster characters appear in American Indian stories. The trickster is a figure that appears in the stories of many tribes. Craig S. Womack observes that "in Creek tradition, the trickster is often the little guy using his wit to overcome a larger, predominant force" (Womack 1999, 152). He is "irrepressible"; he "provides Indian people with road maps for survival in the face of oppression" (162). In addition, as Jace Weaver points out, the trickster assumes "many guises," the most commonly recognized of which is coyote, but whatever guise is assumed, trickster "is a breaker of barriers and an eraser of boundaries" (Weaver 2001, 247–48). Tricksters in most Native societies are represented by animals able to live on the boundaries of human settlements (Weaver 2001). They elude human traps, invade human homes, and play tricks. They are survivors. Trickster walks the borderland, the liminal area in between, and calls it home. The tactics of a trickster are subversive. Tricksters lie, but their lies contain an element of truth, a fiction that reaches the heart of the matter, revealing something people refuse to see about themselves. Thus tricksters aren't all positive; they can destroy, tear down, when necessary. Though many see trickster as a creator, the late Vine Deloria saw the trickster as a "transformer" who brings on "periodic renewal" by purging the old, and forming "order out of chaos" (Deloria 1999, 25–26).

Because of their ability to shapeshift, tricksters are as arbitrary and changeable as language. As Gerald Vizenor points out, in discourse, the trickster is "a comic holotrope, and a sign in a language game" (Vizenor 1989, 187). Trickster discourse "is comic nature in a language game, not a real person or 'being' in an ontological sense" (Vizenor 1988, x). Language play is the signature of trickster discourse, but the play has a serious purpose that carries transformative power. The games trickster uses to communicate messages are often humorous. Because tricksters point out contradictions, Vizenor describes trickster narratives as "ironic survivance" (Vizenor 1994, 170).

It is, of course, difficult to determine Boudinot's intentions with regard to the *Phoenix*. He appeared to favor accommodation. However, as

Womack points out, "Disguises are necessary against an enemy with more power—one cannot win by means of brawn, so more subversive methods are employed" (Womack 1999, 152), and evidence suggests Boudinot was using the paper in subversive ways. The way he transformed the word *savage* in the paper by identifying Georgians who committed criminal acts against Cherokees as "white savages" is exactly the kind of language trick often used by those who employ trickster discourse.

Even the masthead and name of the *Phoenix* have tricksterish overtones. The phoenix symbol would give Europeans the impression that Cherokees had adopted a European myth, but to Cherokees, the masthead meant something more spiritual. Rennard Strickland claims that the selection of the phoenix as the emblem for the paper was fitting. He writes:

> The power of that ancient mythical bird who was consumed by fire and arose from his own ashes seems to be inborn in the soul of the Cherokee people. There is an eternal flame of the Cherokees—a fire so carefully guarded that it has continued to burn for them through forcible removal, civil war, and tribal dissolution. According to the ancient legend, as long as that fire burns, the Cherokees will survive. (Strickland 1975, 3)

My position is that the emblem of the phoenix rising out of the fire doesn't represent a Nation that sold out; it is a depiction of the meaning of the name of the Cherokee Nation, the "wise ones," the "possessors of the divine fire" (Weaver 1997, viii).[19]

Therefore, the *Cherokee Phoenix*, and all material from it, is an excellent example of accommodationist rhetorics and protest rhetorics. But Boudinot himself is an even more complex figure. Because he was such a superb rhetorician, Boudinot's rhetoric has been the focus of many of the studies of the *Cherokee Phoenix*. Boudinot was skilled in European rhetoric, but he was also very trickster-like. As Theda Perdue points out, Boudinot was careful to present only what he thought the white audience should hear in his efforts to persuade them; he even resorted to misleading the white audience by exaggerating Cherokee progress toward European notions of civilization (Perdue 1977). This manipulation is consistent with trickster tactics.

But Boudinot is also a confusing and complex figure because of his role in the removal; his change of position has been the topic of controversy. In 1887, George E. Foster argued that Boudinot had good intentions. Foster uses Boudinot's previous experiences to prove his intent must have been for the good. He writes:

> Whether he and his comrades did betray their countrymen for gain cannot now be determined, but it hardly appears possible that one who had

served his people so faithfully should at the late day have done so with traitorous intent. Indeed, a careful reader of history must feel that, while Boudinot acted not according to the will of the many, that he did what he thought to be for their future welfare. . . . Let the mantle of charity surround his memory; let us not believe him a traitor to the people whom he had so long served; let us revere his memory for the great work he performed. (Foster 1887, 67–68)

Theda Perdue takes an opposite approach, reading all of Boudinot's deeds as assimilationist. She argues that "throughout his life, Boudinot maintained that the preservation of his people depended solely upon abandonment of their own traditions, culture, and history" (Perdue 1996, 3). Bethany Schneider takes a different tack, arguing that Boudinot strove to redefine sovereignty in order to save the Cherokee Nation; to do so, he attempted to separate the idea of sovereignty from the land (Schneider 2008). Steve Brandon suggests that Boudinot's trickster-like nature, which helped make him a good rhetorician, also became his downfall. Brandon notes that Boudinot's Cherokee name, Galagina, which means "the Buck," is a clue to his motivation. Brandon elaborates, noting that the Deer does serve the role of a trickster in some traditional stories; in one story, the Deer even tricks Rabbit, the main trickster figure. Brandon suggests that Boudinot identified with tricksters because of his name, masking his true identity in an effort to fool Europeans. But, as Brandon cautions, "Tricksters are dangerous creatures with whom to identify" (Brandon 2003, 174). In the end, Boudinot's own hubris led him to attempt to make choices for his people, even ones that went against their wishes.

Whatever the reason for Boudinot's switch, he clearly made mistakes. Boudinot went on to become an infamous historical figure because he signed the Treaty of New Echota on December 29, 1835. The treaty, often called the *Minority Treaty* because it was endorsed only by a small number of middle-class Cherokees, allowed the United States to remove the Cherokees to the West (Perdue 1996). After the Treaty of New Echota was ratified, a petition was signed by fifteen thousand antiremoval Cherokees in an attempt to stop the Senate from ratifying the treaty; the petition was unsuccessful, and the treaty was authorized in 1836. The Treaty of New Echota allowed for the forced removal of the Cherokee Nation in 1838 (Perdue 1996). Boudinot is an ideal example to provide for students because he demonstrates all three kinds of resistance—fight, flight and accommodation—and he is an historical figure who resists stereotypes because he is so very human.

ᏞᎰᎭᏉᎤᎥᎠᎬ[20]

> *A study of almost any topic dealing with Natives involves a look at history. A discussion of the cycles of history is imperative to students' understanding that history is often an author's creation of stories of past events. (Mihesuah 2003, 467–68)*

History is often messy, and Boudinot's story illustrates that reality vividly. In the classroom, I discuss Boudinot's impacts, both positive and negative, on the Cherokee Nation. Students are at first confused by Boudinot because of his dramatic change to proremoval. They want to find a reason for his actions. But history doesn't provide them with clean, simple answers. The complexity of Boudinot's story helps convey some of the difficulties every contemporary Native in the academy must face. Boudinot, because of his notoriety, was seen as a representative of his tribe. But he was a very real human being with human strengths, fears, and weaknesses. Students expect me to have an answer that satisfies them, but I do not. I leave them with more questions than answers. In this unsettled atmosphere, we read Jace Weaver's (2001) chapter "Trickster: The Sacred Fool" in *Other Words: American Indian Literature, Law, and Culture* and Malea Powell's (1999) discussion of trickster discourse in "Blood and Scholarship: One Mixed-Blood's Story."

After we discuss trickster discourse, I introduce students to excerpts from the *Cherokee Phoenix*. The issues of the *Cherokee Phoenix* that were published prior to the forced removal contain many articles filled with linguistic trickster turns. I present students with an article from a December 16, 1829, issue of the *Phoenix* entitled "Savage Hostilities." In this article, Boudinot[21] writes that there were three incidents in which "parties of whites from Georgia" engaged in "savage hostilities" toward Indians (Boudinot 1829c, 3). Students read and analyze this article. I ask students to comment on the article's language, and at least one student always comments on the use of the word *savage* in the article. I ask students what the use of this word means, and we begin discussing the way the term has been used against Indians. I don't tell students the answers; I let them discover them. As we discuss this piece, I remind them of bits of history. Because of his writings, Boudinot began to receive death threats, and by 1832, he changed his position on the removal question (Perdue 1996, 25). Students begin to see Boudinot's sudden change in a different way. They begin to see him as a wannabe trickster who masterfully used language but who ended up becoming too prideful, believing he knew what was best for his community.

We go on to examine other editorials from the *Phoenix* that used similar language. One issue describes "savage whites who have outstripped the Indians in deeds of blood" (Boudinot 1829b, 2). Yet another issue includes the following statement: "It is not the Indians that are so savage, quarrelsome and such lovers of blood. It is the whites who reside near them that are merciless and cruel. It is their meanness of spirit which causes in most instances what is termed the 'Indian Outrages'— their skill in getting from the red man all he has that is valuable for a mere song" (Boudinot 1829a, 2). In the process of our discussions, students come to realize that this rhetoric served two purposes. First, it reversed the meaning of the term *savage*, a term that had been used against Cherokees and other Indians. It separated the term *savage* from *Indian*, whereas previously many whites had considered the two terms synonymous. This strategy was vitally important, especially for gaining support from antiremoval whites. The message was clear: any "civilized" person should defend the Cherokees' right to sovereignty. Second, the use of the term *savage* derided Georgians, implying that they were less civilized than Cherokees. Boudinot redefined savage as a state of being. According to this definition, Indians are not inherently savage. Instead, those who love violence and intentionally do harm to others, whatever their race, are savages. Thus whites can be, and often are, savages by this definition.

All of these instances include the juxtaposition of white expectations of savagery against the actual actions of whites and their hostilities toward Indians. This act of conflating two opposing views of *savage* uses "dominant discourse" to position Cherokees not just as "victim[s] subject to it" but as "subject[s] within it" (Powell 1999, 425). In effect, these articles use the language of the oppressors and turn it back against them. In doing so, the true motives of the whites are exposed. As one article states, "But we again put it to the good sense of the public, who have the best claim to be protected from savages, the frontier whites or the Cherokees? . . . Since Gold has been discovered in this nation, a very strong incentive for intrusions has been offered to the frontier inhabitants of Georgia. We understand several hundreds of these people are now busily at work, digging for Gold on the sources of the High Tower River" (Boudinot 1830, 2). Thus, the notion of Indian savagery is exposed as an excuse, an insidious ploy to justify greed and outright theft.

I present the *Phoenix* as a battleground. I do not consider this war to be one that was lost. It was a rhetorical battle that didn't prove effective in the way it was intended, but it did produce positive results. The importance of history lies in its impact on the present, so I like to show students how the *Phoenix* changed the Nation. As Devon Mihesuah reminds us, "We have to talk about the realities of life and not just teach history, for example, as if everything happened in a vacuum and no longer relates to the present" (Mihesuah 2006, 136). I explain what happened after the Trail of Tears and tell the students that the newspaper is currently being published by the Cherokee Nation of Oklahoma. I then exhibit current issues of the paper. Typically, students are, at first, surprised to see the paper is still in circulation. Because of the *Cherokee Phoenix*, Cherokees are seen by non-Indians and by other Indian groups as "the Indians who write." It sets Cherokees apart from other tribes because the popular stereotype of the Indian warrior hunting buffalo and living in a tipi doesn't fit with the Cherokee scribe image. Every element of the story of Boudinot and the *Phoenix* defies stereotypes. Boudinot is not a noble savage. He spoke against savagery, and his actions are often far from noble. Yet he was able to create a newspaper that fostered National pride, and it has been a constant, apart from a few gaps during times of upheaval in the Cherokee Nation.

ᏅᎥᏗᎦ ᎦᏬᏯ[22]

Although the eagle sighting I describe in the introduction of this piece was my first, I have been blessed with many more. I live in the country in an area that has many small waterways and ponds. I imagine eagles nest here because of the low population density and the plentiful food supply (many of the ponds have fish). They are my sacred neighbors, and I have made it my goal to get to know them. I have done all I can to not just read about them but to watch them (a delightful task). In the air, they are graceful and awesome flyers. There is nothing more beautiful than an eagle in flight. But I also watch them eating roadkill because that is a part of who they are. Now, they are more than sacred to me. They are real. They are not separated from me by some imagined glass case, but are right here, right now. The more I understand them, the more I respect and honor them.

It is my hope that I can foster the same kind of understanding in my students. I hope they will be awakened by learning about Indians who do very human things that contradict stereotypes and idealized images and that they will begin to see us as human beings, not as noble images of the past.

Notes

1. Harjo doesn't specify whether she saw a golden or bald eagle, but the Salt River area is a nesting site for bald eagles, so it is possible that the eagle described in the poem is a bald eagle (Corman and Wise-Gervais 2005).

2. At the time, I didn't know much about eagles, but I had the idea that it was probably a bald eagle because I didn't see a golden band of feathers on the back of its head (which a golden eagle would have had). I later found out my assessment was accurate. Young bald eagles often look similar to golden eagles; they range in color from solid dark brown to mottled brown and white. Bald eagles take five years to mature, and it isn't until they reach maturity that they develop their characteristic white head and tail feathers (US Fish and Wildlife Service 2007).

3. Although bald eagles are well known to be expert fishers, they also will eat small mammals and carrion (US Fish and Wildlife Service 2007).

4. I was later able to confirm that this eagle was a young bald eagle because I noticed the eagle's legs were almost completely featherless. Golden eagles have feathers down their legs, but bald eagles only have feathers at the tops (US Fish and Wildlife Service 2007).

5. Though there is no way to know for certain, the eagle was probably male. Female bald eagles are larger than males, and this one was small in comparison to many I have seen since then.

6. ᎠᎵᏍᎪᎵᏍ means *golisdiyi,* "understanding."

7. See Berkhofer 1979.

8. The racism that exists in post-civil rights movement America can best be described as a *new racism,* or *color-blind racism.* For more information on this, see Bonilla-Silva 2002, McPhail 2002, and Villanueva 2006.

9. By "others" I mean all other people who are not students, including professors, friends, and other American Indian people, all of whom can believe stereotypes about American Indians.

10. ᎠᎵᏪᎯᏙᎸᎢ means *nulitanidolv,* "history."

11. See Chrystos 1988.

12. ᎠᏗᎶᏫᏗ means *adisvsdi,* "struggle."

13. ᏣᎳᎩ ᏗᏣᎦᏚᎣᎯ: means *Tsalagi Asdeliski,* "*Cherokee Phoenix.*"

14. Boudinot's Cherokee name was ᎦᎳᎩᎾ, or Galagina, which means "buck" (Malone 1950). The spelling of his name is questionable. Boudinot's name appeared as *Boudinott* in the first issue of the *Phoenix* but as *Boudinot* in all following issues.

15. Of course, the division wasn't cleanly split along racial lines. There were full bloods who learned English and mixed bloods who remained traditional. But the vast majority of full bloods called themselves traditionalist, and mixed bloods were more likely to be progressives (Brandon 2003).

16. Boudinot's great-grandfather was Scottish (Gaul 2005, 69n18).

17. The excerpt here was unsigned in the English version of the text, but I am attributing it to Boudinot because in the Cherokee syllabary version that follows it, the signature ᎠᏴ ᎦᎳᎩᎾ (*Ayv Galagina,* "I Buck") follows the text. Boudinot's Cherokee name was Galagina.

18. ᏥᏍᏚ means *tsisdu,* "rabbit," the Cherokee trickster.

19. There is a debate about the history and meaning of the term *Cherokee.* It is not a word Cherokees used to describe themselves; the name used prior to contact was Ani Yun Wiya, which means "principal or real people" (Mooney 1992). At one time, there were as many as fifty ways to spell the word *Cherokee* (182). Some scholars believe the word came from a Choctaw word indicating that Cherokees lived in a land filled with caves (Mooney 1992). Others argue that the name comes from "the Muskogean word

tciloki, which means 'people of different speech'" (Mankiller and Wallis 1993, 17). The meaning of the word I'm referencing here comes from Cherokee scholar Jace Weaver, who writes, "The name Cherokee may derive from cheera tahge, the term for wise ones, meaning 'possessors of the divine fire'" (Weaver 2001, viii). I'm using Weaver's definition here because, whether or not it is the "correct" origin of the word, the meaning is truer to the national consciousness of Cherokee people.

20.   ᏞᏃᏛᎤᎥᎬᎢ means *dadeyohvsgv,* "teaching."

21.   This article is unsigned, but Boudinot was responsible for writing most of the editorials in the *Phoenix,* so most scholars assume he is the author of all unsigned *Phoenix* articles.

22.   ᎤᎥᎫᏋ ᎾᎣᎯ means *udohiyu nasgi,* "real."

References

Awtrey, Hugh R. 1941. *New Echota: Birthplace of the American Indian Press.* Washington, DC: United States Department of the Interior. National Park Service.

Berkhofer, Robert, Jr. 1979. *The White Man's Indian: Images of the American Indian from Columbus to the Present.* New York: Vintage.

Bonilla-Silva, Eduardo. 2002. "The Linguistics of Color Blind Racism: How to Talk Nasty about Blacks without Sounding 'Racist.'" *Critical Sociology* 28 (1–2): 41–64. http://dx.doi.org/10.1177/08969205020280010501.

Boudinot, Elias. 1828a. "Prospectus." *Cherokee Phoenix,* Feb. 28.

Boudinot, Elias. 1828b. "To the Public." *Cherokee Phoenix,* Feb. 21.

Boudinot, Elias. 1829a. "Indians and the Outrages." *Cherokee Phoenix and Indians' Advocate,* Sep. 23.

Boudinot, Elias. 1829b. "Indian/White Conflict." *Cherokee Phoenix and Indians' Advocate,* Aug. 5.

Boudinot, Elias. 1829c. "Savage Hostilities." *Cherokee Phoenix and Indians' Advocate,* Dec. 16.

Boudinot, Elias. 1830. "Intruders on Cherokee Lands." *Cherokee Phoenix and Indians' Advocate,* Feb. 24.

Boudinot, Elias. (1983) 1996. "An Address to the Whites." In *Cherokee Editor: The Writings of Elias Boudinot,* edited by Theda Perdue, 67–83. Athens: University of Georgia Press.

Brandon, Stephen. 2003. "Sacred Fire and Sovereign Rhetorics: Cherokee Literacy and Literature in the Cherokee and American Nations, 1760–1841." PhD diss., University of North Carolina, Greensboro.

Castillo, Edward D. 1991. "Review of *Dances with Wolves* by Kevin Costner: Jim Wilson." *Film Quarterly* 44 (4): 14–23. http://dx.doi.org/10.2307/1212760.

Chrystos. 1988. *Not Vanishing.* Vancouver, BC: Press Gang.

Conley, Robert J. 2005. *The Cherokee Nation: A History.* Albuquerque: University of New Mexico Press.

Corman, Troy E., and Cathryn Wise-Gervais. 2005. *Arizona Breeding Bird Atlas.* Albuquerque: University of New Mexico Press.

Deloria, Vine Jr. 1969. *Custer Died for Your Sins: An Indian Manifesto.* New York: Macmillan.

Deloria, Vine Jr. 1999. "The Trickster and the Messiah." In *Spirit and Reason: The Vine Deloria, Jr., Reader,* edited by Barbara Deloria, Kristen Foehner, and Sam Scinta, 17–31. Golden, CO: Fulcrum.

Foster, George E. 1887. "Journalism among the Cherokee Indians." *Magazine of American History* 18 (1–5): 65–70.

Gaul, Theresa Strouth. 2005. Introduction to *To Marry an Indian: The Marriage of Harriett Gold and Elias Boudinot in Letters, 1823–1839,* edited by Theresa Strouth Gaul, 1–76. Chapel Hill: University of North Carolina Press.

Harjo, Joy. 1990. *In Mad Love and War.* Middletown, CT: Wesleyan University Press.

Hudson, Angela Pulley. 2006. "'Forked Justice': Elias Boudinot, the US Constitution, and Cherokee Removal." In *American Indian Rhetorics of Survivance: Word Medicine, Word Magic*, edited by Ernest Stromberg, 50–65. Pittsburgh: University of Pittsburgh Press.

King, Lisa. 2012. "Rhetorical Sovereignty and Rhetorical Alliance in the Writing Classroom: Using American Indian Texts." *Pedagogy* 12 (2): 209–33. http://dx.doi.org/10.1215/15314200-1503568.

Lippmann, Walter. 1922. *Public Opinion*. New York: Macmillan.

Littlefield, Daniel F. Jr., and James W. Parins. 1984. *American Indian and Alaska Native Newspapers and Periodicals, 1826–1924*. Vol. 1. Westport, CT: Greenwood.

Malone, Henry T. 1950. "The Cherokee Phoenix: Supreme Expression of Cherokee Nationalism." *Georgia Historical Quarterly* 34 (3): 163–88.

Mankiller, Wilma, and Michael Wallis. 1993. *Mankiller: A Chief and Her People*. New York: St. Martin's.

McPhail, Mark Lawrence. 2002. *Rhetoric of Race Revisited: Reparations or Separation?* Lanham, MD: Rowman & Littlefield.

Mihesuah, Devon A. 2003. "Basic Empowering Strategies for the Classroom." *American Indian Quarterly* 27 (1/2): 459–78. http://dx.doi.org/10.1353/aiq.2004.0068.

Mihesuah, Devon A. 2006. "'Indigenizing the Academy': Keynote Talk at the Sixth Annual American Indian Studies Consortium Conference, Arizona State University, February 10–11, 2005." *Wicazo Sa Review* 21 (1): 127–38. http://dx.doi.org/10.1353/wic.2006.0008.

Mooney, James. (1891) 1992. *James Mooney's History, Myths, and Sacred Formulas of the Cherokees*. Asheville, NC: Historical Images.

Perdue, Theda. 1977. "Rising from the Ashes: The *Cherokee Phoenix* as an Ethnohistorical Source." *Ethnohistory)* 24 (3): 207–18. http://dx.doi.org/10.2307/481695.

Perdue, Theda, ed. (1983) 1996. *Cherokee Editor: The Writings of Elias Boudinot*. Athens: University of Georgia Press.

Perdue, Theda. 2005. *Cherokee Removal: A Brief History with Documents*. 2nd ed. Boston: Bedford/St. Martin's.

Powell, Malea D. 1999. "Blood and Scholarship: One Mixed-Blood's Story." In *Race, Rhetoric, and Composition*, edited by Keith Gilyard, 1–16. Portsmouth, NH: Heinemann.

Schneider, Bethany. 2008. "Boudinot's Change: Boudinot, Emerson, and Ross on Cherokee Removal." *ELH* 75 (1): 151–77. http://dx.doi.org/10.1353/elh.2008.0008.

Strickland, Rennard. 1975. *Fire and the Spirits: Cherokee Law from Clan to Court*. Norman: University of Oklahoma Press.

US Fish and Wildlife Service. 2007. "Bald Eagle: Haliaeetus Leucocephalus." http://ecos.fws.gov/speciesProfile/profile/speciesProfile?spcode=B008

Villanueva, Victor Jr. 2006. "Blind: Talking about the New Racism." *Writing Center Journal* 26 (1): 3–19.

Vizenor, Gerald Robert. 1988. *The Trickster of Liberty: Tribal Heirs to a Wild Baronage*. Minneapolis: University of Minnesota Press.

Vizenor, Gerald Robert. 1989. "Trickster Discourse: Comic Holotropes and Language Games." In *Narrative Chance: Postmodern Discourse on Native American Indian Literatures*, edited by Gerald Vizenor, 187–211. Norman: University of Oklahoma Press. http://dx.doi.org/10.2307/1409216.

Vizenor, Gerald Robert. 1994. *Manifest Manners: Postindian Warriors of Survivance*. Hanover, NH: Wesleyan University Press.

Weaver, Jace. 1997. *That the People Might Live: Native American Literatures and Native American Community*. New York: Oxford University Press.

Weaver, Jace. 2001. *Other Words: American Indian Literature, Law, and Culture*. Norman: University of Oklahoma Press.

Womack, Craig S. 1999. *Red on Red: Native American Literary Separatism*. Minneapolis: University of Minnesota Press.

6

HEARTSPEAK FROM THE SPIRIT
Songs of John Trudell, Keith Secola, and Robbie Robertson

Kimberli Lee

These survival songs
put us back together
　　　　　　　—Qwo-Li Driskill (2005)

For centuries indigenous peoples in this hemisphere have raised powerful voices of resistance to the unjust treatment and outright genocide they have received at the hands of colonizers. This resistance has been, and continues to be, manifested through a variety of rhetorical venues: speeches, stories, poems, songs, and at times, when other avenues were exhausted, outright confrontation. But it is song I am interested in exploring here, specifically the genre of contemporary Native music of the last fifty years. Since the early 1960s, Native American music has been bringing a unique fusion of the written word and oral traditions while also syncretically blending traditional instrumentation with modern electronic technologies. While the forms and styles of contemporary Native American music are always changing, the medium of song still serves, as it has for millennia, to transmit and process information important to Native communities: histories, philosophies, political concerns, social values, and stories. Likewise, they may be sung as expressions of joy, sadness, victory, defeat, love, or anger—any emotional or spiritual feeling can be addressed in song. As Simon Ortiz points out, "The substance [of a song] is emotional, but beyond that, spiritual, and it's real and you are present in, and part of it. . . . A song is made substantial by its context—that is its reality, both that which is there and what is brought about by the song" (Ortiz 2003, 240). Let's think about that for a moment—the context and how that becomes a song's reality. Honor songs, prayer songs, love songs, and encouragement songs are all sung with powerful words meant to do something significant for the People. Not only are songs "texts," but they are also active sites that can

DOI: 10.7330/9780874219968.c006

and do bring about change. I view them as valid Native texts for serious study in a variety of academic venues, from the classroom to national conferences. While some may think of these songs only as entertainment or amusement, their purposes are more complex if one really takes the time to listen. In fact, these songs contain viable educational elements—sometimes subtle, sometimes direct.

Excellent Native musicians are active in all genres of the industry: jazz, blues, heavy metal, hip-hop, rock, country, punk, powwow, pop, folk; the list is endless. Many innovative, creative Native songwriters contribute to the contemporary Native music scene these days. Award-winning artists such as Buffy St. Marie, Joy Harjo, Jim Boyd, Joanne Shenandoah, Rita Coolidge, John Trudell, Keith Secola, and Robbie Robertson are dedicated musicians whose work is a testament to the variety of excellent music available today. This chapter, however, focuses on the work of Trudell, Secola, and Robertson. All three are songwriters who incorporate viable messages of survivance into their songs designed to make us think and give us strength, demonstrating how Native oral traditions are evolving and continuing to function for Native people. In addition, these songs can be excellent sources for engagement in Native American studies classes.

JOHN TRUDELL

Dakota activist, artist, actor, poet, prophet, and free thinker John Trudell has led an extraordinary life dedicated to sovereignty, indigenous human rights, land, and language issues, carrying on evolving Native American oral traditions and keeping them alive so we may all learn from them. Born in 1946, Trudell spent his early years living on the Santee Reservation in northern Nebraska. After serving in the US Navy from 1963 until 1967, he briefly attended college, thinking he would go into radio and broadcasting. In 1969 Trudell became deeply involved with Indians of All Tribes and the takeover at Alcatraz, putting his broadcasting skills to use by hitting the airwaves on *Radio Free Alcatraz*. This period is when he first attracted national attention—from both the public and the US government; the FBI began a file on Trudell that now exceeds seventeen thousand pages. In 1973 he became the national spokesperson for the American Indian Movement, a position he held until 1979 when Trudell suffered the loss of his wife, Tina, three children, and mother-in-law on the Shoshone/Paiute reservation in Nevada. Trudell and many others believe the house fire that killed them was deliberately set to intimidate and silence both him and Tina (who was a powerful activist in her own

right). Trudell describes it as an "act of war." Since that time, he has been
giving voice to his pain and the politics that brought it on through writing poetry, or "lines," as he called them during a March 2005 interview
with me. His poem in honor of Elvis Presley, entitled "Baby Boom Che,"
has recently been anthologized in *Reading Our Histories, Understanding
Our Cultures* (McCormick 2002). In addition, he occasionally works in
film, playing roles in such feature films as *Thunderheart* (1992) and *Smoke
Signals* (1998), as well as the documentary releases *Incident at Oglala: The
Leonard Peltier Story* (1992) and *Alcatraz Is Not an Island* (2001). In 2005,
a documentary about his life entitled *Trudell*, directed by Heather Rae,
debuted at the prestigious Sundance Film Festival. Now a recognized
international spoken-word recording artist, Trudell is still speaking out
for decolonization and continued resistance to the oppression of Native
peoples. Interestingly, he blends these spoken lines with musical backgrounds—both contemporary sounds and traditional Native music.
Through his recordings, speeches, and published materials, Trudell
powerfully fuses written literature and oral traditions and brings that
fusion into the twenty-first century.

Foremost among the topics Trudell returns to in his discourse is the
Earth and our relationship to Her. For example, in his song "Listening/
Honor Song," Trudell (1983) highlights the significant connection
between human beings and the Earth, but the political message to stay
active and involved can't be missed.

Mother Earth embraces Her children
in natural beauty to last beyond oppressors' brutality . . .
we are the spirit of natural life
which is forever
the power of understanding
real connections to spirit is meaning
our resistance, our struggle is not sacrifice lost
it is natural energy properly used.

This story is told in order to promote and sustain people's connections to Earth, which is of ultimate importance to the survival of Native
people. Indeed, it is of paramount importance to the survival of all life.
His are words of encouragement and fortification, not just empty talk
of tree spirits, soaring eagles, or tipis by the river. Trudell speaks to our
responsibilities toward Earth and helps us understand it is not ours to
do with as we please. Above all, he wants people to understand that we
are an extension of Earth; the reality is that our human forms are made
up of the same natural elements found in Earth, and whatever treatment
we impose on Earth will ultimately be treatment we receive in return. As

responsible citizens of Earth, people must acknowledge and protect the intricate relationship shared by all life forms. We must understand on a fundamental level that we are related. Trudell states that we must move beyond human rights:

> We must step into the reality of natural rights because all of the natural world has a right to existence and we are only a small part of it. There can be no trade-off. We are the People. We have the potential for power. It takes more than good intentions. . . We are going to have to find a way to communicate our thoughts and our resistance and our consciousness that we will not accept the nuclearization of the earth; this struggle for our survival is absolute and complete. (quoted in Igliori 1994)

Trudell emphasizes that we must find a way to communicate to those who may not always be willing to listen; we must find "ways to be communication ourselves" (quoted in Igliori 1994). I interpret this to mean we need to set examples and use our intelligence at every opportunity as teachers in our classrooms, in our homes, or anywhere we have the chance to convey the message that we have a responsibility to Earth and a responsibility to future generations. We must speak things into reality.

As Craig Womack reminds us in his introduction to *Red on Red: Native American Literary Separatism,* "As often as not Indian writers are trying to invoke as much as evoke. The idea behind ceremonial chant is that language, spoken in the appropriate ritual contexts, will actually cause a change in the physical universe. This element exists in contemporary Native writing and must be continuously explored . . . language as invocation that will upset the balance of power, even to the point . . . where stories will be preeminent in land redress" (Womack 1999, 17). We hear this type of invocation in many of Trudell's poems. For example, in "Rant and Roll" he identifies the daily frustrations brought on by the oppressive dominant society and suggests how to deal with these, calling upon us to "Rant and Roll":

> Religions of men heavy with fear
> Industrial war against the land
> Every woman knows the fugitive
> Rich men keep living off me poor
> The soul is what's left after they eat your spirit
> When every act is an act of self-defense
> We have to do something or perish in the pretense
> Rant and roll
> Heartspeak from the spirit
> Say it loud so everyone can hear it

Say what you mean
Mean what you say
Rant and roll when you feel that way. (Trudell 1994a)

This poem is a call to resistance; the poet advises that we should not be silent when these situations arise. We don't have the option to be depressed and inert about these issues—to take that path is to perish. We must speak things into reality—we must act.

Trudell's songwriting also addresses kinship and gender roles. In "Shadow over Sisterland," the poet talks about both, again advocating for resistance, this time to the male dominant society's violence toward women. He reminds us that women are still treated unfairly in the judicial system because the "laws of justice are business decisions/gender and class [are] cut with surgical precisions." Likewise, in "See the Woman," Trudell (1994b) reminds us to respect women:

She carries herself well in all ages
she survives all man has done
in some tribes she is free
in some religions she is under man
in some societies she's worth what she consumes . . .
in all instances she is sister to Earth
in all conditions she is life bringer
in all life she is our necessity . . .
see the woman spirit daily serving courage with laughter
her breath a dream and a prayer. (Trudell 1994c)

In this song, several different societal views of women are presented, but at the end, Trudell suggests that we need to retrieve traditional Dakota views of women and uphold them. As we know, in most precontact Native societies across the Americas, women were honored for their contributions as nurturers and conservators of cultural values. Trudell is calling for a recovery and reassertion of this honoring. Recovery of this kind of traditional thinking and action will help all women, especially Native women, to survive and thrive in such diverse situations as the home, the business world, and the academy. Trudell freely acknowledges that in the past women have been kinder to him than he has been to them; and perhaps, as he has matured, he seeks to make amends and remind others of the importance of women in our societies (Caldwell 1999, 3). We must think of women as our relatives, as our necessity; they are spiritual beings, not just sexual objects who are under men.

Language is a topic Trudell returns to repeatedly. He approaches language respectfully and chooses his words carefully, as one would expect a poet to do. He thinks about words, language, and the construction of both. Trudell composes his songs in English, for the most part, although there are occasions when a Dakota word serves where it seems appropriate. He advocates understanding the words we speak, reminding us that "if we really look at the words, not just frivolously use them as a convenience, . . . if we really take time to look at the language we speak, and take some time to identify ourselves, we can use the information and we can create the way we need to go . . . we need to pay attention to the systems we are surrounded by. . . . [There is a lot of talk] about freedom of speech, but what about freedom of thought or being?" (quoted in Igliori 1994). Many well-known Native authors and scholars have addressed the power of the spoken word; among them is Kiowa author N. Scott Momaday, who writes in *The Man Made of Words*, "In the oral tradition one stands in a different relation to language. Words are rare and therefore dear. . . . Words are spoken with great care, and they are heard. They matter and must not be taken for granted; they must be taken seriously and they must be remembered. . . . Perhaps the most distinctive and important aspect of oral tradition is the way in which it reveals the singer's and the storyteller's respect for and belief in language" (Momaday 1997, 15). Momaday's thoughts on language seem to apply directly to the work Trudell is doing through his spoken-word lyrics. Trudell's words are powerful expressions advocating for resistance and decolonization. If we listen to him carefully, we cannot help but sharpen our awareness of the situations we need to address in Native studies. As he has said many times, we must use the power of our intelligence responsibly—in the most clear and coherent manner we can—to bring about positive change in our realities. Knee-jerk reactions will do us no good, he related to me in a March 2005 conversation; we need to think clearly about how we resist oppression so our motion isn't just motion—it has a direction and a force.

In his twenty-three-year recording career, John Trudell has worked with many prominent musicians, both Native and non-Native, including Jackson Browne, Jesse Ed Davis, Jeff Beck, and Robbie Robertson. He continues his work in contemporary Native music and is slated, along with Keith Secola, for the forthcoming Peter LaFarge tribute project. Designed by Cherokee journalist Sandra Hale Schulman, this project is still in the finishing phase, but several well-known Native artists have signed on to cover some of LaFarge's all-but-forgotten songs (a topic to which I will return later in this piece). In addition, Trudell has just completed *Madness and the Moremes*, a new work with his current band, Bad Dog. Concerts, speaking engagements, and promotion for the documentary *Trudell* (now available on DVD) have kept him on the road quite a bit these days; however, Trudell still finds time to write lyrics that challenge us to think about and express our lives.

KEITH SECOLA

Bois Fort Band Anishinabe songwriter and musician Keith Secola deals with several issues that affect Native communities through his songs. Born in Cook, Minnesota, in 1957, Secola was raised in the nearby Mountain Iron area. Encouraged to take up a musical instrument early in his life, Secola, along with his siblings, would later join the Mountain Iron High School band. Since that time music has been an integral part of his life. Although Secola never strays far from his indigenous roots, his music is actually quite eclectic, spanning a wide range of musical styles: blues, jazz, folk, country, and rock. Into this mix Secola successfully blends traditional elements, including tribal drum, chants, and the occasional 49 tune or perhaps a flute instrumental. Add to this the powerful lyrics Secola pens, and his work makes quite an impression. He has won multiple awards and has toured extensively in both Europe and North America since the early 1990s with such notable artists as the Indigo Girls, David Bowie, the Neville Brothers, and Pearl Jam. Further, his work has been featured in several Native films and documentaries, including Norman Jewison's *Dance Me Outside* (1994); Chris Eyre's *Skins* (2002); the Philomath documentary about homelessness on Pine Ridge Reservation, *Homeland* (1992); and Plutte and Fortier's *Alcatraz Is Not an Island* (2001). He is also a featured musician in *Rockin' Warriors* (1998), a little-known documentary about contemporary Native American musicians. An artist and activist, Secola truly works for the good in Native communities—especially while touring—often holding music workshops for youth on and off reservations. In addition, he regularly performs benefit concerts throughout North America to raise awareness about Native issues and environmental concerns.[1] Secola holds a highly respected position on the Native American music front, although he remains virtually unknown in popular American mainstream music.

Land claims, racism, imprisonment, cultural and intellectual property rights, and other Native realities are just a few of the many topics Secola addresses through his songs. All these are serious issues that continue to affect Native people in the western hemisphere today. And while these issues are formidable ones, Secola sometimes uses humor and wit as a vehicle for getting his message across. He says that rather than "being overcome with anger when hearing of the history and situations of American Indians," he wants his audience "to get to the deeper meaning of his words" and perhaps initiate a healing process (pers. comm.). In fact, Native peoples have often used humor as a form of survival and resistance. Vine Deloria Jr., arguably one of the most prolific Native survivance writers/scholars of the twentieth century, dedicates an entire chapter in his celebrated *Custer Died for Your Sins* to humor: "Humor has come to occupy such a prominent place in national Indian affairs that any kind of movement is impossible without it. . . .The more desperate the problem, the more humor is directed to describe it. Satirical remarks often circumscribe problems so that possible solutions are drawn from the circumstances that would not make sense if presented in other than a humorous form. . . . Often people are awakened and brought to a militant edge through [humor]" (Deloria 1988, 147). "Humor," says Secola, "warms the blood and lightens the heart and encourages a higher level of thinking" (pers. comm.). Insightful truths can be found and pondered in such language and laughter, truths that appreciate with time.

One such song that employs humor to deal with the serious issue of land claims is from Secola's (1996b) CD *Wild Band of Indians*, entitled "Wide Open Spaces." Embedded within the song is the story of a Native American man who gets involved in a radio talk show, debating with the host about the concepts of ownership, fences, signs, and land. After giving a Native perspective on these issues, the narrator is met with a long period of silence, and then the talk show host pontificates:

> What's the matter man, are you some kind of commie?
> This here's America,
> Land of the Atlanta Braves, Home of the Washington Redskins.
> Red, White and blue, America, and if you don't like it here in America,
> why don't you just get back to where you came from?

The narrator replies: "So I did. I camped out in his backyard!"[2] The song's chorus continues:

> From the land of the blue sky water
> there's a voice calling out to you
> your soul needs refreshing
> souls need regressing, too—
> Wide open spaces
> Wide open heart
> Back to the spirit
> Back to the start.

This part of the song is significant because the radio show host's attitude toward the Native caller is something many American Indian people face every day of their lives—denigration, racism, ignorance, and disregard for their rights in this country. When Secola sings the phrase "Red, White and blue, America," the listener may first think of the American flag—but there is another, more nuanced feeling one gets as well: that the existing dichotomy and polarization between Red and White is making America blue. We must never forget the past, but we must enact a new future: open our hearts (and our minds), refresh our spiritual selves, and move forward. This song is a persuasive call for unity and alliance building. This song is designed to make people think and act to change the status quo, while the interplay between seriousness and humor helps heal and refresh our souls. I view this as a manifestation of what Cherokee writer and scholar Marilou Awiakta calls "art for life's sake" (quoted in Justice 2004, 109).

Yet Secola maintains a serious side as well, as we see in his rendition of Peter LaFarge's graphic song "Crimson Parson," a song that addresses the Sand Creek massacre of 1864. Penned in the early 1960s, years before Native American civil rights issues were brought to the attention of mainstream America, this song is a powerful indictment against the dominant narrative that often spoke of the "battle" at Sand Creek as a US military victory. Peter LaFarge was on the forefront of what we might call *contemporary Native musicians.* Of Narragansett descent, Peter was the son of Oliver LaFarge, the author of *Laughing Boy* and a trained anthropologist and writer who lobbied for Native rights during the horrific termination years of the 1940s and 1950s.[3] In his short career, Peter wrote many songs that addressed American Indian issues and historical truths, and "Crimson Parson" stands strong among them. LaFarge spared no details in the song; it is part history lesson, part social critique, and full-on protest song. Secola's version is a "softer" one—more melodic with expanded instrumentation and a few lyric and tune changes. But the historical truths still resonate.

> They call him the Crimson Parson
> The Rev'rend Chivington
> History books don't recommend him
> For all the trouble he'd begun
> Make die, take out Indians
> Was his battle cry
> The Rev'rend Colonel Chivington
> With a Bible by his side.
> In the valley of the Sand Creek, lived a peaceful tribe

Chivington knew them for their peace, but glory was his pride
In the middle of the night he fell upon the place
Commenced his victory dance in disgrace
The Rev'rend Colonel Chivington
With a long knife by his side
All the way up to Sitting Bull
They told their mournful tale
War pipes smoked like they hadn't smoked since
They cut the Oregon Trail
For the next twelve years
Indian wars scattered across the land
The Rev'rend Colonel Chivington
Started all with his little band
They call him the Crimson Parson
The Rev'rend Chivington
History books don't recommend him
For all the trouble he begun
Make die, take out Indians
Was his battle cry
The Rev'rend Colonel Chivington
With a Bible by his side. (Secola 1992a)

The massacre of Cheyenne and Arapaho families at the hand of Chivington and his vigilantes remains vivid in the minds of many Native people today, although a majority of Americans have never heard of the traumatic ordeal that precipitated the Plains Indian wars. Contrast this with the amount of attention garnered by the US military's attack on the camp at Little Big Horn, which had a decidedly different kind of ending. Historians reveal that just after the Sand Creek massacre, Chivington and his 100-days men were celebrated and toasted throughout Denver; the militiamen were later mustered out with honors. Although he was later investigated for the murders he perpetrated there, Chivington was never charged with war crimes. Interestingly, the only man who called attention to the atrocity, Lieutenant Silas Soule, would soon become the victim of an unsolved homicide himself in the streets of Denver after he testified against Chivington.

One thing I like about this song is that it isn't all about the Cheyennes as victimized people. It portrays them as agents in their own survival and resistance—enacting survivance Yes, the massacre was devastating, and yes, hundreds fell victim to Chivington's psychotic violence. But the survivors found allies and retaliated—they did not vanish or fade off into the sunset. The song also points out that Chivington, a Methodist minister, was really a murderer of women and children, a man who did so "with a Bible by his side." This song has impact and certainly gives students something to think about besides a pretty tune or poetic language. In the documentary film *Making a Noise: A Musical Journey of Robbie Robertson* (1998), Cherokee singer and songwriter Rita Coolidge points out that "many of our truths are yet to be told. If we can tell these truths and stories in songs, then that's how we'll do it." "Crimson Parson" is an outstanding example of how these truths can be told through song.

Another issue Secola addresses that reveals his resistance to the oppressive status quo in America is his support and honoring of American Indian Movement leader and political prisoner Leonard Peltier. Peltier is a member of the Turtle Mountain Chippewas who has been incarcerated since 1976 on fallacious murder charges. These charges stem from federally supported violence and intimidation that took place on Pine Ridge Reservation during the mid-1970s. Whatever may have occurred at Oglala, South Dakota, that day in June, Peltier's actions were clearly self-defense. Peltier's struggle for a fair trial has been successfully thwarted for almost forty years by the US government, but he has not been forgotten, thanks in part to many Native American musicians such as Trudell, Secola, and Robertson, among others. In "Innocent Man," Secola honors Peltier by singing of Peltier's dedication to traditions in the confinement and isolation of a federal prison:

> There wasn't a microphone
> But he felt like singing
> To a pale moon, hear him singing.
> He's an innocent man
> He's an innocent man.
> In the ancient rain, hear him saying
> That the price you pay
> Ain't worth the taking.
> He's an innocent man
> He's an innocent man. (Secola 1996a)

This song resonates for many because Peltier has taken on something of an iconic status as an activist symbolic of Native resistance and endurance. But the imagery and reality presented in this song are worthy of serious study—especially in the context of Native American oppression and the fact that Native American inmate populations are rising dramatically nationwide. And, even though this song is dedicated to and focused on Leonard Peltier, the expressed sentiments can apply to all who suffer from emotional, psychic, or physical imprisonment.

In "Kokopelli's Blues" (a 2002 Native American Music Award [NAMA] winner), Secola (2000) takes on the issue of Native intellectual

and cultural copyright. This song speaks to the fact that the image of
Kokopelli has been so thoroughly appropriated that his real identity and
purpose have become unrecognizable for most mainstream Americans.
In the bluesy shuffle, Kokopelli sings that he has the blues because of
all the "cheap imitations out there." He tells us hucksters are "using
[Kokopelli's] image to depict a new age," and no one really wants to
know about the "real cat." And, indeed, that is the case. Most people
think of Kokopelli as a whimsical little cartoonish character who brings
happiness by playing his flute, but for many tribal people he is a revered
deity of fertility. We find the image of Kokopelli plastered on everything
from oven mitts to high-dollar jewelry with little or no respect for his
Hopi origins or the true meaning of his image. Secola addresses this
trivialization of Kokopelli with insight and humor, yet he never loses the
focus that this appropriation is wrong.

Secola is probably best known for his song "NDN Kars," which some
people have called a Native American anthem. This song, which was
highlighted in the film *Dance Me Outside*, has become a favorite in Indian
country and is a poignant testimony to resisting dominant culture values and celebrating modern Native realities. Again, Secola draws us into
a serious (and some would say sad) situation through humor and good
feelings; it's a situation that almost anyone can relate to on some level.
The song tells the story of a poor powwow singer out on the "powwow
trail" in his ramshackle "rez car":

> I've been driving in my NDN car
> The sound of the wheels drumming in my brain
> The dash is dusty, the plates are expired
> Please Mr. Officer, let me explain
> I got to make it to a powwow tonight
> Singin' 49s down by the river side
> Lookin' for a sugar, ridin' in my NDN car
> . . .
> My car is dented; the radiator steams
> One headlight don't work
> But the radio screams
> I got a sticker; it says NDN Power
> I stuck in on the bumper; that's what holds my car together. (Secola 1992b)

The song starts off with a familiar musical refrain—something on
the order of the old "Indian Drumbeat Song" that everyone has heard
at one time or another. And for a moment, one wonders if this song is
going to be some sort of musical stereotype. But upon the first crunch
of the electric guitar punctuated with a powwow beat, the confusion

dissipates and the song resituates that old tune in something new and decidedly Native. Secola has a knack for imagining new spins on old themes. As the song progresses and the story comes to light, the listeners are drawn into a "circuit of an Indian dream/We don't get old/We just get younger/Flyin' down the highway, ridin' in our NDN cars" (Secola 1992b). This song is about the richness of cultural connections, the restorative power of music, and the ability to make the most of what one has. It is about surviving and resisting in a dominant society that, in large part, measures success and happiness with materialistic gauges—people are most often valued for what they consume and how much money they spend. It also addresses the class system that has segregated the "haves" and the "have-nots," an issue that needs further attention.

Now based out of Arizona, Secola is currently recording and touring extensively. His CD of new work, entitled *Native Americana*, was released in March 2006 and won three 2006 NAMA awards. His work with Karen Drift, *Anishinabmoin*, was been nominated for two NAMA awards in 2007.

ROBBIE ROBERTSON

Robbie Robertson is best known for his work (some would say legendary) in American mainstream music, but only a few people know he is of Haudenosaunee, or Mohawk, descent. Robertson was born in Toronto in 1943, and like Secola, he was encouraged early on to become involved with music. As a child he spent his summers with his mother's people on the Six Nations Reserve, and that is where he began learning guitar from his relatives. Robertson relates in the documentary film *Making a Noise* that the "whole family" was musical in some form or another and that the guitar skills he learned there were largely blues based. By age sixteen Robertson was writing original music and had begun as lead guitarist for Ronnie Hawkins and the Hawks, the core group that would evolve into The Band. By 1965, Robertson and The Band were touring with Bob Dylan, a relationship that would span several years and produce many critically acclaimed works now considered classics. After The Band disbanded, Robertson began a lengthy and productive collaboration with film director Martin Scorsese, scoring the music and soundtracks for *Raging Bull* (1980), *The King of Comedy* (1983), and *The Color of Money* (1986). In 1994, Robertson was asked to score a soundtrack for Turner Broadcasting Company's documentary *The Native Americans: Behind the Legends, Beyond the Myth* (1993–1996). For this effort, Robertson brought together a virtual who's who of contemporary Native musicians, a collective known as the Red Road Ensemble. Artists contributing to this project included John Trudell, Rita Coolidge and Walela, Floyd Red-Crow Westerman, Bonnie Jo Hunt, Ulali, and Kashtin. This project brought Robertson back in touch with his indigenous roots and served as a catalyst for his efforts to recover and reclaim his Mohawk relations. After an absence of thirty years, Robertson returned to the Six Nations Reserve to renew and reeducate himself in Haudenosaunee ways. This experience was the impetus for his critically acclaimed recording *Contact from the Underworld of Red Boy*, a work containing songs that address Native concerns. Robertson continues as an activist and advocate for Native people, in part by promoting new and unknown Native musicians as well as by lobbying on their behalf in the music industry.

Robertson's approach to concerns such as land claims is a bit more confrontational than Secola's, and it contains some serious resistance themes. For example, the groove-driven song "Making a Noise" advocates for Native unity and strong presence. Robertson (1998a) sings in the chorus:

Making a noise in this world
Making a noise in this world
You can bet your ass I won't go quietly
Making a noise in this world.

He then confronts the dominant society:

I don't want your promise
I don't want your whiskey
I don't want your blood on my hands
Only want what belongs to me.
I think you thought I was gone
I think you thought I was dead
You won't admit that you was wrong
Ain't that some shit that should be said?

No vanishing Indian here; on the contrary, we have a forceful Native voice addressing the heart of the issue, resisting the status quo. New York rock critic Jeff Apter (1998) writes that "Making a Noise" is a "beat driven celebration . . . without a trace of World Music condescension" (2). This comparison to World Music, a favorite category of aging new agers, reminds us that mainstream American music critics still view Native American artists as something other than American. Perhaps the hard truths are difficult to deal with directly.[4] Interestingly as well, Robertson includes a portion from a Sherman Alexie poem during a spoken-word interlude within "Making a Noise." In fact, Robertson credits Alexie and Joy Harjo for inspiration on *Contact from the Underworld of*

Redboy, both artists have built successful "bridges" between literature and music.[5] I predict we'll witness more of this trend in the coming years— Native literary artists blending "borders" between genres (music, poetry, art, all creative ventures).

Like Secola, Robbie Robertson (1998b) calls our attention to Peltier's situation in a song aptly entitled "Sacrifice." At the center of this song is the voice of Leonard Peltier telling his own story of the events that led to his imprisonment. Robertson and Peltier collaborated on this song by recording a phone conversation Robertson later underscored with music. Robertson relates that the phone call from Peltier ended with a sacrifice as well: "He didn't call me back for some time after [that] and I was [later] told that his phone privileges had been taken away for 90 days. I don't know if it was because they had monitored our conversation" (*Hollywood and Vine* 1998, 1). During the song, Peltier reminds us that Native people have long been making these sacrifices: "The sacrifice I have made, when I really sit down to think about it, is nothing compared to what our people of a couple hundred years ago, or fifty years ago, or twenty-five years ago have made. Some gave their lives, some had to stand there and watch their children die in their arms. So the sacrifice I have made is nothing compared to those. I've gone too far now to start backing down." "Sacrifice" has been described by various music critics as "tragic" and "haunting," but in my view, it is a powerful piece of spoken-word artistry every student of Native American literature should experience. It is a statement of the power of Native voice and survivance.

Perhaps Robertson's strongest statement of survivance comes in his song "Ghost Dance," from the CD *Songs for Native Americans.* This song deals with the Wounded Knee Massacre of 1890 in which at least three hundred Lakota men, women, and children were shot down by the US military on a cold December morning. In Robertson's hands, this song addresses one of the darkest, deadliest days in Native history, yet he reminds us that this was not the "last day" or the "end" of a culture. I quote here at length because Robertson (1994) actually gives a miniature history lesson that can become the impetus for larger discussion:

> Crow brought the message
> To the children of the sun
> For the return of the buffalo
> And a better day to come
> You can kill my body
> You can damn my soul
> For not believing in your god
> And some world down below

Chorus:
You don't stand a chance
Against my prayers
You don't stand a chance
Against my love
They outlawed the Ghost Dance
They outlawed the Ghost Dance
But we shall live again
We shall live again

My sister above
She has red paint
She died at Wounded Knee
Like a latter-day saint
You got the big drum in the distance
The Blackbird in the sky
That's the sound that you hear
When the buffalo cry

[Chorus]
Crazy Horse was a mystic
He knew the secret of the trance
And Sitting Bull the great apostle
Of the Ghost Dance
Come on Comanche
Come on Blackfeet
Come on Shoshone
Come on Cheyenne
We shall live again
We shall live again
Come on Arapaho
Come on Cherokee
Come on Piegan
Come on Sioux
We shall live again
We shall live again

[Spoken]
We used to do the Ghost Dance
We don't sing them kind of songs no more

Many may at first find these lyrics incongruous with the prevailing
narratives of what happened at Wounded Knee—love, prayers, and life
connected with such devastation? But for myself and many others, this
song is an affirmation of life and living—why should we dwell on the

darkness of that day? This is not to say we should ever forget what happened there, but we must dismantle the dominant narrative of Wounded Knee as the "end" or "last days" of "authentic-traditional" Indian life, as many non-Native historians would have us believe. In *Red on Red*, Womack (1999) points out that "the process of decolonizing one's mind, a first step before one can achieve a political consciousness and engage in activism, has to begin with imagining an alternative" (230). This song imagines and promotes that alternative. It speaks of love and prayers as spiritual forces—active resistance to hate and despair.

The song also points out significant historical facts—that the Ghost Dance was done in order that the participants might survive the intense starvation (both physical and spiritual) they were facing and that the dance had indeed been outlawed (as had all Native ritual and practice; participants were routinely arrested and jailed). Nicholas Black Elk relates in Raymond DeMallie's (1984) *The Sixth Grandfather* that Ghost Dancers did in fact use red paint, a signifier for healing and happiness in Lakota culture. And even though Crazy Horse did not directly participate in the Ghost Dance (he had been murdered in 1877 at Fort Robinson, Nebraska), he was known to have gone often to lament or cry for visions in order to help his people.[6] Sitting Bull, on the other hand, was a physical participant in the Ghost Dance early on, and even though in time his enthusiasm for the dance began to wane, he knew the dancing helped sustain the People's hope. It was in response to Sitting Bull's assassination that Big Foot's band of Miniconjous were fleeing for sanctuary in Red Cloud's camp at Pine Ridge in December 1890 and were "apprehended" at Wounded Knee. By including pertinent facts such as these, Robertson reminds us that what happened at Wounded Knee was not an event that happened in isolation—it is a reality linked to past events as well as future ones; it is something we must remember.

Near the end of the song, there is a sort of pantribal call for unity and cultural renewal among Native nations—many of whom had their own variations of the Ghost Dance in their communities and perhaps still do. I like to think about the possibility of songs and dances to pray for resurgence, renewal, and a new Native world to come.[7] At the end of the song is a spoken segment: "We don't sing them kind of songs no more." This may seem to be the last word on such a possibility—but isn't Robertson's own Ghost Dance song here evidence to the contrary?

While this particular chapter focuses on three indigenous male singer-songwriters, there is a varied and wide array of Native women who are also amazing and active musical artists. Foremost among them is Buffy Sainte-Marie (Cree), who since the early 1960s has been writing and performing her music with an immense consciousness about Native American and First Nations' rights. She has never wavered in her support for indigenous peoples worldwide and advocates for alliances between them. Sainte-Marie has won numerous awards in both the United States and Canada for her music, education advocacy, and activism. Rita Coolidge is another Native singer/songwriter who has been an influential and popular Native songwriter and performer in the vocal group Walela. Also, Pura Fe, probably best known for her award-winning work with the all-Native women's vocal group, Ulali (with Jennifer Kreisberg and Soni Moreno), has recorded several solo projects and continues her music and activism. She travels often, performing live in both Europe and the Americas. With an amazing vocal range and songs that tell the histories and philosophies of her Tuscarora peoples, Pura Fe's delta-bluesy feel and tone is a feast for the ears. Other Native women artists include Annie Humphrey, who has worked with John Trudell on music projects and writes songs full of historical truth. Joanne Shenandoah, Joy Harjo, Martha Redbone, Star Nayea, Eekwol Knight, and Crystal Shawanda are all Native women musicians and singers who are working in a profusion of genres—from country-folk to jazz to hip-hop—and all of whom keep the stories of the People central to the songs.

Native American music has been studied in some capacity since contact; however, most people wanted to analyze it for its exoticness or "primitive beauty" rather than to listen for the stories or lessons it might teach. Numerous books on Native music exist, but most researchers (many of whom are non-Native) tend to concentrate on the older songs, the more "traditional" music.[8] Most believe that "authentic Native music" is only the old war songs and honor songs sung in tribal languages. And certainly, study in that venue is valuable. In fact, calls for inclusion of Native American music in college curricula have been made before, but almost invariably the call has been for study of "authentic" or "traditional" music or chants.[9] My contention is that many Native studies scholars are overlooking or ignoring the most accessible music—that of current contemporary Native musicians. They are a resource we must pay attention to and respect. I see them as "alter/native discourses" not only vital to our study of Native literatures but also as important texts in thinking about decolonizination. As Malea Powell (2002) points out in her essay "Listening to Ghosts," writing alternative discourses and listening to them are acts of survivance (21).

Trudell, Secola, and Robertson are just three of the many Native musicians who are currently releasing new work we can use in our classrooms. These singers are sending their voices into the vibratory

universe as Native singers have done for millennia. They are addressing important issues that concern Native people today, issues that
should concern every American citizen. But beyond that, these works
function as texts of Native literature and should be given serious con-
sideration as such both at academic conferences and, perhaps more
importantly, in the college classroom. These texts will work well on
several levels in any Native American studies classroom—especially in
any Native American literature (indeed, any American literature) classroom for a variety of reasons.

First, and perhaps most important, these songs teach students to
really listen to what is being said. Listening is quickly becoming a lost
art. We do not want to take the time to listen and think—we are rushing
our lives away, hearing only about half of what is being said and rarely
taking time to think about what it is we are hearing. We often encourage
our students to speak in class—to participate in discussions, add their
voice—and such participation holds a fundamental place in our pedagogies. It is tremendously important that we teach students about listening
to words as well; we must show them that listening and contemplating
the words they hear are worth the time it takes to consider what is being
said. We must slow down a bit and think about the words and language
we are hearing.

Second, students relate well to this kind of poetry because it is more
accessible to them, blended as it is with music. As we know, music is
a major concern for many of our students—they pay attention to it.
We witness this every day, students all around campus with iPods or
Walkman earphones practically cemented in their ears. And, it seems to
me, we can implement their love for music to remind them that music
and poetry are actually relatives in the creative realm. Listening to these
works can also encourage them to listen to their own favorite kinds of
music in new ways. These kinds of texts can aid students in learning
about evolving oral traditions and the rhetorical strategies inherent in
such endeavors.

In addition, many students find these kinds of texts less intimidating
than some other forms of poetry or literature simply because music is a
part of their daily lives. When I incorporate contemporary Native musical forms such as the songs of Trudell, Secola, or Robertson into my
teaching, our transition into other Native writers is accomplished more
smoothly; many students spend more time with the texts and engage
with them on a new level. The students are more receptive and begin
to read poetry and literature differently, relating to it with more imme-
diacy; they become aware that they are "listening" to the words printed

on the page rather than just reading them. Equally important, however, is the fact that these texts acquaint students with crucial Native issues such as cultural survival, decolonization, and resistance. Studying song texts like these encourages critical thinking about those issues. As many Native scholars already know, songs are alive and powerful, and we can be listening to, thinking about, and learning from these texts.

Notes

1. This information is included in Secola's press kit from Akina, his production company.
2. I am not certain, but I think this particular joke was used as a result of collaborating with Native comedian Charlie Hill.
3. See Darcy McNickle's (1971) biography, *Indian Man: A Life of Oliver LaFarge.*
4. Although not well known in the United States, many Native American musicians have a global following; they regularly headline venues and festivals in Europe. In America, they only seem to get airplay on tribal radio stations or public radio stations.
5. Alexie has collaborated with NAMA award-winning musician Jim Boyd (formerly of the Native band XIT) in writing songs (see soundtrack for *Smoke Signals*). Harjo performs regularly with her band Poetic Justice, and her new CD, *Native Joy For Real,* won a NAMA award for 2004.
6. See Mari Sandoz (1992), *Crazy Horse: Strange Man of the Oglalas.*
7. Along with others, I am confident that the current revitalization in Native languages and cultural practices is the manifestation of prayers offered by the ancients long ago. They prayed for the People to live and know their ways, and I think we see this coming to fruition, even against long odds.
8. The list here is quite lengthy, and these books focus on powwow music or "traditional" songs and are mostly written by anthropologists or ethnomusicologists. See, for example, Frances Densmore's (1992) *Teton Sioux Music and Culture,* Alice Fletcher's (1970) *Indian Story and Song,* William K. Power's (1990) *War Dance: Plains Indian Musical Performance,* Judith Vander's (1988) S*ongprints,* and Severt Young Bear and Ron Theisz's *Standing in the Light* (Young Bear and Theisz 1994) Contrast this with works on contemporary Native music, most written by music journalists: Sandra Schulman's (2002) *From Kokopellis to Electric Warriors* and a one-page essay by J. Poet (2001) in *American Roots Music* (the 2001 publication that accompanied the PBS documentary of the same name).
9. For example, see Olsen (1986).

References

Alcatraz Is Not an Island. 2001. Dir. James M. Fortier. Pacifica, CA: Diamond Island Productions.

Apter, Jeff. 1998. "Robbie Robertson: Making a Noise." *New York Rock,* May. http://www.nyrock.com/features/robbie_robertson.htm.

The Color of Money. 1986. Dir. Martin Scorsese. Burbank, CA: Touchstone Pictures.

Caldwell, E. K. 1999. *Dreaming the Dawn: Conversations with Native Artists and Activists.* Lincoln: University of Nebraska Press.

Dance Me Outside. 1994. Produced by Norman Jewison and Sarah Hayward. New York: Rez Films.

Deloria, Vine Jr. 1988. *Custer Died for Your Sins: An Indian Manifesto.* Norman: University of Oklahoma Press.

DeMallie, Raymond. 1984. *The Sixth Grandfather: Black Elk's Teachings Given to John G. Neihardt.* Lincoln: University of Nebraska Press.

Densmore, Frances. (1918) 1992. *Teton Sioux Music and Culture.* Lincoln: University of Nebraska Press.

Driskill, Qwo Li. 2005. *Walking with Ghosts.* Cambridge, UK: Salt.

Fletcher, Alice. (1900) 1970. *Indian Story and Song.* Boston: Small Maynard.

Hollywood and Vine. 1998. www.capitolrecords.com. Site now discontinued.

Homeland. 1992. Dir. Jilann Spitzmiller and Hank Rogerson. Santa Fe, NM: Philomath Films.

Igliori, Paola. 1994. *Stickman: Poems, Lyrics, Talks, A Conversation.* New York: In and Out.

Incident at Oglala: The Leonard Peltier Story. 1992. Dir. Michael Apted. Santa Monica, CA: Lion's Gate.

Justice, Daniel. 2004. "Reading (and Seeing) Red: Indian Outlaws in the Ivory Tower." In *Indigenizing the Academy: Transforming Scholarship and Empowering Communities,* edited by Devon Mihesuah and Angela Wilson, 100–23. Lincoln: University of Nebraska Press.

King of Comedy. 1983. Dir. Martin Scorsese. Los Angeles: Twentieth Century Fox.

Making a Noise: A Musical Journey of Robbie Robertson. 1998. Dir. Dana Perry. New York: Perry Films.

McCormick, Kathleen. 2002. *Reading Our Histories, Understanding Our Cultures: A Sequenced Approach to Thinking Reading and Writing.* 2nd ed. Upper Saddle River, NJ: Longman.

McNickle, Darcy. 1971. *Indian Man: A Life of Oliver LaFarge.* Bloomington: Indiana University Press.

Momaday, N. Scott. 1997. *The Man Made of Words.* New York: St. Martin's Griffin.

The Native Americans: Behind the Legends, Beyond the Myth. 1993–1996. TNT. Atlanta, GA: Turner Broadcasting Company.

Olsen, Loran. 1986. "Native Music in College Curricula." *Wicazo Sa Review* 2 (2): 59–65. http://dx.doi.org/10.2307/1409019.

Ortiz, Simon. 2003. "Song/Poetry and Language-Expression and Perception." In *Speak to Me Words: Essays on Contemporary American Indian Poetry,* edited by Dean Rader and Janice Gould, 235–46. Tucson: University of Arizona Press.

Poet, J. 2001. "Native American Music." In *American Roots Music,* edited by Robert Santelli and Holly George-Warren. New York: Harry N. Abrams.

Powell, Malea. 2002. "Listening to Ghosts: An Alternative (Non)argument." In *Alternative Discourses and the Academy,* edited by Christopher Schroeder, Helen Fox, and Patricia Bizzell. Portsmouth, NH: Heinemann.

Power, William K. 1990. *War Dance: Plains Indian Musical Performance.* Tucson: University of Arizona Press.

Raging Bull. 1980. Dir. Martin Scorsese. Los Angeles: MGM.

Robertson, Robbie. 1994. "Ghost Dance." *Music for the Native Americans.* CD. Capitol.

Robertson, Robbie. 1998a. "Making a Noise." *Contact from the Underworld of Redboy.* CD. Capitol.

Robertson, Robbie. 1998b. "Sacrifice." *Contact from the Underworld of Redboy.* CD. Capitol.

Rockin' Warriors. 1998. Dir. Andy Bausch. Luxembourg: Lynx Productions.

Sandoz, Mari. 1992. *Crazy Horse: Strange Man of the Oglalas.* Lincoln: University of Nebraska Press.

Schulman, Sandra. 2002. *From Kokopellis to Electric Warriors.* Portland, OR: First Books Library.

Secola, Keith. 1992a. "Crimson Parson." *Circle.* CD. Akina.

Secola, Keith. 1992b. "NDN Kars." *Circle.* CD. Akina.

Secola, Keith. 1996a. "Innocent Man." *Wild Band of Indians.* CD. Akina.

Secola, Keith. 1996b. "Wide Open Spaces." *Wild Band of Indians.* CD. Akina.

Secola, Keith. 2000. "Kokopelli's Blues." *Kokopellis Blues.* EP. Akina.

Skins. 2002. Dir. Chris Eyre. Century City, CA: First Look Pictures.

Smoke Signals. 1998. Dir. Chris Eyre. Santa Monica, CA: Miramax.

Thunderheart. 1992. Dir. Michael Apted. Fairfield, NJ: Tristar Studios.

Trudell, John. 1983. "Listening/Honor Song." *Tribal Voice.* Peace Company. CD.

Trudell, John. 1994a. "Rant and Roll." *Johnny Damas and Me.* Rykodisc. CD.

Trudell, John. 1994b. "See the Woman." *Johnny Damas and Me.* Rykodisc. CD.

Trudell, John. 1994c. "Shadow over Sisterland." *Johnny Damas and Me.* Rykodisc. CD.

Vander, Judith. 1988. *Songprints: The Musical Experience of Five Shoshone Women.* Champaign: University of Illinois Press.

Womack, Craig. 1999. *Red on Red: Native American Literary Separatism.* Minneapolis: University of Minnesota Press.

Young Bear, Severt, and Ron Theisz. 1994. *Standing in the Light.* Lincoln: University of Nebraska Press.

7

MAKING NATIVE SPACE FOR GRADUATE STUDENTS
A Story of Indigenous Rhetorical Practice

Andrea Riley-Mukavetz and Malea D. Powell

Malea: This is a story.
Andrea: LOL, you always say that.

What follows is a series of stories in which we theorize our experiences collaboratively teaching a graduate seminar, American Indian Rhetorics. In offering these stories, we're trying to focus on the *how:* how we used indigenous rhetorical practices to develop a syllabus and strategize (usually on the fly) an indigenous pedagogy appropriate for graduate education; how our students—mostly graduate students from diverse humanities disciplines—learned to practice indigenous rhetorics; and how we've processed and reflected on the experience of this course to accumulate some advice for others. Especially significant here are the stories of our collective struggles in accumulating an indigenous rhetorical practice that lives in balance with the demands of the academy. These stories, then, constellate the space from which our theorizing arises—the intersection of our experiences as both teachers and learners in the shared space of an academic course. We'll begin, then, where the course began, with some fairly mundane details about the course itself, a story about what we mean when we say *indigenous rhetorical practices,* and one that shows how our own network of relations came together to build our pedagogical practices. Then we'll move to a story crafted around the four central points of our pedagogical practice—body, place, culture, making—and a shared dialogue about what actually happened in the course. Our final story focuses on the teachings we took from our experience together in this particular classroom community. During these tellings, sometimes we speak with one voice, sometimes as our individuated selves; we do this to parallel the conversations and convergences *we* experienced as teachers, scholars, friends, students.

DOI: 10.7330/9780874219968.c007

THE COURSE

The course we cotaught was a graduate level American Indian Rhetorics seminar that met once a week, three hours per meeting, for fifteen weeks.[1] Malea had taught versions of this course many times, as a regular semester-long graduate seminar at Michigan State University, as a week-long intensive course for the CIC American Indian Studies Consortium (June 2009),[2] and for the North Dakota State University English department's Summer Scholar program (June 2010).[3] We planned this course together around a kitchen table, making decisions about structure and context and strategizing pedagogical approaches. During the course itself, we continued to work collectively, tackling on-the-fly planning and troubleshooting around a conference table in a research center[4] at the university. Throughout the course, we both provided comments for students' weekly written work[5] and project plans, both met with students during office hours, both acted as facilitators during class meetings. Although the course was listed under the rhetoric and writing program's course offerings, students who enrolled came from a broader array of disciplines and fields—philosophy, Chicano/a studies, and museum studies. One English education student from a nearby university audited the class, and we waived one undergraduate into the course because of his deep commitment to Native rhetorics as a field of study. Because we had access to the enrollment list as we planned the course, we knew we needed to take their disciplinary experiences into account.

One of the things it's *not* safe to assume when teaching Native rhetorics at the graduate level is that students already have experience in navigating and learning from Native writers and rhetors. Or that the experiences they *do* have go beyond a simple acknowledgment that Native writing and rhetoric exists, that it's a form of resistance, and that it can be quite beautiful. Because we wanted our students to get far enough beyond simple "appreciation" for Native rhetorical practices to be able to use indigenous theoretical approaches in their own scholarship, our course would need to layer a radical demythologizing with an intensive focus on the theoretical outcomes of the seemingly simplistic storytelling methodologies favored by many of the writers we chose for the course. Early in our planning and discussions, we decided to construct a course with a strong historical background grounded in the particularities of the Eastern Woodlands and Northern Great Lakes, and to then build a web around this geographical center with contributions from writers/rhetorics situated across North America. Our strategy was suggestive rather than comprehensive and followed the advice of Lisa Brooks to map Native space over/into/around/under academic and other dominant spaces. When we talk about mapping native space and forming relationships with the land, we are invoking Brooks's observation: "What I am talking about here is not an abstraction, a theorizing about a conceptual category called "land" or "nature," but a physical, actual, material relationship to 'an ecosystem present in a definable place' that has been cultivated throughout my short life, and for much longer by those relations who came before me, which, for better or for worse, deeply informs my work" (Brooks 2008, xxiv). Into each piece of the course we wove stories about indigenous rhetorical practices and theoretical/methodological frames from specific indigenous locations alongside our own storied practices as scholars and teachers who were situated both within the academy and within our home communities.[6]

So, let's back up a moment and retrace some of the intellectual trade routes we've suggested so far. What do we mean when we say *indigenous rhetorical practices*? What does it mean to strategize and enact such a set of practices in a graduate classroom? To build this indigenous groundwork,[7] we'll need to tell some stories.

WHAT WE MEAN WHEN WE SAY *INDIGENOUS RHETORICAL PRACTICES*

These days, a lot of folks resist claiming that a generalized set of indigenous rhetorical practices can even be invoked. The past decade of scholarship in tribally specific practices has shown the degree to which the details of a specific tribe's traditional cultural practices, linguistic relationship to reality, relationship to land bases (both originary and diasporic), and historical experiences of colonization and the resulting contemporary political structures still make for a distinctive and traceable set of literary, historiographical, artistic practices.[8] However, we believe there are commonalities across those distinctive tribally specific practices worth exploring and worth teaching about. It's true that many of these commonalities come from our collective experience of colonization, but we see those connections as arising out of something larger than just centuries-long experiences of violence and victimry. In fact, the indigenous connections that matter most to us arise from our common relationships to this land base—the American continent—and from the practices of making that arise from those relationships with the land, animals, people, and spirits who persist here. Imagine a kind of four-part layered web that situates the body in a particular place across historical time, rooted in cultural practices that arise from—and are responsible to—a land base. This orientation to that set of relations, and the responsibilities that arise from maintaining "right" relations, then forms the ambiguous boundaries of something we call *indigenous rhetorical practices.*

Clearly, then, we're not just talking about practices that find their end in alphabetic text, nor in ones necessarily visible to the eye of the general public. We believe even the most highly published and critically acclaimed Native writings are rooted in the everyday practices of Native peoples, not as "authentic" anthropological representations of "real" Native cultures but as orientations, inclinations, approaches that reflect body, land, culture, history in particular ways. For us, all of the land in North America is Native land. Indigenous lives, relationships, spirits, and practices form the foundations on which *all* of us live and work each day. They lace together, a strong matrix of roots that surrounds us. One of the goals of any course on Native rhetorics is to visibilize this truth. We know, we know. This sounds both grandiose and vague. Give us a minute and let us show you how this works.

ALL OUR RELATIONS

Everyone in the classroom that semester brought different histories with them. One of the teachings we asked our students to take was the practice of visibilizing the web of relations in which their own stories were situated. This is where we began.

Malea

I never had a single course in Native studies in all of my educational experiences—only the occasional Native text sprinkled into other curricula. All of the work I did to gain Native mentors and work with Native scholarship was done outside my university, on my own time and my own dime. I read as much as I possibly could of American Indian studies scholarship when I wrote my thesis in 1994, then my dissertation in 1998. One of the most distressing memories I have of my graduate education was a seminar on storytelling. I was so excited about this course! And, as it turned out, so naïve. Instead of actually studying storytelling as a methodology, or storytellers as theoretical, this course focused on representations of storytelling in European literature and theory. We read Foucault, Benjamin, Calvino, Vargos Llosa, Deleuze, Guattari and Lacan—you get the idea. We were assigned to bring our own expertise to the course by providing a reading for the whole class to read. I chose Gerald Vizenor's (1993) *Narrative Chance* for "my" day near the end of the course. Throughout the semester, I patiently and diligently slogged through all those course readings, all the similar kinds of things my classmates provided, all the conversations that seemed to me to be about everything *but* the practice of storytelling. I offered alternative views and arguments at every turn—usually to a mixed audience of folks who were genuinely trying to understand what I was saying as valid and folks who thought I simply didn't want to do the "real" work of learning European continental theory. When we got to the Vizenor reading, the classmates from the latter category claimed that he "didn't make any sense." Many admitted to having stopped trying to understand his argument by the end of the second page of the reading. Unlike their readings of Deleuze and Guattari, they cited Vizenor's lack of clarity as proof of unintelligible thinking. The professor agreed. I argued back and spent the remaining years in graduate school embattled and at odds with most of my peers and many of my professors. Now, of course, I realize the degree to which my education was mired in the muck of colonialism and in racist stereotypes about the intelligence—and intelligibility—of Native peoples.

Andrea

From an early age, my parents made it clear to me that the only way I could attend university was by receiving funding from our band's postsecondary fund and the Michigan Indian Tuition Waiver. By benefitting from my ancestors' difficult decisions, I didn't have to take out a single loan until I pursued a PhD. Of course, I heard all the critiques from my friends about how lucky I was to go to school for "free." Since I was the first person in my family to attend a four-year university, I was pretty much in it alone. I started to form relationships with the women in charge of the Michigan Indian Tuition Waiver and the postsecondary fund. They encouraged me to use this extremely complicated gift to better understand American Indian issues—to get in touch with American Indians on campus. So, I listened to them. I took courses in Michigan Indian history and Ojibwe language. By the time I finished my second year as a doctoral student, I understood how to find my people. And yet, it *still* took me a long time to learn how to ask for help, to understand that people wanted to help me, and to see that there were allies in the university. I learned a lot of hard lessons along the way. These relatives used indigenous rhetorical practices to mentor and professionalize me. Now, I use these practices to mentor students and help them find their people. In this way, I believe I am continuing the work of my scholarly elders and ancestors—of the women who initially encouraged me to use this gift to benefit our people—to make a space for young people to survive institutional spaces.

Whenever I visit with my family, especially my Native side, they are always interested in how so much has changed from when they went to school: that I could be "out" as an American Indian, take courses in American Indian studies by Native faculty, and *now* teach courses using American Indian knowledge practices. I hear a lot of "I wish I could have taken that class." When I completed my dissertation, my father made it clear that he wanted to read it and share it with the Native people he knew. In so many ways, my formal education paved the way for opportunities to hear about what it was like for my father, aunts, and uncles growing up in Detroit. Before I attended university, I never heard these stories—I knew little of our history.

Despite the radical differences in our specific life experiences, Malea and I share some core beliefs and practices that arise from our common experiences as mixed Native women that have had a profound effect on how we strategize and practice pedagogy in a classroom. We've both taken teachings from communities of Native women and learned to hear in those stories the theoretical frames that construct our own approaches to teaching and scholarship. Out of those teachings, we've built our scholarly identities on decolonial practices rooted in indigenous studies, a set of practices that take into account the necessity of providing space for students to experience both discomfort and love in a Native-centered classroom.

Andrea

I never truly understood what it meant to nurture or be nurtured in a classroom until halfway through doctoral study. Before, as a creative writing/English studies/American studies student, my experiences in the institution were centered on being criticized for not being intellectual enough, for not understanding traditional academic writing, or for having to constantly defend how I understand theory. But, when I entered a classroom focused on American Indian issues, especially pertaining to American Indian women, I had a wholly different experience. My professors *noticed* me. They saw aspects in me I never knew existed. They didn't treat me as a model or representative. These professors (all women) took the time to listen to me, to work with me, to help me identify what came easily for me and what I had to continue practicing. I have learned from these experiences—the teachings passed down to me—to take the time to show students that I see them and hear them—that I know they are *there*. Yet, *I* learned how to listen from working with (and for) a group of urban, Native women. These women created collective and multigenerational theory through telling stories about their lived experiences. They used their relationships to each other, to me, to space, as the weaving component—as the tool. This idea of relationships—relationality—is not a new idea, especially in decolonial and indigenous theories. It's given me a way into identifying and expressing what felt intangible—inexpressible—embodied. And yet, it's something I have known how to do all along. Our collective work has provided me with an understanding of how practice is central to indigenous worldviews; that relationships are material and we must work (with) them every day. In class, I try to emphasize that a way into making something—whether it's a five-page research paper, a prospectus, or a basket—is by understanding and examining one's relationship to the world, that it's a point of deeply complex inquiry.

Malea

It was a long way from my experiences in graduate school to my first "a-ha" moment a few years ago when I realized that what my beadwork teachers were doing was a critical piece of the theory I'd been trying to find for years. It would be a few years even further down the line when I had my second "a-ha" moment when I watched Robin Scott theorize material practices in a way that definitely paralleled what I'd been seeing in the practices of nineteenth-century Native writers. I now understand that while I spent decades learning from the teachings of indigenous women tradition-bearers and artists, it's only in the past few years that I've learned to take a teaching from them. The distinction between what we're taught in the academy is a teaching/learning relationship and what indigenous communities call *taking a teaching* is such a huge one, it's really hard to explain. That teaching/learning relationship is one in which a teacher makes their own knowledge and rhetorical expertise available to help a student do something they want to do—write an article, bead a bracelet, make dinner, and so forth. To take a teaching implies a greater level of responsibility to hold knowledge that's being passed down in order to make it available for future generations. So, in the first configuration, teachers help you do things for yourself (and maybe, if you're a nice person, you pass it on); in the second configuration, you are gifted with knowledge in order to pass it on. The learner is a vessel for the teaching, not the other way around, and this relationship makes the teacher a tradition-bearer—a person who's carrying knowledge in order to share it. Trying to reconfigure this dynamic in my own classrooms is one of the most difficult things I've ever had to do because it has forced me to confront my own ego and my own motivations for becoming a scholar.

BODY, PLACE, CULTURE, MAKING

Okay, maybe you're thinking all these stories about us are perfectly nice and interesting—reminiscent of that whole "positioning yourself" thing we all learned to do in the '90s—but isn't the focus here supposed to be on graduate pedagogy? Our teaching here is focused on precisely that! We've been giving a teaching that sketches the web of our relations—a practice we expected students to see in the writings/practices we selected for our course, one we practiced, and one we expected them to practice as well. More than simple "positioning," telling the stories that form a web of relations is a deeply critical, deeply reflective practice. It asks participants to recognize learning—and their participation in it—as a fluid process, always in motion, rather than as a static, unchanging set of facts. We learn to see others in particular ways because of how we've been taught to think of them, and of ourselves in relation to them. These sedimented layers of belief must be unpacked, examined, *and* decolonized in order for students to arrive at a different space of practice.

To Get to Space, You Must Start with Place (At Least, That's How We're Interpreting Brooks's Theoretical Work Here)

Because this course took place in Michigan—aka Three Fires territory—we decided to root the course in that web of relations. Three Fires Great Lakes → Northeastern Woodlands. We did this for two reasons. First, we wanted to tell a story about Michigan Indian rhetorical history. As scholars whose research and ancestral relationships are linked to the Great Lakes, we wanted to undo, or push against, the idea that Indians exist only in the West (and in the past) in order to emphasize the "here-ness" of both historical and contemporary indigenous peoples and practices. By acknowledging the physical geography in which we were located, we were also acknowledging the historical events that happened in these places, the cultural and spiritual practices that lived there. Second, we wanted to make clear that relationships to land bases are central to understanding indigenous rhetorics. In this way, we were able to ask our students to draw upon their own relationships to the land and to theorize those relationships to what we were reading.

Through this theorizing, students found their own connections to indigenous rhetorical practices—connections we found to be more meaningful than simple literary and/or artistic appreciation. Further, the constant reminders of real places we could drive to, and of real people who were, quite literally, all around us, helped us be attentive to our textual practices in a different—more responsible—way. Textual practices—like material practices such as beadwork and basket making—arise from somewhere, they happen in relation to some place, and they are experienced by readers who are also situated in a specific place. And, again like material practices, when textual practices travel, they take their "home" with them. This way of organizing the course to focus on rhetorical practices influenced by the shared space/place/land of particular makers provided some glue to hold those local materials together across more diversely geographied readings. For example, we assigned Andrew Blackbird's historical writings situated in Michigan alongside contributions from Chrystos, Qwo-Li Driskill, Deborah Miranda, and Shawn Wilson.

To Understand How Place Is Practiced into Space, and To Operationalize That Knowledge Rhetorically, You Have To Tell Some Stories

Because we take seriously Thomas King's invocation, "The truth about stories is that that's all we are" (King 2008, 2), we designed our syllabus to begin with Native stories. As we've already modeled throughout this narrative, stories and storying practices are central to how we *do* native rhetorics as scholars and teachers. We began the semester with different kinds of stories:[9] academic stories, literary stories, a children's book, and a lot of poetry. What we hoped to make visible was how stories function methodologically and theoretically. By beginning with *our* own stories—as we've done in this chapter—then moving to different published Native stories, we tried to demonstrate how story as methodology is one of the common features of indigenous rhetorical practice *and* to emphasize story as a central theoretical practice for the course. While, as we said earlier, we knew what programs/fields our students were coming from, what we didn't/couldn't know was what stories and relations our students would carry with them: stories from Texas, Michigan, Chicago, Kenya, Sierra Leone, Virginia, Indiana, Ohio, California, and other places/spaces. We *did* know the course would need have a theory of movement. In other words, we'd have to be willing to travel through time and space. We'd have to make space for folks to linger, to dwell, to practice, to teach, to learn.

ON TRAVELING, AND STANDING STILL: OR, WHAT HAPPENED

we read poetry out loud
Andrea

I remember poetry. I remember how poetry helped us form and sustain relationships with each other. Malea and I assigned a lot of poetry, short stories, and teachings by elders. And, we read these pieces for how the writers theorized and enacted indigenous rhetorical practices. We read them as tribal histories and theories.

Early in the semester, we noticed that the class struggled with the course objectives. We tried to get them to believe that theorizing the struggle was crucial to experiencing and practicing indigenous rhetorics. The students were not yet willing to be vulnerable, to experience, and to story. You know, those difficult things we ask students to do. I remember sitting with Malea and talking about what we were witnessing in class. We talked a lot about how we might solve this problem, whether it was solvable or a consequence of the material we were reading. We wondered if this resistance was a result of early relationship building.

And, in the same moment, I felt as if one of us said something about how we wanted more stories. And that was our "oh, crap" moment. We realized we needed to make space for more opportunities to make stories—to story. Poetry didn't magically solve all of our problems. Instead, this "oh, crap" moment represented a realization that we, too, were having difficulty enacting indigenous and decolonial practices and that it is easy to fall back into teaching models that assume a single norm and experience. What this conversation made visible is that storying as an embodied, relational practice created opportunities to collaboratively theorize and talk about the "texts" in a way that moves beyond summation or deconstruction. Since we both identify as writers, we decided to ask the students to select a poem from the required readings: *Sovereign Erotics*, an edited collection of two-spirit writing, or *Not Vanishing*, by Chrystos (1989). We and the students took turns reading our selected poems aloud. Then, after each speaker finished, we spent time writing about the poem: our reaction to the poem, to it being read aloud, to our relationship to the poem. I began with Paula Gunn Allen's piece "Some Like Indians Endure": "so dykes/are like indians/because everybody is related" (Allen 2011, 23). I don't remember much from this experience except good, healing feelings. I remember what came after; I remember that something shifted.

[handwritten marginalia: MAKE SPACE TO STORY]

Malea

I remember the day we read poetry out loud. We were sitting around the long table in 2 Olds that day and we asked who wanted to start. E[10] volunteered. I remember thinking "wow" and "oh, crap" simultaneously—partly because E was the only undergraduate in a room mostly full of PhD students and partly because the poetry we were asking them to choose from was from Chrystos, Joy Harjo, and the edited collection of two-spirit writing *Sovereign Erotics*. The week before E had gushed at how much he loved Chrystos's (1989) erotic imagery, so I really expected him to read some of that poetry. But he didn't. He chose "For Eli," a six-page poem about a boy who was beaten to death by his father. It would take at least twelve to fifteen minutes to read. I did a quick time calculation and nodded my head. E began to read, haltingly, without the affective rhythms of someone used to reading poetry out loud. I watched those doctoral students put on their polite teacherly smiles, knowing—as I did—that this would be a long haul. He got about a third of the way through the poem when he began to tear up; halfway, he had to stop and sob. We—the whole class—soothed him, encouraged him to keep reading.

Andrea

And, as he started to cry a little, I cried a little. I remember feeling happy and relieved that the students did not shame him. Instead, they respected his vulnerability. I respected his willingness to make himself both visible and vulnerable—to let us learn something about him that we didn't know before. For me, these moments when a relationship shifts—when we open ourselves to trust, to be trusted, to share, and to learn something new—are important theoretical moments whether we are in the classroom or doing fieldwork. I believe these experiences can give us a better language to articulate the *how* of indigenous rhetorical practices.

Malea

He said this poem was hard for him because he felt he had so much in common with Eli. We all nodded our encouragements. He kept reading. He finished the poem. Repeated that he chose it, "even though it's long," because it spoke to him. Because he felt he was "just like" Eli except he didn't die. I think I said something inane about how poetry is supposed to build these kinds of connections. Or something.

Anyway, we kept going around the table. Everyone picked a poem to read out loud. All the more experienced students picked poems that were shorter, sometimes more political or more erotic. Some of them clearly felt connected to the poems; others clearly chose them because they could be distant, academic, analytical. All of them modeled different kinds of scholarly relations. I still don't know how to process that moment with E, though. I could say, in that detached scholarly way, that in that moment E became a relation of Chrystos and Eli, that in his connection . . . his choice . . . he imbricated himself into the web that holds them together in more than a textual way. He became their relative through shared experiences, shared emotions—terror, fear, grief. Maybe he liked that poem for the same reason Chrystos wrote it—because he survived. And the guilt and joy of that survival forged a bond between a not-quite-not-white straight boy from Grand Rapids, Michigan, and a radical indigenous lesbian poet from California. And maybe that's it—that human connection. Maybe that's part of what indigenous pedagogy looks like: the revelation of that web of relations that *isn't* part of the stereotype. That shows the real cost of colonial violence, of patriarchy. Maybe.

we struggled through/without students
Andrea

But there are other costs our students felt because of colonialism. We felt them too as we tried to give the students space to transform and decolonize their scholarly practices. While trying to convince the students that it is possible to enact indigenous methodologies, I was reminded of how difficult it was for me to begin doing this work. One student in particular reminded me of what it was like to struggle with using the very knowledges deemed inappropriate to deconstruct and then recast the institutional training that helps one survive academe. S, a PhD student in Chicano/Latina studies, approached the reading and discussion in that traditional liberal humanist model: to deconstruct arguments. Many of us have had similar training and we know that this scholarly approach is still considered an intellectual and theoretical form of critique. Malea and I encouraged S to open up to the idea of enacting indigenous rhetorical practices. But who could blame him for not wanting to when he already had developed a scholarly practice for survival? One day, S came into my office to talk about Shawn Wilson's (2009) *Research Is Ceremony*. We assigned this book with an excerpt from my dissertation since I had tried to model Wilson's research paradigm. We talked a lot about how to approach texts with a good heart, how to form relationships with texts that reflect indigenous rhetorical practices. But S was still struggling. As he went to certain passages in the book, I noticed how he marked up and wrote in his book, replicating that deconstruction model. I showed him my copy with very few markings in it. I said Wilson discouraged me from that annotated reading strategy. As I read Wilson, I heard him telling me to participate with him and the text similarly to how indigenous folks hear teachings. I think S heard me because we started to talk about how he could theorize his struggle to enact indigenous rhetorical practices in his final project.

Malea

And we weren't the only ones S talked to about his struggles. A Xicano from Texas, S had acquired perfectly good traditional academic practices in his journey to the university. These practices were his protective suit of armor, his proof that he was, in fact, smart enough/good enough to get a PhD. S always reminded me of Charles Eastman's taking on the "bows and arrows of the whitemen" in gaining a traditional, Eurocentric education. Both Eastman and S knew the lie of those tools. Even so, S still found it hard to deliberately walk away from their affordances, even for a semester in one seminar.

At any rate, S's advisor talked with me because she was worried we'd give him a bad grade. She said, "S has had a hard time with some of his courses in the English department and he really needs to get a good grade." This plea came during an unplanned conversation in the hallway when I said, "Hey, we have one of your students in our seminar." Because S had gotten bad grades in classes in which he'd written about his heritage, she was worried that we were trying to "trick" him into showing his indigenous side in order to give him a bad grade. This treatment of S was infuriating to me since he was in a Chicano/Latina studies (CLS) PhD program. Why *wouldn't* he be writing about his field of study—which coincides with his heritage—in all of his courses?! Of course, I know all the answers to that question. Wendy Rose knew them way back in the day as well. What really got to me, though, was that this was a Chicana colleague—the director of CLS—was asking me, an indigenous colleague, these questions. She didn't trust me to not be like all the rest of the faculty despite the fact that all of my scholarship advocates for S's ability to build his scholarly work from his own experiences. Sigh.

Andrea

One night after class, S showed us a version of his final project. He had created a video that further examined the conversation we had in my office. He modeled a deconstructive/destructive reading and then enacted a relational and participatory reading by creating a talking circle between him and his two young sons. In the video, S let us see himself as a father. He let us see his sons. As the audience, we weren't supposed to know what was said during the talking circles. We were supposed to see how S and his sons interacted with each other. I remember one scene in particular when S put the talking-circle stick in his youngest boy's hands. The young one kept playing with the stick, and S put his hand over the child's hand. I loved how the boys kept giving the camera these funny little boy looks like "this game is so much fun" or "what's going on?" I learned so much from (and about) S while watching him teach his sons. I knew S wanted feedback about the video. But he left me speechless. As I struggled to say something meaningful, I realized my struggle—my emotional reaction—*might* be enough.

we paid attention to costs

Malea

The seminar was based on a similar one I'd taught during the summer of 2009 but offered in an "immersion" format of five days. One of the most successful and powerful moments during that summer came during a visit to the Cranbrook Institute. In some ways, the visit was a fluke. I'd promised we'd do "rhetorical fieldwork," but the financial support for those experiences had quickly disappeared. So when Kevin Kelly, the collections manager at the Cranbrook Institute, offered to set up a group tour for us and let us into the collections space, I decided to just pay for it myself. Money well spent and all. So we piled into cars and agreed to meet at the museum. Some folks decided to take a trip to Sonic on the way—it was that kind of group experience. We arrived. We checked in. I paid. We did the tour. Kevin and Mike Stanford, the museum director, were quite thoughtful as they led us through the Native exhibits and talked about their process and their theory of that stuff. Then we went into the collections.

Andrea

We went into the collections. It was a small space. Our bodies rubbed up against each other, the cupboards, the door handles. Kevin spoke about what the collections contained, how the museum came to "own" the materials, and how the materials were cared for. While he was speaking, I remember Malea being really excited that the collection held Miami regalia—this particular regalia was very rare. A, one of the doctoral students, asked Kevin about how the Native American Graves Protection and Repatriation Act (NAGPRA) would affect the collections. Kevin let us know that the museum had prepared the remains for travel and ceremony. He said something like "they are right there" and pointed above us. All eleven of us looked up and saw the bones in marked cardboard boxes. Immediately, I felt this sense of dread and immense sadness. I know many of my peers did too as some asked to leave and some turned away, looked down, or covered their mouths. We were silent for a while. I think Kevin felt weird too because in order to break the silence, he let us touch things while he opened the cupboards. I found an Odawa-made strawberry quill box. As I ran my finger over the design, I remembered hearing stories about collecting quills and harvesting strawberries.

Malea

I got to see and feel the Miami ribbonwork leggings and moccasins I'd only seen pictures of—the same materials that prompted Scott Shoemaker to revive ribbonwork traditions in our tribe. Ancestors were everywhere. When A and the other students left, they had to be let out—the collections are behind an airlock of two doors. I knew they were gone. And I knew it would take a while for the reality of what the students had seen to sink in. I stayed with my ancestors as long as I could. Then the rest of us left the collections room. I thanked Kevin and Mike and joined the students outdoors. I had tobacco in the car with me (I always do), so I offered it to the students. I encouraged them to take some time in the sunshine to process, think through, pray, whatever they needed to do. We did. We drove home. The next morning in the classroom, I began, "You all seemed a little shocked when Kevin told us where the human remains were kept. So where did you think they kept the bones?"

Andrea

And, that was a good moment. More than anything, Malea and I wanted to replicate that experience in the course we planned together.

so, we really wanted to go somewhere . . .

Andrea

We had a few plans: we could go to Cranbrook Museum (south), Ziibiwing Center (north), or Harbor Springs (way northwest). We quickly (and regrettably) ruled out Harbor Springs because it would cost a lot of money and we couldn't find a good time to go. Next, we tried to go to the Ziibiwing Center, a museum and cultural center run by the Saginaw Chippewa Tribe in Mt. Pleasant. In Anishinaabemowin, *ziibiwing* means "down by the river." Mt. Pleasant is about an hour's drive from East Lansing. We figured that we could make this a day trip that would happen over spring break or on a Saturday.

I remember talking to one of the directors from Ziibiwing. She was incredibly helpful and accustomed to having groups of students visit to the center. But she had never worked with graduate students or professors—the center rarely organized events for an adult educational audience. I believe this focus on children s most likely typical of many museums and indigenous cultural centers in local areas. Museum events are often associated with arts and crafts: dreamcatchers or pony-bead key chains. The Ziibiwing Center's events for youngsters are incredible. Right now, one activity is a make-your-own Anishinaabe valentine's card, which is a part of their language revitalization program.

But we wanted something different. We wanted to walk around the museum, which would take ten to fifteen minutes, and to talk to someone associated with the museum or listen to stories by one of the community elders (another service they provided). But it just cost so much money.

Malea

It started to feel like some force in the universe just didn't want us to take a trip together. Before talking to Ziibiwing, we'd tried to plan a visit to the Cranbrook, but the scheduling was completely off since the seminar met from 5:00 to 7:50 p.m. The museum would be closed by the time our class even started. Earlier in the day was impossible because of students' teaching and other course obligations. We could go on the weekend, but none of the collections staff could be there to let us have the experience in the collections room that had proved to be so profound at the Cranbrook during the summer. . So we were really hoping that a visit to the Ziibiwing center would work. Andrea did the groundwork and, like she said, we ran up against sheer cost. We could tour the museum on our own for $4.50 per person. Easy, but the ten-minute walk-through hardly seemed worth the two-hour drive. Ziibiwing could provide a speaker or guide for us, but we'd need to pay for the room ($100/hour) and for the speaker (cost determined by availability and topic). We estimated $50/person, which, for the graduate students who had already spent over $100 on books, seemed like a lot of money.

Andrea

These moments teach me something about the community in the classroom. It teaches me about the complex relationship of experience, practice, and shared beliefs. I recognize that many of the students didn't seem into the possible experience. Admittedly, I might not have been into the possible experience. I remember the constant exhaustion and struggle in the course. I remember trying to manage teaching my own course, the dissertation, the job market, and all of the transitions that occur while preparing to graduate from doctoral study. It was good exhaustion and good struggle, but it still affected me—my body. Malea and I were gently pushing the students to theorize and enact indigenous rhetorical practices, and maybe that was enough work for the semester. Maybe, for this class, that's all we could ask them to do.

Malea

I remember the moment we gave up trying to go somewhere—February 12. Not because we didn't have more ideas on our back-up list but because it suddenly just seemed too hard to make it all work out. Every plan pushed us up against barriers put in place by the institution— either the places we wanted to visit or the university—or by the students themselves. Like Andrea said, it just seemed as if we had pushed them as far as they were willing to go.

Taking a teaching.
On wanting consensus
Malea

Like I said before, this idea of physically going somewhere was one of two places where we seemed to hit a wall with our students (the other was the second making project—no one could decide what kind of thing we should make). Maybe this resistance was their way of letting us know we'd pushed them too far off the familiar academic grid, so they dug in the only way they knew how—by pushing responsibility onto their teaching schedules, their course schedules, their lack of funds. In retrospect, I could've behaved differently. I could've set up a Saturday visit to the Cranbrook even though we wouldn't be able to see the collections. I could've insisted that we drive to Mt. Pleasant, do the museum tour, and then go over to the tribe's casino to see a different kind of Native installation. I could've made my own reservations in Harbor Springs, reserved a block of rooms at the Best Western, and invited folks to take advantage of that time by coming up and looking around at all the places we'd be reading about later in the semester. I could've been a bigger cheerleader, a more directive leader. But I was reluctant to do that then and am still reluctant to think about it now because the impact it would've made on my positionality in the course is problematic for me in terms of the learning goals, the processes, and the practices we wanted to encourage throughout the course. We wanted consensus. And sometimes that meant giving up on the ideas we had (Andrea and I) and giving over to the will of the whole. To what they seemed to be telling us they needed/ wanted in that moment.

And there's a part of me that realizes I put too much focus on going someplace and not enough on the place where we already were—the university, the local geography, the land on which we were meeting and taking/teaching classes. In retrospect, I understand that while we tried hard to create a space inside the university for students to imagine Native space and practice Native rhetorics, we didn't do much to reimagine the *place* on which the university was built as indigenous . . . or as indigenizable.

On making
Malea

I remember a moment I think about as the "oh yeah, stories" moment. We were a handful of weeks into the course and were having a confab about what was happening—more precisely about what *wasn't* happening—during class discussion and in the weekly writings. We saw students holding the materials at arm's length, or engaging with them in the usual de(con)structive ways that are rewarded in grad seminars, or treating them as "special" in an especially grumpy-making way. The this-isn't-really-about-me-but-it-is-quite-interesting approach alongside the critique-for-its own-sake approach alongside the academic version of "beads and feathers and flute music, oh my." We were unhappy and had made a number of attempts to intervene in these practices with our students. Some of those attempts had worked a little bit for a while, some others seemed to work pretty well for specific students, most hadn't worked well at all. So we were talking, frustrated, wondering what to do. Our discussion just happened to occur as we were sitting in our lab space, waiting for folks to show up and help scaffold an article were writing collectively. On the whiteboard—above all the other writing and drawing—were two sentences written in purple marker: "The practice of story is integral to doing cultural rhetorics. If you're not practicing story, you're doing it wrong." We were both staring right at this whiteboard during our entire conversation. I don't remember who said it first, but one of us said, "Maybe we should have them tell some stories." Then we both laughed. And the other one of us said, "Omigod, you mean we should practice what we've been preaching?!" And we both laughed again. And that day, we went into class and told some stories and asked students to tell some stories.

After that, things started to break open. We let go a little bit and let ourselves relax into a different relationship to folks in the course. I'd like to think we settled into the kind of community roles we have outside the university in which Andrea is an important listener and participant with the Circle ladies and Malea is a friend and student of many women artists and tradition-bearers. In retrospect, it's clear to me that I was trying hard to model a kind of pedagogical scaffolding Andrea would find useful for other graduate seminars—more mainstream theory, history, methodology—and I let that felt responsibility intrude on my usual approach to teaching Native rhetorics. And it's also clear that my previous two experiences with the course influenced my approach to this seminar. Those experiences had both been intensive summer courses where we met every day from nine in the morning until four in the afternoon and had immersion experiences with one another as well as with the course materials—something nearly impossible to reproduce in a regularly scheduled seminar setting. My expectations, then, were deeply colored by the intimacy of those former pedagogical spaces and by my own desires to recreate them in another time/place/community. A completely impossible task. So it helped when I was able to take my own teaching *as* a teaching and let *this* community make its own story.

WE COME TO YOU WITH A GOOD HEART

For Native peoples, that phrase indicates an orientation to whatever work we find in front of us. A "good heart" is an open heart, one attuned to the responsibilities we all share as relations and inhabitants of the continent. It is an orientation that tries to pay attention to the needs of the whole community instead of pushing the agenda of a single individual. It is almost exactly opposite of everything we're taught to be in the academy. Academic ideologies that tout a single individual as holding power and authority of any kind, or that encourage competition for scarce resources, are anathema to the idea of a good heart. As people who live at least part of our lives within academic communities, these are difficult ideologies to resist. We're the first to admit that any kind of decolonial and/or indigenous pedagogy is difficult to enact in a university setting. It takes time, patience, and understanding and encourages a shift in student/teacher roles that can feel disorienting. While undergraduates who engage with Native rhetorics often profess discomfort with new knowledge or new ways of understanding, graduate students who do so are often literally facing a crisis of investiture. Their very identities as scholars—the ones they're working so hard to build—are threatened when we ask them to practice indigenous rhetorics.

Practicing indigenous rhetorics requires a recognition of the degree to which the entire university system—the categories it enables, the knowledge it values, and the practices we've used to survive its violences—is a tool for the continued colonization of indigenous peoples. To teach graduate students, then, for us, means to be willing to risk just as much as they are: to share the stories of our own struggles with negotiating the tensions and risks of practicing Native rhetorics as scholars and teachers. To acknowledge supremely humbling moments when we had to remind ourselves to listen to our ancestors, or when we let our own needs and desires get in the way of what the community wanted/needed. We tried to be good aunties in this classroom— to clear a path for the students' own stories, to honor their struggles, and to find ways to build relationships between, among, around those stories and the physical space of their tellings. None of this was easy. It never is. But we hope what we've shared here shows you why it's always worth the work.

mihši neewe
miigwetch

Notes

1. This course was offered as one of the cultural rhetorics concentration courses in the rhetoric and writing PhD at Michigan State University during the spring semester of 2012.

2. CIC stands for the Committee on Institutional Cooperation, a consortium of Big 10 universities (plus the University of Chicago) through which these "world-class research institutions have advanced their academic missions, generated unique opportunities for students and faculty, and served the common good by sharing expertise, leveraging campus resources, and collaborating on innovative programs." (See http://www.cic.net/about-cic for more information.) The American Indian Studies Consortium (AISC) of the CIC has since morphed into the Newberry Consortium for American Indian Studies (http://www.newberry.org/darcy-mcnickle-center-american-indian-and-indigenous-studies-programs). One of the longstanding features of the CIC-AISC, though, was a summer seminar comprised of one or two students from each of the CIC campuses.

3. Our coteaching arrangement came about as part of a pilot for a graduate-level teaching internship program in the rhetoric and writing graduate program at MSU. The basic idea behind these internships is to give advanced PhD students practice in teaching graduate courses without violating their union contract and with appropriate levels of faculty support. For Malea, these internships also model the Native teaching practices she's experienced from tradition-bearers (beadworkers, basket makers, quillworkers, etc.) in Native communities where one learns an art by engaging in it instead of through sheer observation.

4. Almost all of our on-the-fly work was done sitting at the conference table in the Cultural Rhetorics Theory Lab, where we'd frequently read students' weekly responses together, commenting back and forth, discuss how to respond to the posts, and talk about how to arrange our approach to the class each day.

5. Though in different forums—Andrea published comments on the course discussion list and Malea wrote comments on hard copies of the weekly writings.

6. Andrea is a mixed-blood of First Nations Chippewa, Chaldean, and Lebanese ancestry. She is an enrolled member of the Chippewa of Thames band in Muncey, Ontario. Malea is a mixed-blood of Indiana Miami, eastern Shawnee and Euro-American ancestry (mostly Welsh, English, and French).

7. For an explanation of *indigenous groundwork*, see Clark and Powell 2008.

8. See Lisa Brooks (2008), Louise Erdrich (2006), Daniel Heath Justice (2006), Maureen Konkle (2006), and Craig Womack (1999; 2009).

9. For details and specific readings, see the Materials appendix to this chapter.

10. We chose to include our students' initials in this piece. Andrea contacted the students, requested their permission, and shared a draft of this chapter. Both students enthusiastically decided they wanted their names in the chapter. We do use one pseudonym for a student in Malea's CIC version of the American Indian Rhetorics course.

References

Allen, Paula Gunn. 2011. "Some Like Indians Endure." In *Sovereign Erotics: A Collection of Two-Spirit Literature*, edited by Qwo-Li Driskill, Deborah Miranda, Daniel Heath Justice, and Lisa Tatonetti, 21–24. Tucson: University of Arizona Press.

Brooks, Lisa. 2008. *The Common Pot: Mapping Native Space.* Minneapolis: University of Minnesota Press.

Chrystos. 1989. *Not Vanishing.* Vancouver: Press Gang.

Clark, D. Anthony Tyeeme, and Malea Powell. 2008. "Resisting Exile in the 'Land of the Free': Indigenous Groundwork at Colonial Intersections." *American Indian Quarterly* 32 (1): 1–15.

Erdrich, Louise. 2006. *Books and Islands in Ojibwe Country.* Washington: National Geographic.

Justice, Daniel Heath. 2006. *Our Fire Survives the Storm: A Cherokee Literary History.* Minneapolis: University of Minnesota Press.

King, Thomas. 2008. *The Truth about Stories: A Native Narrative.* Minneapolis: University of Minnesota Press.

Konkle, Maureen. 2006. *Writing Indian Nations.* Chapel Hill: University of North Carolina.

Vizenor, Gerald. 1993. *Narrative Chance: Postmodern Discourse on Native American Literatures.* Norman: University of Oklahoma Press.

Wilson, Shawn. 2009. *Research Is Ceremony: Indigenous Research Methods.* Nova Scotia: Fernwood.

Womack, Craig. 1999. *Red on Red: Native American Literary Separatism.* Minneapolis: University of Minnesota Press.

Womack, Craig. 2009. *Art as Performance, Story as Criticism.* Norman: University of Oklahoma Press.

8

REMAPPING SETTLER COLONIAL TERRITORIES
Bringing Local Native Knowledge into the Classroom

Joyce Rain Anderson

(May 2011) It's quiet as I write this early morning, the sun rises and light peers through the trees. A few birds begin their morning song. But it is mostly quiet. Before the sun gets too high, I will gather the tools, start my car, and head off to the garden. Driving from Brockton, I pass through East Bridgewater then into Bridgewater past an old and partially rusted sign which registers "Bridgewater: Incorporated in 1656." In four miles, I turn off route 18 onto an unassuming road which winds through large oaks, maples and smaller trees and bushes. For a moment, I am taken to a space different from the clutter of everyday. Sometimes Rusty Grump, as my grandfather used to call red squirrel, comes out to chatter before making his way to forage. A bit beyond the trees in a marshy area, this season's cattails are beginning to grow while a few from last year still stand bursting and fluffy. Soon, my dreaming is ruptured by the barbed wire and brick buildings of the Bridgewater Correctional Facility. A brick tower rises on my right but I turn left past a recreational yard driving several yards down the road to the Bridgewater Growing Spaces: nine acres of beautiful land leased by the state to the university. Though mostly a hayfield, a small portion of these lands has been turned into community gardens. It is here that my cousins and I grow a Three Sisters Garden. Our 20 x 20 foot plot sits on a small rise. Yet in past years, the grass was so high that I was hidden while I sat among the three sisters weeding. So peaceful were those moments where I understood our relationship to the land. The pull of gravity bringing my body that much closer, the way I moved—sitting, kneeling, crawling, pulling—among the mounds of corn, beans and squash. All around redwing blackbirds, bob-o-links and crows called out. Hoof prints in the dirt indicated that the deer had been around to visit. As the sun rose higher into the sky and I was finishing my weeding, I would rest and marvel at how my female ancestors would each have tended two to three acres of traditional garden. It was the way of planting that made the work lighter, the way each of the three sisters nourished the other.

DOI: 10.7330/9780874219968.c008

This place is where stories live. Throughout the planting season, this land offers itself to the community. Our garden nourishes by giving traditional foods and offering stories. In the introduction to *The Land Has Memory*, John Paul Jones writes, "There is no place without a story. Every plant, every animal, every rock and flowing spring carries a message. Native peoples of the Americas learned over thousands of years to listen to messages, and we know every habitat. We know the earth; we know the sky; we know the wind; we know the rain; we know the smells. We know the spirit of each living space. The spirit of each place is deeply embedded within us; we are connected to something larger than ourselves" (Blue Spruce and Thrasher 2008, 1). This understanding of how we are connected to the land, how we are an extension of the land, how story is integral to all we know is critical to understanding how we teach indigenous rhetorics.

The Algonquian name for the Bridgewater area is *Satucket*, which means "great-pouring-forth-stream place." The Satucket River served as a passageway from the Taunton River to the North River and into Massachusetts Bay. Place names often were given based on landscape features. As Keith Basso notes in *Wisdom Sits in Places*, "Places . . . are as much a part of us as we are of them" (Basso 1996). According to Bridgewater's historical documents, On March 23, 1649, at Sachem's Rock (now in East Bridgewater), Ousamequin (Massasoit) signed over Satucket (Bridgewater) to the English for "7 Coats; 9 hatchets; 8 hoes; 20 knives, 4 moose skins; and 10 yards of cotton." The deed was written by Miles Standish, signed by Massasoit, and the original still exists (Kingman 1866). This deed, then, marks the beginning of a replacement narrative for the peoples of Satucket.

While many areas have been victims of settler colonial tactics, it is clear that New England is a prime example of the intent of settlers to stay and replace the indigenous populations with themselves. Thus it is vital for me to remind all my students in all my classes that we are on indigenous lands and, thus, must respect those upon whose blood and bones we now have built our university. Colonial histories of "firsting" and "lasting" (O'Brien 2010b) have attempted to write out the continuous presence of Native peoples. That is, these settler colonial tactics erase both any history prior to their settlement and the continued presence of Native peoples. Jean O'Brien's book, which focuses on southern New England, explores the settler colonialists who made the "boldest claims" of "origin stories of the nation" (xii–xiii). In *Firsting and Lasting: Writing Indians Out of Existence in New England* O'Brien (2010b), opens her introduction with a story about the bicentennial of Bridgewater,

Massachusetts. She writes that on this occasion, former Governor Emery Washburn stepped forth to celebrate New England ancestors; however, "The original inhabitants of the land before it became Bridgewater barely registered in his address, although the way they did turn up is telling" (O'Brien 2010b, xi). Washburn mentions the transaction at Sachem's Rock, then says the following: "But it is sad to think that of all the race who peopled this region nothing now but tradition remains." Further, Washburn states that there is no trace of Indian blood left in the Bridgewater region even as those listening knew they lived among Indian people. In her study, O'Brien examines multiple town histories and other town publications and asserts that her "aim is to understand how non-Indians in Southern New England convince themselves that Indians there had become extinct even though they remain as Indian peoples—and still do to this day" (xii). As one who is descended from these Indians, I too struggle with such claims as Washburn and others make; these sweeping claims of firstings have made it difficult to recover some of my ancestors.

Because of these firstings, students often ask me why they haven't heard the stories I tell in my classrooms. It is then *necessary* that I as a Native educator work with my students to provide a past, present, and future that includes Native peoples—a continued *presence*. It's not enough to simply require students to read about Native peoples and histories. They have been thoroughly soaked in a history that has told them a single story of how this nation began. In New England territory, it is the grand narrative of the pilgrims in 1620. This single story is reinforced in their elementary classrooms when students reenact the so-called first thanksgiving and continues to this day as they drive around this area and see sign after sign like those announcing the incorporation of Bridgewater. Many are unaware of how the land they walk upon each day was "acquired," and many are unaware of the survival of Native peoples. It is my responsibility to tell them that this university and every other university in this country are built on the lands of Native peoples (Gould 1998) and that Native peoples still live here and across America despite these attempts at erasure.

To that end, I include local knowledge in my class. In part, I consider what Sandy Grande claims as "Red Pedagogy," which "necessitates (1) the subjection of the processes of whitestream schooling to critical pedagogical analysis; (2) the decoupling and dethinking of education from its western, colonialist contexts; and (3) the institution of indigenous efforts to reground students and educators in traditional knowledge and teachings" (Grande 2004, 56). While Grande sometimes leans toward nationalism in *Red Pedagogy*, I align myself with her views on critical pedagogy and challenges to colonialist education. Similarly, my teaching aligns with Scott Lyons's suggestions in his germinal essay, "Rhetorical Sovereignty: What Do Indians Want from Writing?" In it, he writes that we must provide our students with knowledge of "Indian peoples' ongoing struggles for sovereignty" and the relationships to that sovereignty. He continues by suggesting that work take place on "local and community levels" (Lyons 2000, 464).

In her book *The Common Pot: Recovering Northeast Native Space,* Lisa Brooks provides a metaphor for weaving Native curriculum and programming into education so that we all benefit. Brooks describes the Abenaki *a-wik-hig-an* as tools we use in "transmitting an image or idea from one mind to another" and something that "operates within particular, tangible spaces" (Brooks 2008, xxii). Brooks explains that many indigenous-language words are active. These tools, then, involve activities that are ongoing and at the same time rooted in a particular place. I carefully and respectfully honor this concept by incorporating multiple ways of "transmitting" to the students in my Native Women Writers and Native Rhetorics courses and to colleagues and community members in university programming.

This chapter discusses ways to incorporate local Native knowledge into courseworks. In collaboration with local Native communities, I invite local Native knowledge into the classroom so students can witness firsthand the continued presence of Native peoples. Since coming to Bridgewater State, I have made it a priority to bring Native programming to the university in a variety of ways because it *must* be part of the institution—and at times, like the powwow, transform BSU into Native space. I also recognize I have not brought about these changes alone but in collaboration with some of my colleagues and, most important, with local Native communities.

I often begin my Native studies classes with an exercise that asks students to read series of terms like *savage, Indian giver, mascot, captivity narrative, cowboys and Indians.* I ask the students what words are familiar to them, in what contexts, and how they think about these words. Reactions vary from guilt (e.g., if they frequently use phrases like *low man on the totem pole*) to confusion to awareness. Some words are fuzzier: *Satuket, Massasoit, Titicut, Nippenicket, Pometacom, Nemasket, Patuxet,* and more. Students have heard them, even see them on signs around their communities, but they are not quite sure about them or what they mean. We then begin talking about the ways in which Native histories and peoples have always been and are still present; we talk about survivance.

The histories of America's indigenous peoples are complex; the history of one people affects all of us. Those histories do not fit easily between the covers of a book. They slide off the pages, seep through the covers, and reappear in current histories, at tribal councils, in human-rights forums, at conferences, in discussions of sovereignty, in classrooms, at powwows, in political arenas, in prayer, and in our homes. For me, claiming these histories is how I learn and grow in my teaching.

When I came to Bridgewater State in 2008, classes were being taught in several disciplines as part of a US Ethnic Studies Program, yet from my perspective, there was not a sustained Native studies program. While speakers had been brought to campus to celebrate Native Heritage Month, Native heritage was usually celebrated only during that month. There had been few attempts at a reciprocal connection to our local Native communities, and the attention to Native peoples was an old model of celebrating culture rather than integrating ways of knowing. While some of the faculty were teaching classes about local Native history, archeology, and literature, not having indigenous peoples present on campus just reinforced the ideas of erasure and replacement. Working with my colleagues, I began inviting Native peoples from our surrounding Native communities to speak in our classes and at the university on a regular basis. We also worked on establishing a powwow with the Massachusetts Center for Native American Awareness (MCNAA), on which I currently serve as advisory councilmember. When integrating indigenous programming and pedagogy into my university's strategic plan, I particularly focus on goals that maximize learning relationships between Bridgewater State and the broader community in southeastern Massachusetts. In my correspondence to the administration, I am vigilant in connecting these goals to local Native communities to gain support for my programming. It is vital for anyone starting up a program to weave it into existing structures. Because BSU has cultivated other partnerships with Native peoples locally and in South Dakota, we have developed cultural-competencies training for our employees and students.

This kind of work involves building relationships with local Native communities; it's as much about trust building as it is anything else. You need to get out and support Native communities by attending their events and offering yourself only if they need your assistance—and then follow through. As Lyons (2000) reminds us, we should "lend support to what's already being done there . . . every university or school exists in a place, on a land, with a history and a community of struggles: every place has its peoples" (464). Thus it is important to attend Native events, listen to the people, and respect their points of view. It is important to remember that the relationship between Native peoples and institutions has been fraught with tensions. The systems have treated Native peoples unjustly, histories have been erroneous, assumptions have been made, and sometimes you may be the target of anger and distrust. But listen, and let them know you are listening. Let them know you want to welcome them to the campus to tell their stories. Most important, be willing and able to honor and form reciprocal relationships with those who do come. For example, at BSU we provided a local Native artist with her first pottery display; following her show, I helped her write a small grant, which she received. In another case, a Native speaker was asked to come to campus, and I argued to get an honorarium for him. Too often, Native peoples are asked to speak and not offered the same remuneration as other speakers; this behavior is not acceptable. I also gift our speakers, often with a blanket and tobacco. It will take time to build your reputation, and you often do so by being willing to give back.

Furthermore, begin to find ways to interest faculty from a variety of disciplines in attending and participating in some of this programming. In 2009, we purchased the film *Rocks with Wings* and encouraged our movement arts and physical health and leisure studies (MAPHLS) faculty and students to attend the screening or to use the film in their classes; we followed up by screening *Crooked Arrows* in 2013. In 2010, we started a new tradition, and we now cosponsor, with the Pride Center, two-spirit event each year; speakers have included Qwo-li Driskill, Kianoa Blackeagle, and Harlen Pruden. In November 2009, we held the first powwow. Its success has gained the attention of the administration, and it has become an institutionalized event; the powwow has brought many Native alumni who are pleased to have BSU recognizing a Native presence. Conversations with these alumni, powwow vendors, dancers, and drummers also helped increase the network of Native peoples we could connect with. We also worked on displays for Native Heritage Month and have exhibited them in Boyden Hall and Maxwell Library. It was a great pleasure to display the work of Wampanoag artist Kerri Helme for the first time. In addition to Kerri's work, the works of Troy Philips, Casey Figueroa, and Deborah Spears Moorehead have been featured. We now have dedicated time and space for these exhibits. Currently, we are working on developing a permanent exhibit, one that tells a story of Native peoples here. In 2010, with a small grant from the Center for Research and Scholarship at my institution, we started a three-sisters garden to demonstrate to students and the public how our ancestors grew food; we continue to create this garden each year. In April 2013, Urban Thunder, a Native drum group, performed on World Music Day. For now, I argue these programs assist Native peoples in resituating themselves in an institution built upon their lands, and students can witness firsthand the survivance of Native peoples in New England. This programming has been infused into classes as students and faculty attend as part of their courses. Native students have just started the first Native student club, the Native American Cultural Association (NACA). Their hope is to expand the club to include alumni. This year, for the first time, Native stoles were given to Native students to wear at graduation.

But more significantly, I am always respectful of the teachings of ancestors and elders. In *Indigenous Storywork*, JoAnn Archibald discusses core principles in doing indigenous work: respect, responsibility, reciprocity, reverence; this work is also holistic and interconnected (Archibald 2008). In wrapping indigenous curriculum around students and the university, these principles are key. In planning, I want to be sure Native peoples are getting something in return for their contributions to the programming. Archibald's work brings me back to thinking about *The Common Pot*. Brooks (2008) writes, "[The common pot] is the wigwam that feeds the family, the village that feeds the community, the networks that sustain the village. . . . Inherent in the concept of the common pot is the idea that whatever was given from the larger community of inhabitants had to be shared within the human community . . . sharing space meant sharing resources" (4–5). It is how I envision weaving together the curriculum and programming at BSU so we all benefit.

CLASSROOM PRACTICES

In addition to understanding names and phrases, I ask students to participate in a mapping project (see companion teaching resources website). Using Jill Lepore's (2002) *Encounters in the New World: A History in Documents* and Joy Harjo's (2001) poem "A Map to the Next World" as well as historical maps of the area, students are asked to make their own maps. We delve further into place names that were discussed earlier. Students complete a rhetorical mapping project, which asks them to plot out the area where they live, then create an overlay of Native space. By doing so, they explore the complex histories and the ways in which Native spaces are recovered within their communities. In addition, they explore the current representations of Native peoples through naming and realities. Students continually comment that they had little idea of the connections to Native space that still exist in their communities.

Like other indigenous ways of knowing, these activities connect and educate the mind, heart, body, and spirit. Indigenous peoples understand theory and research as evolving from these ways, which include writing, orality, bodies, and makings—connecting the whole—contrary to Western ways of knowing. As Malea Powell (2010) says often, *I am where I think and do.* So when I applied for the small grant, I began to imagine the Indigenous Garden and Wetu Project at the Bridgewater Growing Spaces as bringing these concepts together. Local Native people came in as consultants on the project and created this Native space to become a teaching space for BSU as well as for Native communities. The garden helps to bring indigenous knowledge to the classroom and helps foster relationships between BSU students and local Native communities.

When we can, classes come out to the garden. When we run into conflicts with the weather, we bring the garden to the class, showing pictures of how the garden is progressing and how it connects the body to the land. We explain that each of the mounds is made to be the size of a pregnant woman's body, as Earth is about to give birth. Corn is planted when the oak leaves are the size of a mouse ear, and beans and squash are planted around them once the corn is a hand high. Our tools have been made from deer and moose scapulas. We tell the story of the three sisters whose mother prayed for them to help one another, so they became these plants. We tell how the crow brought corn to us, so we always plant five corn seeds—for the four directions and one for the crow. We talk about how these plants enact with one another: the corn takes nitrogen from the soil, but the strong stalks provide a climbing space for the beans, which put nitrogen back. The squash leaves, broad and prickly, protect the roots, keep the mounds moist, and keep small animals away. In my classes, we read Cherokee scholar Marylou Awiakta's (1994) *Selu: Seeking the Cornmother's Wisdom* and create cornhusk dolls while I tell cornmother stories. This making activity shows students how all aspects of the plant are used. I tell an Iroquois story of the cornhusk doll and explain why the doll's face is left blank so children can see their own beauty reflected in the doll. Awiakta also tells a Cherokee story of how corn came to the people, and she discusses our relationship to land and how it has been endangered. We talk about the important ways all resources are used with little waste. We read Winona LaDuke and discuss how GMOs are destroying corn as a staple.

The students also have experiences with quilling, beading, and creating small clay pots. Students not only gain knowledge from the readings and our guests, but also learn how writing and makings are important to the transmission of this knowledge. These makings, as Malea Powell writes, "are significant for understanding Native rhetorical traditions because *as things* they provoke, create, and prompt the stories that tell us who we are in relation to one another. They instruct us about our responsibilities to each other, and to the land" (Powell 2010).Thus students are able to examine these makings, from a corn-leaf basket to pottery to finger-woven pouches, as well as experience creating their own to see the "possibilities of this rhetorical work" (Powell 2010, 7). In their making, they, too, make stories, which are connected to the stories of other makers, of place. These are tied into the numerous readings and the experiences of Native peoples and woven into the fabric of student learning. By the end of the semester, students come to understand, as Duane Blue Spruce writes, "For Native people, the process of creating something—a meal, a basket, an article of clothing, a dance, a song—is as important as that which is being created" (Blue Spruce and Thrasher 2008, 11). At the end, we share the students' work at a potluck. Once more, we invite our Native speakers back. As a class, we form relationships with one another, with the Native communities, and with the land. Students then conduct their final research projects with all this in mind.

There is a relationship of the body to the land and to the histories connecting us all. Shawn Wilson (2008) writes in *Research is Ceremony*, "Relationships don't just shape Indigenous reality, they are our reality. Indigenous researchers develop relationships with ideas in order to achieve enlightenment in the ceremony that is Indigenous research. Researchers must be accountable to all our relations, make careful choices in ways we select and present information" (Wilson 2008). So as students engage in their own research, they are considering how this work will affect others. Many of my students are planning on being K–12 school teachers, and they learn strategies in my classes to bring more accuracy to what and how they teach about Native peoples. I am grateful to be able to help reground these potential teachers within indigenous pedagogical practices.

> *I'm driving on Route 24 South, heading to the women's circle. On my left Wattupa Lake appears and my body seems to be free of gravity as I hear ancestors' voices talking of this space. It's a familiar feeling that calls when I am taking notice of space: Awashonks Woods or the Great Blue Hill. They urge me on. I am always grateful for how they have led me to the work I do today, how they help me think about its importance . . . ancestors speak when you listen.*

References

Archibald, Joanne. 2008. *Indigenous Storywork: Educating the Mind, Heart and Body.* Vancouver: University of British Columbia Press.

Awiakta, Marylou. 1994. *Selu: Seeking the Cornmother's Wisdom.* Golden, CO: Fulcrum.

Basso, Keith H. 1996. *Wisdom Sits in Places: Language and Landscape among the Western Apache.* Albuquerque: University of New Mexico Press.

Blue Spruce, Duane, and Tanya Thrasher, eds. 2008. *The Land Has Memory: Indigenous Knowledge, Native Landscapes and the National Museum of the American Indian.* Chapel Hill: University of North Carolina Press.

Brooks, Lisa. 2008. *The Common Pot: The Recovery of Native Space in the Northeast.* Minneapolis: University of Minnesota Press.

Grande, Sandy. 2004. *Red Pedagogy: Native American Social and Political Thought.* Lanham, MD: Rowman & Littlefield.

Harjo, Joy. 2001. *A Map to the Next World: Tales and Poems.* New York: W. W. Norton.

Kingman, Bradford. 1866. *History of North Small New England Town from Its First Settlement to the Present Time with Family Registers.* http://freepages.books.rootsweb.ancestry.com/~blackwell/ma/SmallNewEnglandTownNorth/brdgwtrintro.html.

Lepore, Jill. 2002. *Encounters in the New World: A History in Documents.* New York: Oxford University Press.

Lyons, Scott Richard. 2000. "Rhetorical Sovereignty: What Do American Indians Want from Writing?" *College Composition and Communication* 51 (3): 447–68. http://dx.doi.org/10.2307/358744.

O'Brien, Jean M. 2010b. *Firsting and Lasting: Writing Indians Out of Existence in New England.* Minneapolis: University of Minnesota Press.

Powell, Malea. 2010. *Rhetorical Powwows: What American Indian Making Can Teach Us about Histories of Rhetoric.* Purdue University Hutton Lecture Series.

Wilson, Shawn. 2008. *Research Is Ceremony: Indigenous Research Methods.* Halifax, NS: Fernwood.

9

RHETORICAL SOVEREIGNTY IN WRITTEN POETRY
Survivance through Code-Switching and Translation in Laura Tohe's Tséyi'/Deep in the Rock—Reflections on Canyon de Chelly

Jessica Safran Hoover

Analyzing American Indian[1] literature for its rhetorical prowess and prominence is the first step in gaining acknowledgment, respect, and awareness for the rhetorical sovereignty still very much ignored and disregarded in not only our society but also in various classrooms throughout our school systems. Simply reading American Indian literature will not encourage students to appreciate the significance of the voices in the texts—the rhetorical sovereignty of the author and the resistance within the language and the stories need to be foregrounded. Kimberli Lee, in her article "Heartspeak from the Spirit Songs of John Trudell, Keith Secola, and Robbie Robertson," makes the prudent assertion that "for centuries Indigenous peoples in this hemisphere have raised powerful voices of resistance to the unjust treatment and outright genocide they have received at the hands of colonizers. This resistance has been, and continues to be, manifested through a variety of rhetorical venues: speeches, stories, poems, songs" (Lee 2007, 89). We must encourage our students to engage with these creative mediums through either literary or rhetorical analyses, as well as intellectual alliances, so they may understand and appreciate this resistance.

Scott Richard Lyons argues that treaties and federal Indian laws should be taught as rhetorical texts themselves (2000, 464). I agree. However, American Indian literature should also be taught as rhetorical texts, as rhetoric fleshes out concepts that literature portrays through storytelling and images of the American Indian nations as well as provides a space for additional voices. These voices should not be looked at as "Other" but as part of a larger discourse. While multicultural

DOI: 10.7330/9780874219968.c009

pedagogy has aided in bringing marginalized groups to the attention of our students, more needs to be done (King 2012, 210). By bringing rhetorical sovereignty to the forefront of our students' literary foci when engaging with American Indian texts, we can disrupt our students' preconceived notions of who is American Indian, help them see how the English language is privileged through colonial attempts to silence American Indian nations, encourage them to acknowledge the uniqueness of each American Indian nation, and bring their attention to the rhetorical power in the voices of American Indian authors.

The purpose of this chapter is to use American Indian rhetorical theory to examine Diné[2] Laura Tohe's poetry through the lenses of intellectual,[3] cultural,[4] and rhetorical sovereignty and demonstrate how using Tohe's text in the classroom is effective when teaching about sovereignty. In "Coyote Poems: Navajo[5] Poetry, Intertextuality, and Language Choice," Anthony Webster asserts that Navajo poetry has been submerged or hidden. Navajo oral poetry, although recognized as early as the 1880s, has been largely ignored by the dominant society. Only recently has there been an appreciation of Navajo poetry and American Indian literature in general (Webster 2004, 70). One influential American Indian author is Diné Laura Tohe. Tohe is revered for her poetry, as well as for her various texts and plays, and she is increasingly the subject of scholarly studies; her work has been anthologized and often cited. Tohe has also gained recognition among the Diné, as well as among her scholarly counterparts and other Native nations, for her compilation of poetry and short stories, *Tséyi /Deep in the Rock: Reflections on Canyon de Chelly*.

In this chapter, I will first explain how I encourage my students to understand and appreciate American Indian literatures. Next, I will show how I use Tohe's work in the classroom and how in *Tséyi'/Deep in the Rock: Reflections on Canyon de Chelly*, she demonstrates her rhetorical sovereignty through the use of code-switching[6] and rhetorics of survivance and alliance. Further, I will explain how Tohe claims cultural and intellectual sovereignty in her writing by consciously and intentionally choosing to code-switch from English to the Diné (Navajo) language and translate or not translate specific Navajo terms for the non-Navajo-speaking reader (or even for the Navajo-speaking reader). Finally, I will provide a discussion of the reasons instructors should use Tohe's work in the classroom in order to teach students about sovereignty.

In *Red on Red: Native American Literary Separatism*, Craig Womack argues that "Native perspectives have to do with allowing Indian people to speak for themselves . . . with prioritizing Native voices. Those voices may vary in quality, but they rise out of a historical reality wherein Native people have been excluded from discourse concerning their own cultures, and Indian people must be, ultimately will be, heard" (Womack 1999, 4–5). Lyons calls this notion *rhetorical sovereignty*. In "Rhetorical Sovereignty: What Do American Indians Want from Writing," he tells us that what American Indians want from writing is the ability to pursue rhetorical sovereignty, or the "inherent right and ability of peoples to determine their own communicative needs and desires, to decide for themselves the goals, modes, styles, and languages of public discourse" (Lyons 2000, 449–50). Writing provides a means for regaining the sovereignty that has been torn from the tongues and bodies of American Indian peoples after years of colonization, oppression, and resistance. In this chapter, I argue that code-switching and translation are means of exercising rhetorical sovereignty and acts of survivance, or what Gerald Vizenor and Malea Powell explain are acts of resistance and survival.

Survivance denotes the need for both resistance and survival, the need to resist an imposition of being absent and invisible in the colonial imaginary and to survive the ongoing colonial attempts to define, quiet, and ignore American Indian peoples. As Vizenor's work makes clear, Indians are placed into the past as a vanishing or vanished race, one represented neither by own cultures nor by their own nations but by an image created of them by hegemonic forces that sponsor colonization, assimilation, and dominance. However, Vizenor explains that American Indian peoples and "their stories actuate a presence, not an absence" (Vizenor 2000, 14).

Powell extends Vizenor's theories on rhetorics of survivance as she investigates the rhetorics of resistance + survival among late nineteenth- and early twentieth-century American Indian rhetors Sarah Winnemucca, Charles Eastman, Susan La Flesche, and Andrew Blackbird. In "Rhetorics of Survivance: How American Indians Use Writing," Powell demonstrates how Winnemucca and Eastman used rhetoric to both resist and survive and how doing so worked to transform them from object status to subject status, to assert a presence instead of an absence. I use this scholarship to scaffold a deeper understanding of how Tohe's work operationalizes survivance in complex ways, ways that "actuate a presence" in the face of ongoing attempts to render American Indian peoples absent from American rhetorical, literary, and geographic landscapes.

Below, I will explain how I use American Indian texts in my classroom to demonstrate the presence, not the absence, of American Indian peoples. Most important, I will explicate how using Tohe's text helps students learn about, and understand, sovereignty through studying her use of rhetorics of alliance and survivance, as well as her claims of intellectual and cultural sovereignty through her code-switching and translation choices.

PEDAGOGY

In a general education introduction to literature course during the fall 2012 semester, I focused on contemporary ethnic American literatures, with a strong emphasis on American Indian texts. I started the course with Vine Deloria's "Indians Today," Phillip Deloria's "I Am Not a Mascot," and Louise Erdrich's "American Horse." When discussing these readings with my students, I immediately discovered through student feedback and the discussion topics that ensued (stereotypes, assumptions, and the idea that American Indians are *still* here—not set in the past) that the focus on American Indian works was both intriguing and confusing for the students because they were not familiar with American Indian texts: intriguing because the content was so new and confusing because they did not understand the complex and unique historical backgrounds of the varying nations. Most of my students had never encountered an American Indian text, nor had they any knowledge about American Indian peoples. One student even explained she had "no idea that there are such diverse histories" surrounding the varying nations, while another student stated he did not know "Indians even existed anymore." Carol Zitzer-Comfort asserts that many students come with little to no background knowledge of Native peoples and rely on stereotypes they have learned (Zitzer-Comfort 2008, 162). I found that most of my students had never read a piece of literature by, about, or for American Indians, nor had they any knowledge of the stereotypes surrounding American Indian peoples. However, when discussing the demonstration of stereotypes in Sherman Alexie's *The Absolutely True Diary of a Part-Time Indian*, one student made the comment that "American Indians only play pow wow music." Upon hearing this, I brought up Youtube.com and played an American Indian hip-hop group's music. My students were shocked to see and hear an American Indian music group performing hip-hop. Their surprise was satisfying, as they were being confronted with their assumptions surrounding American Indian peoples.

Perhaps the most disturbing realizations I had when teaching this course was that my students did not have any background in the history of relocation and removal of American Indian peoples. This lack of knowledge provided me the opportunity to relate to my students the history of violence, relocation, removal, assimilation, and alienation that took place during the 1800s. The historical-background discussion then led us into identifying and discussing sovereignty and how it is still denied to American Indian peoples today. Many of my students had no understanding of the struggle for sovereignty American Indian nations continue to survive against; so, to encourage their awareness, I asked them to research current events by using the terms *Native American*, *American Indian*, and *American Indian sovereignty*. Students could use additional terms during their search, but I found that these terms provided them with a strong starting point. In the class session following their search, I asked each student to explain to the class what they had found. Some current events included mascot prejudice, adoption issues, tribal citizenship, Victoria Secret's using American Indian ceremonial dress for their models, and the filming of the *Lone Ranger* taking place at Canyon de Chelly.

While these discussions of current events aided in the students' understanding and awareness of the appropriation of, and denial of, sovereignty to American Indian peoples, the students still struggled with seeing American Indian peoples as separate nations—to most of my students, all were the same. The students' ignorance surrounding the differences between nations arose when discussing *Tracks* by Louise Erdrich; students kept using generalisms like "all American Indian people" or "all American Indian groups." Though I lectured the students about the differences between the many American Indian nations as we read texts by differing American Indian authors, I wanted them to discover the unique histories and cultures on their own; simply telling them that Sherman Alexie identifies as Spokane/Coeur d'Alene and Luci Tapahonso identifies as Diné would not help the students understand the immense differences between the nations, nor the differing histories. So, I took my students to a computer lab and encouraged them to research the backgrounds of the authors we had read (up until that specific time in the course)—including Sherman Alexie, Louise Erdrich, Luci Tapahonso, and Vine Deloria. This exercise gave the students an opportunity to learn about the sovereignty of the individual nations and aided them in their learning process as they acquired this information on their own rather than through lecture.

My students were unaware of the prominence of American Indian authors and literary texts, and they had no understanding as to the significance of the term *sovereignty* when encountering Native texts. Students can learn to identify and become aware of sovereignty by paying attention to current events, but they must also read texts about and by American Indians. Before students can fully appreciate the significance of a piece of work authored by an American Indian author, it is necessary for them to recognize and understand rhetorical sovereignty, as, according to Lisa King, this recognition "asks that students dig deeper and try to understand what they do not know and what is not 'about' them" (King 2012, 223). To provide the students with the opportunity to identify sovereignty in manageable texts, I used excerpts from Sarah Winnemucca's *Life Among the Piutes* and Charles Eastman's *From the Deep Woods to Civilization*, as both works are approachable and effective and demonstrate rhetorical sovereignty for the students. After reading these texts, we discussed how Winnemucca and Eastman display sovereignty through their rhetoric, including code-switching. Using this literature was effective because as Womack argues, "Native literature, and Native literary criticism, written by Native authors, is part of sovereignty: Indian people exercising the right to present images of themselves and to discuss those images" (Womack 1999, 14). These texts encouraged the students to ask the question, is the act of writing this text considered rhetorical sovereignty? Furthermore, I provided my students with excerpts from these texts to make them privy to the ways in which literature and rhetoric come together and to help demonstrate the power of the rhetoric used in the storytelling of both Winnemucca and Eastman, and to acquaint them with the history of the United States that both texts exhibit. The students quickly picked up on the different audiences each author was addressing, the strategies of storytelling, and how both authors used their words and language with a specific purpose—to attain a rhetorical goal.

Though Winnemucca's and Eastman's texts provided the students with two examples of rhetorical sovereignty, I also wanted my students to understand the action of code-switching. To encourage this, I asked my students to go to the library and locate an American Indian author who uses both English and another language in their works. This assignment allowed us to spend a class period discussing code-switching and the plethora of examples they had found and showed the students that different American Indian authors use language in varying ways. Finally, after much discussion of code-switching as well as the definition of rhetorical sovereignty, I then assigned Tohe's work.

First, as was typical when starting a new text, my students were provided with some background about the author. In this case, the author was Diné Laura Tohe. Before engaging with her poetry, I discussed with my students the Diné history, more specifically the Navajo Long Walk, as the Long Walk is a significant image in the text. I then asked my students to read Tohe's poem "Many Horses" and, while in groups, come up with a reason for her code-switching in that poem. This activity led into a discussion of rhetorics of alliance as well as cultural and intellectual sovereignty. Another exercise with Tohe's text asked the students to go through her book of poetry and pick out where they found examples of rhetorics of survivance (after we had defined rhetorics of survivance) and alliance. My students first did this on their own, and then in small groups. This sequence allowed them time to read through the poetry once more (they had read it before class as well) and engage with Tohe's use of rhetorics of survivance and alliance. Placing them into small groups allowed them to discuss this in more detail and provided them with a level of comfort, as none of my students had any knowledge of the Navajo Long Walk, which, as I mention above, is a strong focus in Tohe's text. Furthermore, rhetorics of survivance and alliance can be difficult not only to understand but also to identify when students have not had any previous experience with American Indian texts and/or authors or have little knowledge of the terms *alliance, survivance,* or *sovereignty.* The small groups also allowed them a chance to formulate and better articulate their ideas before coming together to discuss their findings as a whole class.

By discussing and analyzing Tohe's text, my students learned about sovereignty and began to see how and why Tohe reflects on what Canyon de Chelly means for the Diné in terms of their roots and deep historical and personal connections to the canyon. In my case study of Tohe's work, found below, I will provide an analysis of Tohe's text to demonstrate how her rhetoric and demonstration of sovereignty can aid in students' understandings of survivance and alliance as well as rhetorical, intellectual, and cultural sovereignty.

CASE STUDY OF TOHE'S WORK

One way survivance is demonstrated and employed is through storytelling (Vizenor 2008). Through her poetic stories of the Navajo Long Walk and the struggles and tragedies surrounding the Navajo Nation— or rather *Diné bikéyah*[7]—Tohe employs her rhetorical sovereignty; she demonstrates rhetorics of survivance through her use of the Navajo language, code-switching, and translation. Tohe writes her poems predominantly in English and weaves her Navajo language into the content. Through her use of the Navajo language, she is "inserting" herself into English-dominant poetry by disrupting the colonial discourse of English with the Navajo language—she is visible through this disruption. Lyons asserts that "from 'sovereign' to 'ward,' from 'nation' to 'tribe,' and from 'treaty' to 'agreement,' the erosion of Indian national sovereignty can be credited in part to a rhetorically imperialist use of writing by white powers" (Lyons 2000, 453). These "white powers" use the English language to dismantle the sovereignty of American Indian nations. Lisa King argues that "English literacy has been a tool of assimilation, a way to destroy cultures, a way to erase the past, a way to promote imperialism, a way to speak as though sovereignty never existed" (King 2012, 213). Tohe is resisting the English colonial discourse by disrupting it with her Navajo language while also demonstrating her survival of such assimilation attempts. She employs the very language used to deplete her Native voice to portray a strong and very present Navajo Nation through her poetry.

Though Tohe's weaving of the Navajo language into her English-dominant text is significant in her act of survivance, even more noteworthy is her focus on the Navajo Nation's animals, nature, and land in her poetry. The focus on the land of the Navajo Nation is significant, as Womack argues that the American Indian resistance movement against colonialism "confronts racism, discusses sovereignty and Native nationalism, seeks connections between literature and liberation struggles, and finally, roots literature in land and culture" (Womack 1999, 11). It is through Tohe's storytelling, via rhetorical sovereignty, that my students learned more about the Diné and their land than they learned through non-Native rhetorics of fugitive poses. Tohe focuses on the history and significance of the land, more specifically Tséyi, or Canyon de Chelly—as it is known, according to Tohe, on "tourist maps"—which lies in the heart of Dinetah and holds the memories of the Diné, or rather those of "who inhabit it today and of the people who came before" (Tohe 2005, xiii). In her introduction, Tohe explains to the reader that Tséyi' housed the Diné, and the Diné and the land accepted each other (xiii). This kinship was threatened in 1864 when the US Cavalry, led by Kit Carson, forced the Diné from their home—from their land.

It is through her poetry that Tohe teaches non-Native students about the Diné's rich culture and values, as well as their uses rhetoric of survivance, to demonstrate a strong nation and land that endured relocation and removal, as she directly or indirectly translates terms significant to the nature and land of the Navajo Nation. One example of this is in the poem "Deep in the Rock." Tohe writes, "Deep in the rock, crows make echoes, gáagii, gáagii. Their name is pure/onomatopoeia. Gáagii/are everywhere" (Tohe 2005, 9). The Navajo word *gáagii* is connected to the English term *crows*. In *Navajo Land, Navajo Culture*, Robert S. McPherson explains that "a medicine man, said that coyote, wolf, crow, and mountain lion were all hunters and friends of Navajo hunters. The crow cries ahead and tells the hunter where the game is located" (McPherson 2003, 25). Though the crows aided in hunting and survival, as well as communicated with the Diné, in the past, in her poem, Tohe tells the reader that now the gáagii "[pick] up the remains of what humans/ leave, even the stuff not intended for them, like the boxer shorts stolen from/the clothesline" (9). Interestingly, the crow is also seen as a trickster figure in the Diné culture. Guy H. Cooper (1987), in "Coyote in Navajo Religion and Cosmology," states that "raven (or crow, the Navajo do not distinguish the two) is linked with coyote in myth" as a trickster culture hero. Cooper also states that hunting is also a form of "trickery requiring cunning" (188). Not only is the crow seen as trickster, but the very act of code-switching is as well. In *Other Destinies: Understanding the American Indian Novel*, Louis Owens explains that code-switching is a trickster sign (Owens 1994, 109). Tohe's act of code-switching, especially in this poem, is significant; in *Mixedblood Messages Literature, Film, Family, Place*, Owens states that "the role of trickster is to dismember all constructions that impose definitions and limit possibilities" (Owens 2001, 86). Tohe's act of code-switching redefines both her own and the Diné's sovereignty and numerous political, economic, social, literary, and personal possibilities. Furthermore, in *American Indian Rhetorics of Survivance: Word Medicine, Word Magic*, Ernest Stromberg suggests that trickster stories can rewrite history as well as aid in a fight for self-determination and self-definition (Stromberg 2006). Thus, the above example shows Tohe's use of rhetorics of survivance through not only her use of the Navajo language in her English-dominant text, which makes her a "subject within [the dominant discourse], not just a victim subject to it" (Powell 2002, 425), but also through her depiction of survivance through the image of the crow and her engagement in trickster rhetoric through her code-switching. Tohe asserts her active, Diné presence through the representation of the crows and is, in a sense, telling the reader "like the crows, we are still here." Perhaps as a connection to the Diné, or even Natives as a whole, as they are here—present, not absent, and yet ignored and taken for granted, this assertion demonstrates Tohe's "active sense of presence over absence, deracination, and oblivion" (Vizenor 2008, 39). Tohe's connection between the Diné and the crows' and trees' sustained presence in the land represents the Diné's continued and active presence; according to Vizenor, "The presence of animals, birds, and other creatures in native literature is a trace of natural reason, by right, irony, precise syntax, literary figuration, and the heartfelt practice of survivance" (Vizenor 2008, 12). This presence is a rhetorical act of defiance against the assimilation, relocation, and removal the American Indian Nations faced in the nineteenth century, for "despite hundreds of years of pressure, first from American colonists then from Euro-Americans, Natives did not disappear" (Powell 2002, 427). This concept was an important one for my students to identify in Tohe's text: that American Indians are not only in the past and absent— they are both present, and in the present.

Tohe's emphasis on the Diné land is significant not only through her actions of survivance but also in her decision to teach the reader the Navajo language, which can be seen in her poem "Many Horses." Tohe directly translates full-length sentences, as is demonstrated in the following excerpt:

> Dził bich 'į' yisháái . . . I am approaching the mountain
> Dził bikáá' haashā . . . I am ascending the mountain. (Tohe 2005, 7)

Tohe uses ellipses to guide the reader to a translation of the Navajo phrases. Tohe clearly demonstrates that she knows her audience includes non-Native readers, as she is outwardly teaching them the Navajo language. Not only does this example demonstrate rhetorics of survivance through her use of both the Navajo and English languages but also rhetorics of alliance, as Tohe is sharing knowledge with the non-Native audience. It is through her "teaching" that Tohe is engaging in rhetorics of alliance, as she is encouraging the reader to become an "ally"; one who works "toward the survival" of their community and the Navajo Nation (Powell 2004, 42). By studying rhetorics of alliance and analyzing Tohe's text, my students quickly learned and understood that Tohe, through her code-switching, was teaching them the language of the Diné. This language learning is especially important because, as Powell asserts in regards to ceasing a struggle between languages and cultures, we "need a new language, one that doesn't force us to see one another as competitors" (41). Using both English and Navajo languages creates that "new language," as both propose their meanings and translations for the audience. Furthermore, Tohe recognizes her audience of non-Natives and thus is presenting to them the idea that in addition to listening to one another, we "must share some understanding of one another's beliefs. We don't have to believe one another's beliefs, but we do have to acknowledge their importance, understand them as real, and respect/honor them in our dealings with one another" (Powell 2004, 42). Respect and acknowledgment are both demonstrated through Tohe's conscious decision to translate the Navajo language for the non-Navajo-speaking reader—she is aiding non-Diné students in learning about the Diné culture and demonstrating that these languages can coexist.

Tohe's expertise in two languages expands as she cleverly continues to teach the non-Diné reader not only about the land of the Navajo Nation but also about the traditions and beliefs of the Diné, which are rooted in the canyon. This teaching can be seen in the poem "Jiní" when Tohe directly translates the Navajo term *jiní* to the English phrase "they say"; she writes, "Jiní, *they say*. We accept jiní as part of our stories on simple faith. It's not important who said it, but that it was said" (Tohe 2005, 11). Tohe's explanation of *they say* is housed within a poem that remembers the past and demonstrates a respect for what *was* said by Diné ancestors—it is nostalgic of a precolonial nation. She is demonstrating the Diné as a people who have endured hardship and as a nation that has great strength. Tohe seems to be educating not only the non-Diné reader but also the Diné as she engages in sharing Diné stories about the past. This move in her work demonstrates both cultural and intellectual sovereignty as she displays self-determination and a motivation to keep alive the Diné past through storytelling, which, according to Robert Allen Warrior, promotes community renewal and keeps alive the American Indian intellectual tradition. We see this through Tohe's work; she engages with both Diné and non-Diné audiences alike, "teaching" them as she both includes and excludes them.

Adding to Philip Deloria's analysis of sovereignty, Warrior argues that part of intellectual sovereignty is American Indians' awareness of the importance of "choosing carefully whom . . . [they] invite into the sovereign space that is . . . [their] intellectual praxis" (Warrior 1994, 123). Tohe is choosing carefully what she discloses to particular audiences. By doing this, she is also claiming her cultural sovereignty, as she keeps some parts of her language and culture sacred and private to only the Diné. These choices are seen in her poems "Female Rain" and "Male Rain." What makes these poems unique is that they are written entirely in the Navajo language, and *then* a direct translation of those poems is written entirely in English. These English translations are placed next to—not above or beneath—the Navajo versions. Again, Tohe is aware of both audiences, and she is placing the languages on equal terms by situating the Navajo language to be just as significant as the colonial discourse of the English language. Tohe separates the Navajo-speaking reader from the non-Navajo-speaking reader with her separate versions. She may blatantly separate these two versions of the same poem to demonstrate the solidarity and communal connection the Diné culture has with the earth and rain at the specific place of Canyon de Chelly. An example of the English version of the poem "Female Rain" is as follows: "Female Rain/Dancing from the south/ cloudy cool and gray/pregnant with rainchild" (Tohe 2005, 26). While *rainchild* may not be a term used in everyday language in Western society, an outsider to the Navajo Nation (or even one within the Navajo Nation) can still understand the overall meaning: there is a raincloud holding a lot of rain. This again shows Tohe's desire to teach the non-Navajo-speaking reader, but it also shows a connection to the Diné culture and her prowess with two languages.

Tohe continues to retain her intellectual and cultural sovereignty through her decision to not translate specific terms for the non-Navajo-speaking reader. While it can be argued that Tohe is teaching the non-Navajo-speaking reader some of the Navajo language through her uses of code-switching and translation, the welcoming of the outsider into the Navajo language is only extended so far. This limitation depicts Tohe's cultural sovereignty; it is a way of ensuring that her culture does not continue to be appropriated by non-Natives in irresponsible ways. Tohe is keeping some parts of her language and culture sacred to only the Diné, which clearly demonstrates her cultural sovereignty, as Amanda Cobb defines cultural sovereignty to be acting in "self-definition" and ensuring "cultural continuance" (Cobb 2005, 502). Tohe does both. This lack of translation in Tohe's work, according to Martha Cutter, means a non-Navajo-speaking reader "*must* become a translator if she or he hopes to gain meaningful access to these texts" (Cutter 2005, 177). Tohe's lack of translation of specific terms and demonstration of cultural sovereignty not only encouraged my students to understand how the Diné are different from other American Indian nations but also led them to question what the terms she does not translate represent.

Tohe teaches the non-Diné reader about the Navajo language and Diné history and shared culture, but she does not, interestingly, translate any references to "the people," or rather, she does not translate the term *Diné* (Tohe 2005, xiii). While she does not provide a direct or an indirect translation of the term, the reader can still understand that the term *Diné* is connected to a group of people or a person. For example, in her poem "Jiní," Tohe writes, "'It's best to take time to listen to the stories and not be in a hurry,' the Diné elder/says" (11). The phrase *Diné elder* allows the non-Navajo-speaking reader to make the connection that the term *Diné* is connected to a person. However, while the non-Navajo-speaking reader can see *how* the term is being used, the reader still does not know the meaning of the term, or rather, *why* it is being used. *Diné* is a term used for self-identification. One must be an insider to use it and understand it appropriately. Furthermore, some Navajo words cannot be expressed in English, according to Diné Luci Tapahonso, as she states that "there are things that can be said in each [language] that cannot be said in other [languages]" (quoted in Brill 1997, 136). Webster too claims that code-switching allows the self to be reflected in the creative work and that "we do not say something new, rather we insert ourselves into the implicated and entangled history of our language" (Webster 2004, 2). The term *Diné* does, indeed, have a deeply "entangled history";[8] it represents struggles with violence, loss, and removal during the Navajo Long Walk.

Diné is not the only Navajo term Tohe chooses not to translate. The term *Hwéeldi* is also never translated into English in Tohe's poem "What Made This Earth Red?" *Hwéeldi* is what the Diné call their relocation place of Bosque Redondo, also known as *Fort Sumner*. The memories, meaning, and pain behind the term cannot possibly be displayed in an English translation; however, most Diné know what the term stands for in regards to the Diné themselves. In 1864, 8,354 Diné were forced to walk from Dinetah to Bosque Redondo in southern New Mexico, a distance of three hundred miles. They were held there for four years until the US government declared the assimilation attempt a failure. More than 2,500 Diné died of "smallpox and other illnesses, depression, severe weather conditions, and starvation" (Tapahonso 1993, 7). *Hwéeldi* displays the pain and suffering the Diné endured during their incarceration at Bosque Redondo; thus, it is considered a place of "great hardship," according to Tohe (quoted in Webster 2006, 540). This suffering can be seen as she writes in her poem, "What made this earth red? . . . Is it all the trails we took upon ourselves or that were forced upon us, beginning with our blood trails to Hwéeldi and back?" (Tohe 2005, 3). By not providing a translation, Tohe is holding the meaning sacred, or she may be making a statement that this history is something all people should already be privy to—that the suffering and history of the Diné *should* be known. Moreover, by including references to the Navajo Long Walk, Tohe is engaging in cultural sovereignty, as she is "modeling the survivance strategies that have enabled . . . [the Diné] cultural continuance" by providing the reader with not only information about the Navajo Long Walk but also testifying, "Look what we have been through, and yet, we are still here" (Cobb 2005, 502), as can be seen when she writes "to Hwéeldi *and back.*" The Navajo Nation is strong and surviving, as Tohe clearly demonstrated to my students through her poetry.

As can be seen above, analyzing Tohe's text was significantly beneficial to my students' understanding of sovereignty and the Navajo

Nation. To wrap up our focus on Tohe's work, I encouraged my students to write a three-to-five-page response paper on their understanding of Tohe's text and their ideas as to what Tohe is "doing" in her poetry and why. Not only had we focused on code-switching, rhetorical sovereignty, and rhetorics of survivance and alliance, but we had also discussed Tohe's display of intellectual and cultural sovereignty. We had covered a number of topics while discussing Tohe's text, and these response papers provided the students with an outlet to share their understanding of Tohe's demonstration of her own, as well as the Navajo Nation's, survivance—in addition to the other rhetorical moves in her work. Some students focused on Tohe's rhetorics of alliance, noting her teaching the non-Navajo-speaking audience the Navajo language. One student wrote, "I had no idea that the Navajo had their own language. However, I am glad that Tohe taught me the difference between English and Navajo. I feel like I am in a privileged group—learning how to read Navajo." Another student noted, "My favorite part of Tohe's poetry was learning how to read Navajo. Seeing the two languages next to each other made me realize how we say things differently in our different languages. I wonder how the meanings change." These examples of my students' writing demonstrate that the students appreciated learning about the difference in languages and that they valued Tohe's teaching them the language of the Diné. Such learning processes promote alliance.

Many students also recognized Tohe's prowess with two languages, but one student noted that "Tohe's use of both English and Navajo [languages] is a weapon in her arsenal of survival strategies that help her show her presence in literature." Though the student notes Tohe's presence in only literature, they acknowledge the idea of presence and the fight for continued sovereignty through the idea of "survival strategies." Also focusing on sovereignty, another student wrote, "In history class we never learned about the Navajo Long Walk, nor did we learn about American Indians struggling with their sovereignty. What does this tell us about sovereignty today? Leaving out this vital information tells us that there is still a struggle for sovereignty—to be heard." That my students would recognize sovereignty and the constant struggle for it was one of my goals in teaching Tohe's text—she demonstrates this sovereignty through her poetry, and, as can be seen in the examples of my students' responses, she does this well.

As my analysis above shows, Tohe's poetry provides non-Diné students with a glimpse into Diné culture while also displaying the significance of rhetorical, intellectual, and cultural sovereignty. Through her poetry, she shows students, through Diné eyes, the history and culture of the Diné, and through her teaching about her culture, language, and history, she engages students in rhetorics of alliance—she creates allies through her poetry, her storytelling, and her teaching. In the words of Powell, "Maybe as allies, we can spur one another on to even more disruptive tactics" (Powell 2004, 57). By disruptive tactics, Powell means we need to disrupt our students' preconceived notions about American Indians and works authored by American Indians. In addition, for those who have never experienced said texts, we can form a pedagogical framework that both encourages and teaches students to be allies, and I believe texts like Tohe's can help us do just that. Before students can fully appreciate the complexity of American Indian texts, they must understand sovereignty; as Lyons asserts, no student should "encounter a Native American text without having learned something about Indian peoples' historical and ongoing struggles for sovereignty" (Lyons 2000, 464).

CONCLUSION

An American Indian rhetorics pedagogy works to rectify the ways in which colonial educational systems have endorsed problematic ways for both non-American Indians and American Indians to engage with literatures and rhetorics authored by, for, and about American Indians. Encouraging students to read texts like Tohe's that include code-switching not only promotes awareness of American Indian works and voices and requires an understanding of sovereignty still relevant to American Indian nations today, but also calls for students to rethink and reconsider any preconceived notions and stereotypes they may have in regards to American Indians, as well as the English language. Providing students with an understanding of why code-switching is so important in an English-dominant text expands the discussion of sovereignty. Joy Harjo and Gloria Bird state that many American Indian individuals and nations use "the 'enemy's language' . . . to tell our truths, to sing, to remember ourselves" (Harjo and Bird 1998, 21). So, by encouraging a discussion of the connections between sovereignty and language as well as the issue of a dominant discourse, students can come to understand and appreciate code-switching on a deeper level. Furthermore, including additional works that do not include code-switching, such as excerpts from the scholarly articles of Malea Powell or Scott Lyons, or select poems from Luci Tapahonso and Rex Lee Jim, or the work of authors from different American Indian nations, will also enhance the discussion of the differences between the varying nations housed under the umbrella terms *Native* or *American Indian*.

The promotion of the above texts, including Tohe's, does not—by any means—demonstrate a course in its entirety. Rather, I am providing a potential stepping stone for beginning the necessary and complex journey of assisting our students in understanding rhetorical, intellectual, and cultural sovereignty as well as rhetorics of survivance and alliance.

In order to successfully understand and appreciate Native works, students must understand sovereignty. Lyons posits that the "pursuit of sovereignty is an attempt to revive not our past, but our responsibilities" (Lyons 2000, 448). For those of us who are non-Native allies, teaching our students about American Indian nations, the various nations' historical backgrounds, and the significance of and struggle for sovereignty, is our responsibility. The alliance between American Indian authors and texts and the classroom provides a means of listening to each other, a way to contribute to each other to maintain a balance of growth and respect for each other's communities, and a place in which future alliances and a respect for sovereignty can be actuated and valued.

Tohe's use of code-switching and translation in her work and an understanding of how those moves evidence rhetorical performances of survivance and alliance—as well as her rhetorical, cultural, and intellectual sovereignty—will hopefully show educators how using a text such as Tohe's is beneficial for promoting American Indian texts in the classroom. In addition, educators can see the necessity of disrupting, adding to, and maintaining our students' acknowledgment, awareness, and understanding of the significance of rhetorical sovereignty and the power of the voices of American Indian authors in claiming that sovereignty and resisting colonial attempts to silence them. Reading these texts in the classroom will encourage our students to not only hear these voices but also to possibly acknowledge, grow, and change their own voices.

Acknowledgments

I would like to thank the editors for this humbling and generous opportunity to add to and engage with the powerful voices of wisdom housed within this compilation. More specifically, I would like to thank Rose Gubele for her support and advice in revising this chapter as well as for her beautiful friendship. I would also like to thank Angela Haas for all of her help in formulating this chapter and for being a wonderful advisor, mentor, and friend. Lastly, I would like to thank Laura Tohe for allowing me to act as her research assistant in 2006 and to continue to experience her eloquent writing.

Notes

1. I use the term *American Indian* instead of *Native* or *Native American* when referring to general American Indian literature; however, tribal designations are preferred when possible.

2. I use the term *Diné* when referring to the tribal designation and identity of Tohe and in instances of discussing the Diné culture, traditions, and beliefs. Though the term *Diné* is the tribal designation, I use the term *Navajo* when referring to the language of the Diné because the terms *Navajo* and *Navajo language* are more familiar to those outside of the Diné culture, as the term *Diné* is not a widely used term by outsiders. Furthermore, I reference the Navajo Nation and the Navajo Long Walk as such, as these too are phrases with which non-Diné are more familiar.

3. In *Tribal Secrets: Recovering American Indian Intellectual Traditions*, Robert Allen Warrior explains intellectual sovereignty as a means for one who is a part of an American Indian nation to promote community renewal, keep alive the American Indian tradition; it also allows non-American Indians to see "the importance of choosing carefully whom we invite into the sovereign space that is . . . [American Indians'] intellectual praxis" (Warrior 1994, 123).

4. In her article "The National Museum of the American Indian as Cultural Sovereignty," Amanda Cobb explains cultural sovereignty as engaging in an "act of self-definition" and protecting one's "cultural continuance" (Cobb 2005, 502).

5. Because Anthony Webster uses the term *Navajo* in his work, I use it in this paraphrase.

6. I use the term *code-switching* as it is used by Holly E. Martin; as she states that: Codeswitching between . . . English and a Native American language, creates a multiple perspective and enhances the authors' ability to express their subjects. Also . . . writers lay claim to the languages of their communities and resist the dominance of English by proposing that these languages can accompany English in the creation of works of US literature. (Martin 2005, 403–4)

7. *Diné bikéyah*, according to Tohe, is what the Diné call their homeland (Tohe 2005, xiv).

8. The entangled history to which I am referring is the relocation and removal of the Diné, including the Navajo Long Walk, from 1863–1868.

References

Brill, Susan. 1997. "Alk'idaa'jini Luci Tapahonso, Irvin Morris, and Della Frank: Interweaving Navajo and English in Their Poems and Stories." *Cimarron Review* 121: 135–53.

Cobb, Amanda J. 2005. "The National Museum of the American Indian as Cultural Sovereignty." *American Quarterly* 57 (2): 485–506. http://dx.doi.org/10.1353/aq.2005 .0021.

Cooper, Guy H. 1987. "Coyote in Navajo Religion and Cosmology." *Canadian Journal of Native Studies* 7 (2): 181–93.

Cutter, Martha. 2005. *Lost and Found in Translation: Contemporary Ethnic American Writing and the Politics of Language Diversity*. Chapel Hill: University of North Carolina Press.

Harjo, Joy, and Gloria Bird. 1998. Introduction to *Reinventing the Enemy's Language: Contemporary Women's Writings of North America*, edited by Joy Harjo and Gloria Bird, 19–31. New York: Norton.

King, Lisa. 2012. "Rhetorical Sovereignty and Rhetorical Alliance in the Writing Classroom: Using American Indian Texts." *Pedagogy* 12 (2): 209–33. http://dx.doi. org/10.1215/15314200-1503568.

Lee, Kimberli. 2007. "Heartspeak from the Spirit Songs of John Trudell, Keith Secola, and Robbie Robertson." *Studies in American Indian Literatures* 19 (3): 89–114. http://dx.doi.org/10.1353/ail.2007.0024.

Lyons, Scott Richard. 2000. "Rhetorical Sovereignty: What Do American Indians Want from Writing?" *College Composition and Communication* 51 (3): 447–68. http://dx.doi.org/10.2307/358744.

Martin, Holly E. 2005. "Code-Switching in US Ethnic Literature: Multiple Perspectives Presented through Multiple Languages." *Changing English* 12 (3): 403–15. http://dx.doi.org/10.1080/13586840500347277.

McPherson, Robert S. 2003. *Navajo Land, Navajo Culture: The Utah Experience in the Twentieth Century*. Norman: University of Oklahoma Press.

Owens, Louis. 1994. *Other Destinies: Understanding the American Indian Novel*. Norman: University of Oklahoma Press.

Owens, Louis. 2001. *Mixedblood Messages: Literature, Film, Family, Place*. Norman: University of Oklahoma Press.

Powell, Malea. 2002. "Rhetorics of Survivance: How American Indians Use Writing." *College Composition and Communication* 53 (3): 396–434. http://dx.doi.org/10.2307/1512132.

Powell, Malea. 2004. "Down by the River, or How Susan La Flesche Picotte Can Teach Us about Alliance as a Practice of Survivance." *College English* 67 (1): 38–60. http://dx.doi.org/10.2307/4140724.

Stromberg, Ernest. 2006. *American Indian Rhetorics of Survivance: Word Medicine, Word Magic*. Pittsburgh: University of Pittsburgh Press.

Tapahonso, Luci. 1993. *Sáanii Dahataał: The Women Are Singing*. Tucson: University of Arizona Press.

Tohe, Laura. 2005. *Tséyi'/Deep in the Rock: Reflections on Canyon de Chelly*. Tucson: University of Arizona Press.

Vizenor, Gerald. 2000. *Fugitive Poses: Native American Indian Scenes of Absence and Presence*. Lincoln: University of Nebraska Press.

Vizenor, Gerald. 2008. *Survivance: Narratives of Native Presence*. Lincoln: University of Nebraska Press.

Warrior, Robert Allen. 1994. *Tribal Secrets: Recovering American Indian Intellectual Traditions*. Minneapolis: University of Minnesota Press.

Webster, Anthony K. 2004. "Code-Switching in Navajo Orthographic Poetry: On Places, the Mythic, and Mythic Places." *Texas Linguistic Forum* 50.

Webster, Anthony K. 2006. "'From Hóyéé to Hajinei': On Some Implications of Feelingful Iconicity and Orthography in Navajo Poetry." *Pragmatics* 16 (4): 535–49. http://dx.doi.org/10.1075/prag.16.4.06web.

Womack, Craig S. 1999. *Red on Red: Native American Literary Separatism*. Minneapolis: University of Minnesota Press.

Zitzer-Comfort, Carol. 2008. "Teaching Native American Literature: Inviting Students to See the World Through Indigenous Lenses." *Pedagogy* 8 (1): 160–70. http://dx.doi.org/10.1215/15314200-2007-031.

10

TOWARD A DECOLONIAL DIGITAL AND VISUAL AMERICAN INDIAN RHETORICS PEDAGOGY

Angela Haas

This is a hypertext—part investigative report on listening to and using theory, looking at Indian simulations and fugitive poses, and exposing colonial education's role in digital and visual manifest manners[1]; part status report on studying digital and visual culture in American Indian studies; part proposal for adopting a decolonial digital and visual rhetorics pedagogy; part lesson plan for redressing colonial scripts that prescribe ways of interfacing with American Indian digital and visual rhetorics.

For centuries colonization has deeply influenced the ways in which peoples of the Americas have been and continue to be educated both formally and informally. In his landmark text *The Darker Side of the Renaissance*, Argentinian decolonial theorist Walter Mignolo (1995) traces the role of writing and the politics of language in the colonization of indigenous Mexican languages, memories, and spaces that began in the sixteenth century. Mignolo describes the colonization of the Nahuatl languages by the Spanish/Castilian Crown, friars, and missionaries who used Western literacy against Amerindians to assimilate them and convert them to Christianity vis-à-vis hegemonic ties between alphabetic writing and civility and strategic combinations of teaching grammar, orthography, laws, and edicts with proselytizing on how to be a good Christian. Further, he ties the celebration of the letter and book to a warranty of Truth and Western assumptions about the necessary relationship between alphabetic literacy and history—a relationship that has worked to dismiss the value of oral traditions and to relegate peoples without alphabetic writing as being without history or prehistoric. Among other things, this colonial relationship has resulted in the re-writing of indigenous histories, the privileging of Western ways of organizing knowledge, the diminished capacity for a coexistence of languages, literacies, memories, and space with indigenous

DOI: 10.7330/9780874219968.c010

knowledges, and the perpetuation of the notion that what is different is wrong or deficient.

Although the scene and actors have changed, this combination of secular education and the teaching of Western religious doctrine has served as the standard operating procedure in the colonization of other parts of North, Central, and South America, and it continues to inform contemporary Western education. To be sure, colonization has greatly influenced the history of education in the Americas. As Linda Tuhiwai Smith (1999) puts it, "The pursuit of knowledge is deeply embedded in the multiple layers of imperial and colonial practice" (2). And this colonial pursuit of knowledge transpires formally and informally and inside and outside the walls of academia. To explain, in *The Rhetoric of Empire,* David Spurr (1993) evidences how colonial discourses in nineteenth- and twentieth-century Western literary and popular journalism, travel writing, and imperial administrative rhetoric prescribed and limited public-sphere knowledge production, consumption, and reproduction about non-Western peoples.[2]

Certainly, these colonial discourses have rhetorical velocity (Ridolfo and DeVoss 2009)[3]—or a strategic and rapid recomposing, promotion, and thus reenforcing of messages across media, spaces, and places—as they continue to pervade mass media today and continue to educate mass audiences about non-Western peoples, including American Indians. For example, there is a long Western rhetorical tradition of constructing American Indians—via print, visual, oral, and digital compositions—in stereotypical, essentialized, and fetishized ways that contribute to a larger, monolithic fiction of who/what is "the American Indian." Think, for instance, of commercial product branding that typically (re)presents "the American Indian" as a headdress-wearing tribeless, nationless, generic warrior and tireless promoter for all things organic, all natural, and ecofriendly. This rhetorical strategy is not unique and is nothing new for mass media and advertising. Executives would rather imagine and (re)construct indigenous peoples interacting with natural, spiritual, and/or exotic worlds than with a technological one. Most of the Western media and educational resources our students interface with, and many just passively consume, never portray American Indians as engaging with computers or other contemporary technologies; American Indians are rarely represented, in fact, as contemporary peoples with complex identities and technological expertise. Indeed, on most occasions, American Indians are visually and textually linked to a past and erased from the present and future.

These simulacra accumulate and contribute to the perpetuation of a colonial rhetorical assemblage, one that situates American Indian peoples and intellectual traditions outside (post)modern society and correspondingly resistant to the tools and technologies that have signified Western (post)modernity. Thus, educators in rhetoric and composition, American Indian, and computers and writing studies have a responsibility to work with our students to interrogate, disrupt, and reimagine how we continue to be informally educated about American Indians via Western popular media and higher education in ways that reinscribe colonial rhetoric about who is Indian and what Indianness looks like. Otherwise, we risk reinforcing a colonial fiction woven into the fabric of nation building in the United States and proven to be a cash cow for media industries that not only allows for but is sponsored by the continued subjugation of peoples and intellectual traditions indigenous to this country.

Given this responsibility, this chapter contributes to other American Indian decolonial pedagogies[4] by offering a decolonial digital and visual American Indians rhetorics pedagogy concerned with redressing colonial scripts that prescribe how we interface with digital and visual rhetorics (e.g., advertising, art, blogs, film, museums, photography, television, video, websites) about, for, and by people indigenous to the Americas. I demonstrate how this pedagogy interrogates the relationships between rhetorics of Indianness and rhetorics of technology (Deloria 2004; Haas 2007; King 2005; 2007; Vizenor 1994; 1998; 2009); privileges rhetorical evidence of indigenous digital and visual survivance (Powell 2002; 2004; Vizenor 1994; 1998; 2009); supports digital and visual rhetorical sovereignty (Lyons 2000; Haas 2007; King 2011); and holds non-Native students accountable as allies to American Indians (Powell 2004). Finally, I provide example approaches to undergraduate and graduate digital and visual American Indian rhetorics curriculum design and pedagogy that work to decolonize hegemonic habits of mind and practices that have historically shaped how we understand American Indians and indigenous rhetorical and technological traditions.

A FRAMEWORK FOR A DECOLONIAL DIGITAL AND VISUAL RHETORICS PEDAGOGY

Decolonial theories, methodologies, and pedagogies are designed to assist scholars, educators, and students in decolonizing Western foundations of dominant thought by investigating and intervening in the histories and rhetorics that sponsor colonial intellectual production and reproduction. To be clear, decolonial theory is an epistemological and ontological approach to examining (1) how we have individually and collectively been affected by and complicit in the legacy of colonialism; (2) how these effects and complicities of historical and contemporary colonialism influence research and educational institutions, theories, methodologies, methods, and scholarship; and (3) how the effects and complicities of colonialism play out in our everyday embodied practices. Further, decolonial theories are rooted in decolonization practices, which two-spirit scholar Qwi-Li Driskill explains involves the "ongoing, radical resistance against colonialism that includes struggles for land redress, self-determination, healing historical trauma, cultural continuance, and reconciliation" (Driskill 2010, 69). Thus, putting theory into action, decolonial methodologies and pedagogies "serve to (a) redress colonial influences on perceptions of people, literacy, language, culture, and community and the relationships therein and (b) support the coexistence of cultures, languages, literacies, memories, histories, places, and spaces—and encourage respectful and reciprocal dialogue between and across them" (Haas 2012, 297).

Ultimately, a decolonial pedagogy interrogates how colonialism has impacted the experiential and formal education of *all* learners and teachers of *all* cultural backgrounds, as colonization has always already shaped our rhetorics and thus has a long history of prescribing personal and community identities and the values associated with those identities: our different ethnicities, genders, sexual orientations, classes, generations, nationalities, abilities, and more. In the sixteenth and seventeenth centuries, universities in the Americas were created and administered by Spanish and British immigrants and their Creole descendants (Mignolo 2003). Given this history, decolonial approaches to education work to (1) uncover how the colonial values of early educators continue to influence the rhetorics and practices of contemporary US postsecondary institutions, our branding, our colleges, our departments, our programs, our disciplines, and our pedagogy and (2) disrupt the rhetorical velocity of neocolonial rhetorics and practices.

The primary goals of a decolonial digital and visual American Indian rhetorics pedagogy,[5] then, is to decolonize our habits of mind when interfacing with digital and visual representations of Indianness and indigeneity and with all representations of American Indian technological practices. One approach includes studying Western and indigenous digital and visual cultures and the rhetorics therein and how these rhetorics, in turn, have influenced how US citizens—native and non-Native—have come to (mis)visualize Indianness and to (mis) understand the technological practices of people indigenous to the Americas.[6] Ultimately, a decolonial digital and visual American Indian rhetorics pedagogy is—among other things—employed to (1) uncover how colonization and imperialism have historically shaped the relationships between visual culture and digital media and the construction of indigenous identities; (2) privilege rhetorics that support digital and visual rhetorical sovereignty and self-determination and evidence digital and visual survivance; (3) design decolonial disruptions in the rhetorical velocity of colonial digital and visual discourses, and (4) imagine new decolonial digital and visual rhetorical trajectories.

DECOLONIAL DIGITAL AND VISUAL RHETORICS PEDAGOGICAL PRACTICES

This section of the chapter offers some decolonial digital and visual pedagogical practices by discussing ways of bridging theory and practice in a variety of undergraduate and graduate courses in American Indian rhetoric, digital rhetorics, and visual rhetorics (see companion website for sample course descriptions). A key approach to each of the areas of inquiry I broach is the push beyond critique. To explain, although I find great pedagogical and personal value in analyzing and critiquing digital and visual rhetorical colonial detritus, a decolonial pedagogy asks of its users a commitment to social justice. Thus, decolonial pedagogues are to facilitate the redressing of injustice when human, animal, and environmental rights are being infringed upon, neglected, withheld, and/ or abolished.

One approach to teaching decolonial digital and visual rhetorics is to study how colonization and imperialism have historically shaped the relationships between visual culture and digital media and the construction of indigenous identities. As Gerald Vizenor's (2009), Thomas King's (2005), and Phillip Deloria's (2004) work makes clear, indigenous peoples in the Americas have always already been rhetorically constructed by Europeans since their conquest of the Americas. These incomplete and inaccurate representations of Indianness have deep and firm roots in the US colonial imaginary, have rhetorical velocity across the globe, and contribute to larger global colonial rhetorics about global indigenous people.

Through colonial oral, textual, digital, and visual rhetoric, global colonial rhetorics work to reduce the plurality of ongoing, contemporary, complex, and diverse American Indian cultures to one uniform, flat, static, prehistoric,[7] and ancient culture. Historically, Western public and private displays of decontextualized Indian "artifacts" (e.g., museum exhibits, personal collections, media representations) and their associated colonial rhetorics endorsed and reinforced misunderstandings of American Indian people and cultures, and the pervasiveness of these misunderstandings is still evidenced today in contemporary museum displays, photographs, portraits, sculptures, children's books, movies, television shows, advertising, websites, and more. Thus, misinformation about who American Indians are and what American Indians look like surrounds us every day.

The prevalence of this misinformation shapes our understandings of Indianness at a very early and formative age. In fact, the research of Debbie Reese (2008), a scholar whose work focuses on analyzing representations of American Indians in children's and young-adult literature, indicates that children raised in the United States—Native and non-Native—develop their understandings of who American Indians are, how American Indians act, and what American Indians look like before entering kindergarten and that those understandings are based on the representations put forth by children's books and other media (most of which are developed by non-Natives). Unfortunately, these understandings can play out in ways that parallel the experiences Joy Harjo (2007)—writer, musician, visual artist, and professor—describes in her blog:

> For most of the world, turkey feathers in the hair and buckskin, equals Indian.
>
> Once years back, in a class, we studied images of Indians. One of the students took sheets of paper and markers to a preschool class in Boulder. She asked the children to draw an Indian. They all drew one of two images: a warrior on horseback brandishing bloody tomahawks, or delicate princesses, most of them on horseback. They weren't human beings, rather symbols, and the children had already internalized them.
>
> When my daughter was just three, just before she went into Head Start, we went to sign her up at a preschool in Iowa City (where I was attending graduate school). The children surrounded us and danced around doing that Hollywood war whoop, you know the one. Their teacher was embarrassed. I was amazed that children that young had already taken in that false image that had nothing to do with being Indian, or Mvskoke, or Acoma, my daughter's other tribal affiliation.
>
> We're still mostly portrayed in those flat images in art, literature, movies, and not just by non-Indians or three-year-olds. (Harjo 2007, 259)[8]

The hypertext woven by these stories demonstrates that not only is "Indian" an ascribed *name*—a romanticized simulation of Indianness—based on Western ethnographic, anthropologic, and rhetorical discovery, surveillance, collection, claiming/naming, (re)presentation, and commodification; "Indian" is also an ascribed *image*—a romanticized simulation of visible Indianness—based on Western ethnographic, anthropologic, and rhetorical discovery, surveillance, collection, claiming/naming, display, and commodification.

As historian Phil Deloria (2004) explains in *Indians in Unexpected Places*, textual and visual simulations of Indianness in popular culture accumulate into a monolithic fiction of Indianness the public sphere expects to read and see in subsequent encounters with representations of American Indian identity. To explain, the fugitive poses captured in Western fiction and dime novels of the mid- to late 1800s, Wild West shows at the turn of the nineteenth century, and first Western films[9] and art of the early nineteenth century paved the way for the consistent and future success of using stereotyped Indian imagery in radio and television westerns and western comic books in the mid-1900s, western-themed computer games of the late 1900s, and most recently empire-building and "playing Indian" video and multiplayer, role-playing games at the turn of the twenty-first century. Further, contemporary satellite and cable television companies continue to commemorate this colonial fiction with channels such as the Hallmark Channel, the Western Channel, and the Classic Western Channel broadcasting marathons of *Little House on the Prairie*, *Gunsmoke*, *The Lone Ranger*, *Bonanza*, and the like. Needless to say, American Indians have consistently been portrayed as what is most wild about the Wild West, outside the (post)modern world, and resistant to the tools and technologies that have signified Western (post)modernity.

As can be ascertained from cultural anthropologist James Clifford (1988), extensive museum cultures were built in the nineteenth century based on the display of national histories, which gave institutional force to the promotion of a unified national culture. Thus, they promoted the colonial agenda via visual rhetoric, both in art (a.k.a. "artifact") choice, placement, display, and textual support, which, according to Tuhiwai Smith (1999), resulted in representations of fragmented indigenous identities—fragmentation caused by imperialism that disconnected them from their histories, homelands, landscapes, languages, social relations and their own ways of making sense of the world. To be sure, museums and people of color have an interesting history, given the tendency for Western museums to perpetuate the collection of "vanishing cultures" or "wards of the state" and the rhetoric of "primitive" artifacts and tribal people, traces of the uncivilized in civilized, Western "masterpiece" culture.

In pedagogical response to this colonial fiction, we can engage students in decolonial critiques of digital and visual representations of

Figure 10.1. Gast's American Progress (1872).

Indianness. To prepare them for this intellectual work, Spurr's taxonomy of the colonial repertoire of rhetorical tropes is a useful framework for analyzing a common colonial work of art. For example, I ask students to look at John Gast's (1872) *American Progress* (see fig. 10.1)—a pictorial, allegorical representation of manifest destiny in relation to colonial rhetorical tropes. Through aestheticization, classification, debasement, negation, and naturalization, the visual rhetoric of empire employed in this artwork (re)establishes how manifest destiny and its love of "progress" relates to people, civilizations, technologies, literacies, and religions. In brief, Gast (re)presents progress as evidence of civilization and ordained by God. An argument that emerges from this colonial rhetorical analysis—as well as visual design analyses that examine the rhetoric of color, proximity, contrast, and so forth—is that God blesses only the colonizers of the Americas with "cutting edge"[10] technology and advanced civilization; in contrast, indigenous peoples are relegated to the darkness of technological illiteracy and the wilderness. Thus, this painting reflects and represents hegemonic ideologies that seek to justify the colonization of the Americas and its inhabitants as a necessary clearing out of primitive peoples and lifeways to make room for more advanced ones. This visual rhetoric of manifest destiny also reveals Western desires to dominate nature (the landscape and its inhabitants) with the use of technology (guns, dams, plows, guns, steamboats, railroad, etc.), which lends itself to interesting discussions on different ideologies that inform how we come to perceive people and communities as civilized and/or uncivilized and technologically and advanced and/or inferior.[11]

After an initial group inquiry like this, we might next ask students to transfer this decolonial critique to other artistic renditions of Indianness found in virtual and/or physical museums. Students could also broaden the scope of their inquiry beyond one specific work of art and consider larger institutional contexts for displaying Indianness. For example, students could visit a local museum and assess how the local indigenous community is/isn't visually represented. The assignment could ask students to (1) research the board of directors and curators for the museum and the goals for the museum/exhibit; (2) consider the ideologies sponsoring the museum/exhibit displays; (3) identify the intended and unintended audiences of the museum and speculate about the effects of the representations on those audiences; (4) assess the risks and affordances of the visual rhetorical strategies employed by the museum in relation to the aforementioned stakeholders; (5) make suggestions for decolonial change and/or sustainability.

To imagine decolonial ways for redressing colonial museum displays, we should initiate class conversations on and investigations into how museums have historically promoted a colonial consciousness of consumption and nostalgia with the visual rhetoric of museums that typically produces ahistorical, fetishized, and simulated rhetorics of Indianness, and then how these fictions have been taken up by both non-Natives and American Indians and are often re-inscribed in culturally destructive ways. In addition, students may learn from examples provided by visual rhetorical sovereignty scholarship. For instance, rhetoric and composition scholar Lisa King (2011) examines the range of rhetorical change and cultural sovereignty practices Native peoples are exercising in three inaugural exhibits at the National Museum of the American Indian (NMAI). In addition, Kate Morris evidences the intensification of two congruent border-zone frictions post-9/11: "an increasing number of references to borders in contemporary Native American art and an increasing occurrence of border-rights conflicts between Native nations and the governments of the United States and Canada" (Morris, 2011, 550–51). To do so, she provides multiple case studies of Native-produced visual (and other multimediated) arts that work to rhetorically claim political and cultural sovereignty in relation to "border" cultures. Karen Ohnesorge (2008) examines how Native artists

Quick-to-See Smith, Hock E Aye Vi Edgar Heap of Birds, and Charlene Teters exercise artistic sovereignty to decolonize colonial ideologies of landscape, including the corresponding displacement of indigenous peoples from it. This scholarship can help facilitate discussions and other student work that extend beyond rhetorical analysis and toward decolonial, social justice work.

As part of my pedagogical agenda to decolonize colonial ideologies and representations of landscape, place, space, and ownership, I ask students to compose an American Indian cultural literacy/autobiography essay that engages digital and visual rhetorical research (see companion website for the full assignment). The assignment has two parts: one that asks students to describe their cultural literacy as it pertains to American Indian literatures, rhetorics, and cultures prior to enrolling in our class, and another part that expands on this cultural literacy by asking students to research and report on the indigenous culture(s) that had (and may still have) a relationship to the land that each student calls home. I facilitate this second portion by providing them with a host of URLs to credible digital maps and research that provide historical, contemporary, and cultural contexts for which indigenous cultures have been stewards to specific geographic locations. I also advocate that students research the contemporary websites of indigenous tribes/nations to learn how the websites are rhetorically representing the geographic placement/s—and oftentimes displacement/s—of their people and how that geography is related to their lifeways.

These assignments seek to engage students in new habits of mind when it comes to understanding and visualizing indigenous peoples and places, specifically asking them to be allies to Native peoples vis-à-vis respecting and supporting digital and visual rhetorical sovereignty and self-determination. Rhetoric and composition scholar Scott Lyons tells us that what American Indians want from writing is *rhetorical sovereignty*, or the "inherent right and ability of peoples to determine their own communicative needs and desires, to decide for themselves the goals, modes, styles, and languages of public discourse" (Lyons 2000, 449–50). I posit that American Indians want *digital and visual rhetorical sovereignty*, too, or the "inherent right and ability . . . to determine their own communicative needs and desires, to decide for themselves the goals, modes, styles, and languages of public discourse" in digital spaces and visual media.

Beyond positioning digital and visual rhetorical sovereignty as an unalienable right, it is long overdue, given the extensive history of racist appropriations of indigenous symbology and stereotypes of indigeneity displayed in Western media. Take, for further example, product design and advertising, like the still-used stereotypical feathered Indian squaws in the Argo Corn Starch and Land O'Lakes Butter logos; the red-faced, headdress-wearing warriors on cans of Calumet Baking Powder and bags of Big Chief Sugar; and mascot branding for major sports teams like the Washington Redskins, the Cleveland Indians, and the Atlanta Braves— among countless others.

While some may argue that primarily older commercial products and corporations engage in this imperial nostalgia, there is ample evidence that newer commercial products and corporations have embraced the use of colonial commodification vis-à-vis visual rhetoric as well. In 2012, Gap—in partnership with GQ—released a line of modern black-and-white t-shirts designed by Mark McNairy that read "Manifest Destiny." Native and allied activists took to writing in *Indian Country Today*,[12] tweets, Facebook posts and messages, and emails to Gap and GQ CEOs, customer service, and to McNairy himself protesting the shirt and its genocidal message and colonial effects. A Change.org petition[13] charged,

> This article of clothing promotes a belief that has resulted in the mass genocide of indigenous people, and it serves to normalize oppression. This shirt is marketed to teens and young adults, and it gives no context for the racism and inequality that persists in our society, to this day, as a result of this doctrine. We are asking that this shirt be discontinued, and that an apology be issued.

GAP eventually listened and pulled the line of t-shirts from its physical and online stores, but not until after McNairy tweeted "Manifest Destiny: survival of the fittest" and then "I am sorry for my survival of the fittest comment. It hurt me deeply to be called a racist as that is not me. I reacted without thinking."[14]

McNairy's design was a result of colonial amnesia and evidence of how ignorant some Americans are about the history of this continent and its inhabitants, and it was not the only unfortunate colonialism-meets-capitalism mishap of 2012 that served to further perpetuate racist and oftentimes sexist stereotypes—and thus oppress—peoples and cultures indigenous to North America. In fall 2012 alone, Gwen Stefani donned a barely there buckskin dress and headdress in No Doubt's television and YouTube release of their *Looking Hot* video; Victoria's Secret dressed runway model Karlie Kloss in a full headdress, buckskin-turquoise-silver-leopard-print bikini, and fringed booties in the grand finale of their NYC fashion show; in her Halloween episode, Ricki Lake dressed up like a stereotypical Indian princess in a long, straight, black wig, fringed buckskin dress and boots, and turquoise jewelry and animal pelts but claimed to be dressed up as Cher (perhaps when Cher appropriated Native culture when promoting her album *Half Breed*).

All this to say that colonial branding unfortunately continues to be ripe for decolonial investigations, discussions, and interventions into indigenous intellectual property. Students could break into groups, further research one of the aforementioned case studies, and then debate the tensions between appropriation, indigenous intellectual property rights, commercialism, and colonization. Several web resources are available to supplement these discussions, which are purposely diverse depending upon the angle and audience you want to engage, such as scholarly blogs—such as the *Native Appropriations* blog,[15] Reese's award-winning *American Indians in Children's Literatures* blog,[16] and Dustin Tahmahkera's *Brady Braves* blog[17]—and major global reports, including the World Intellectual Property Organization's (WIPO) report *Intellectual Property and Genetic Resources, Traditional Knowledge and Traditional Cultural Expressions: An Overview*,[18] the WIPO report *Marketing Crafts and Visual Arts: The Role of Intellectual Property*,[19] and the United Nations Declaration on the Rights of Indigenous Peoples (2007)[20]—just to name a few.

For more extended reading, Michael F. Brown's (2003) *Who Owns Native Culture?* introduces readers to a variety of indigenous case studies that challenge our traditional notions of intellectual property and to stories that teach us about the determination of indigenous peoples working to protect their communities from continued appropriation and theft. Brown engages important heritage-protection legislation and initiatives related to global indigenous intellectual property rights, including Australia's 1989 Aboriginal Torres Strait Islander Heritage Protection Act, the US's National Historic Preservation Act of 1966, the American Indian Religious Freedom Act of 1978, the Native American Graves Protection and Repatriation Act of 1990, and the UN Declaration of the Rights of Indigenous Peoples, among others. Ultimately, Brown's discussions of heritage property, cultural appropriation, biopiracy, ethnocide/cultural genocide, epistemic hegemony, traditional ecological knowledge, cultural integrity, rights of cultural privacy, and repatriation can help us extend our current rhetorics and thus understandings of intellectual property.

These discussions could also be enriched with the inclusion of video[21] informed by American Indian humor.[22] As expressed by writer, theologian, historian, and activist Vine Deloria Jr., "Indians have found the humorous side of nearly every problem. . . . The more desperate the problem, the more humor is directed to describe it. Satirical remarks often circumscribe problems so that possible solutions are drawn from the circumstances that would not make sense if presented in other than a humorous form" (Deloria 1969, 147). To scaffold students toward interrogating colonial appropriations of indigenous cultural patrimony and stereotypical representations of indigeneity, I share humorous videos that broach the issues with a tongue-in-cheek approach. Graham Green's *Lakota Spoof* video[23] pokes fun of commercial appropriations of indigenous symbology and stereotypical perpetuations that all things Indian are all natural. Non-Native allies have gotten in on some American Indian jokes on cultural appropriation, too. The *Daily Show*'s Aasif Mandvi reports on the threat of extinction American Indian mascots are experiencing in his "Trail of Cheers" segment.[24]

However, it's important to connect humorous responses to colonization with ethical implications and decolonial imperatives for action. Once hooked with humor, some resistant students may become more receptive to more forceful critiques, critiques that rhetorically implicate the viewer more directly. More direct video-mediated curriculum suggestions include Jay Rosenstein's (1997) documentary *In Whose Honor?*, which chronicles the lengths some fans will go to—and the rhetorics they will use—to preserve their American Indian mascots and profiles Charlene Teters's activist work confronts the commodification, merchandising, and disrespecting of American Indian symbols. Further, Thomas King's (2007) documentary, *I'm Not the Indian You Had in Mind*, directly challenges viewers to examine the profound role Western media representations have played in shaping perspectives about an entire ethnic group—comprised of thousands of diverse communities—and juxtaposes indigenous actors, dressed in suits, jeans, and contemporary urban attire, against colonial fugitive poses.

This engagement with diverse representations of indigenous identities leads effectively into assignments that ask students to conduct more in-depth research on an American Indian intellectual, organization, or culture and then share that research in effective digital and visual rhetorical ways with the rest of the class and/or a larger audience via YouTube, public Prezi or Wix website, and so forth. I assign an American Indian intellectual/culture/organization class presentation that asks students to prepare a presentation for the class on an important American Indian, tribe/nation, or organization in American Indian history (from ancient to contemporary) (see companion website for full assignment). If presenting on an important American Indian intellectual, they are to provide a sense of who this person is, what they have done/are doing, in what era they lived/live, and why they are important to their tribal community/history, American Indians writ large, and/or other communities. If presenting on an American Indian culture, they are to contextualize the uniqueness of this culture, its language(s), the ways in which its peoples generally see the world and their place in it, its ancestral land base(s), and other information that may help us to see both the uniqueness of this culture and its peoples' relationships with others. If presenting on an American Indian organization, the students are to provide the history of the organization, its mission, important members of the organization, how it has affected the everyday lives of American Indians and other local and global citizens, and so forth. This type of assignment helps students to understand the diversity within American Indian cultures and across American Indian peoples, lifeways, rhetorics, and so forth. Further, the assignment asks students to privilege credible indigenous research sources so as to support rhetorical and cultural sovereignty.

After students have engaged with American Indian rhetorics at this level of complexity, they are better prepared to engage in summaries and critiques of American Indian rhetorics and literatures. I ask students to summarize and critique a "text"—print or other media—written, performed, designed, edited, filmed, produced, and/or told by an American Indian or group of Indians (see companion website for full assignment). The students are to consider their own personal, intellectual, and/or career interests and think about an American Indian literature and/or rhetoric they would like to critique, including novels, films, children's books, critical/theoretical texts, edited collections, autobiographies, books/collections of short stories and poetry, documentaries, CDs, and more. This assignment has several components that scaffold toward a complex, critical inquiry of American Indian texts, rhetorical situations, literary themes, rhetorical tropes, and media: an informal proposal; a summary of the work for peer review; a summary of the work posted to Native Wiki (www.nativeweb.org); a review essay; and—for extra credit—an Amazon.com (or other online merchant) customer-review post. Several decolonial digital and visual pedagogical strategies are at play in this assignment, including complicating the notion of text and flattening any hierarchy between print, oral, digital, and any other text; providing a venue for indigenous peoples to self-determine the representations of themselves, their world-views, their communities, and more in their work; positioning non-Native students as allies to indigenous peoples, the American Indian studies community, and the larger e-community by asking them to contribute to the development of a *Wikipedia* entry that was designed by Native peoples and allies to be a source of credible, Native-focused content.

There are other ways to foster non-Native alliances vis-à-vis a decolonial visual rhetorics pedagogy. I'd also recommend explaining to students that ethical imperatives extend beyond personal and intellectual examinations and alliances and into their professional and civic lives as well. To explain, in 2005, the American Psychological Association (APA) passed a resolution calling for the immediate retirement of American Indian mascots, symbols, images, and personalities used by schools, colleges, universities, athletic teams, and organizations. The APA justified this resolution with the following statement:

> It is especially difficult when American Indian peoples are trying to present their tribal identity as accurately as possible, to have the dominant culture employ symbols, mascots, images and personalities that depict American Indians in an inaccurate and offensive manner . . . [particularly for] American Indian children and adolescents whose identities are still in the formative stage of development. . . . For a group that already occupies an ethnic minority status in this country and is not often depicted in a positive manner within mainstream media, literature, books, and education, the display of denigrating symbols, images, and mascots can be very damaging. (APA 2005, 2)

Furthermore, the APA asserts that such damaging symbology, imagery, and personalities are forms of discrimination because they are inaccurate portrayals of specific cultural groups and thus an infringement on the civil rights of American Indians. In addition, the APA is concerned that dominant visual rhetorics of Indianness have the potential to teach children and adolescents that the stereotyping of American Indians and other ethnic minorities is acceptable, thereby undermining and infringing on the rights of American Indians peoples and nations to self-determination. Moreover, the APA urges, "If not attended to immediately, the continued use of such symbols stands the risk of causing serious harm to future generations of American Indian people," as they convey misinformation to American Indians and non-Indians about American Indian cultures, societies, lifeways, and spiritualities, thereby fostering negative perceptions of those cultures and creating an environment in which one group may be perceived as less than another (APA 2005, 2–3).

On March 7, 2007, the American Sociological Association (ASA) released a statement that recognized that the use of Native American nicknames, logos, and mascots in sports contributes to socially constructed "racial prejudice, stereotypes, individual discrimination and institutional discrimination . . . that undermine education about the lives of Native American peoples . . . [and] harm[s] Native American people in psychological, educational, and social ways." The ASA continues,

> The continued use of Native American nicknames, logos and mascots in sport shows disrespect for Native American spiritual and cultural practices . . . [and the wishes of] many Native American individuals across the United States [who] have found Native American nicknames, logos and mascots in sport offensive and called for their elimination. (ASA 2007)

In addition to the APA and ASA, a host of American Indian advocacy groups and academic, educational, and civil rights organizations condemn the continued the use of Native American nicknames, logos, and mascots in sports, including but not limited to the American Anthropological Association, the Association of American Indian Affairs, the Modern Language Association, the National Association for the Advancement of Colored People, the National Congress of American Indians, the National Indian Education Association, the North American Society for the Sociology of Sport, and the United States Commission on Civil Rights. Perhaps students could research their current and/or future professional organizations and consider how their professional work intersects with indigenous digital and visual rhetorical sovereignty, human rights, and/or intellectual property rights. Advanced undergraduate students and graduate students with workplace experience may be well poised to take this assignment further by proposing, or even drafting, parallel statements for their professional organizations.

INTELLECTUAL OPENINGS TOWARD NEW EXPECTATIONS

I hope this chapter has provided some modest openings toward revisiting what we currently teach in American Indian rhetorics, visual rhetorics, and digital rhetorics courses and how we teach it. There is already so much ground to cover in American Indian rhetorics courses when so many students have no prior exposure to American Indian cultures, histories, literatures, rhetorics, and discourses. Similarly, in visual and digital rhetorics courses, pressing critical discussions are necessary in relation to rhetorical theories, principles, and production of design (e.g., typography, color, etc.) and delivery (e.g., media/materiality). But I argue that we must make room for decolonial digital and visual rhetorics pedagogy in each of these courses—otherwise, we risk ignoring or even unwittingly reinscribing colonial digital and visual rhetorics that have harmful effects on indigenous peoples and lifeways. Moreover, I advocate for undergraduate and graduate courses that focus on American Indian digital and/or visual rhetorics, perhaps couched as the focus of an existing undergraduate or graduate rhetorical course in theory and application, advanced composition, multimodal composition, digital rhetoric, visual rhetoric, or American Indian rhetorics or literatures course—or even as a "special topics" graduate seminar.

In the web companion for this text, I offer several example inquiry activities and project ideas that could work for a range of the aforementioned courses. I do not prescribe specific curricula, assignments, or software for specific classes given the rhetorical nature of the work that we do. I do not know your institutions, your student populations, their histories (or yours), the educational technologies with which you and your students work, and so forth. But I do advocate that in order to do purposeful decolonial pedagogical work, we must be intentional in our course goals. And the same can be said for ensuring that we are doing digital and visual rhetorical pedagogical work.

For example, the goals of a decolonial digital and visual rhetorics approach to an undergraduate American Indian rhetorics or literatures course could be to interrogate the relationships between multiple American rhetorical and literary media—oral, material, visual, (hyper)textual, (hyper)textile, and digital; American Indians composing in digital and visual spaces in contrast to being written in those spaces; the development, use, and proliferation of older and newer American Indian technologies; and the adoption and/or appropriation of non-Indian technologies. Further, this course could study specific colonial, tribal, and community contexts for the reading, composing, and performing of American Indian digital and visual rhetorics. To accomplish these goals, this course might ask how American Indian reading, composition, and performance practices change in digital and visual environments; how the hypertextual dynamics (a convergence of multiple, linked, and layered elements) of digital compositions complement or diverge from other American Indian rhetorical traditions; how to respect and support visual and digital survivance and rhetorical sovereignty; and how colonialism and imperialism have historically shaped and continue to influence American Indian and nonindigenous representations, perceptions, and performances of American Indian cultural, tribal, community, and individual identities (including technological and visual literacies) in digital, visual, and textual spaces.

Ultimately, the goal of a decolonial digital and visual rhetoric pedagogy is to redress the ways in which colonial histories and (mis)representations of Indianness extend to digital and visual spaces and places of inquiry. This pedagogy pays rhetorical attention to, honors, and respects the ways in which American Indians challenge these colonial digital and visual histories by exercising and supporting sovereignty, self-determination, and community building by writing themselves into digital and visual spaces and histories. As a result, in spite of the long-standing tradition of the stereotypical, essentialized, and fetishized digital and visual media portrayals of indigenous peoples based on the colonizers' ascribed simulations of a monolithic Indian identity, con-temporary American Indians and allies are interrupting this hegemonic homogenous fiction by engaging in digital and visual storytelling, where new theories of Indianness emerge: a place for American Indians and allies to draw upon the oral and visual traditions of American Indian storytelling and contribute to the dynamic bricolage of the multiple and varied stories and identities of indigenous peoples. This decolonial digi-tal and visual rhetorics pedagogy, then, may lead to a reimagining of the colonial expectation of a single indigenous experience and identity—a reimagined, more diverse and dynamic notion of Indian-ness rooted in specific histories and cultural contexts. Thus, building upon Vizenor's (1998) assertion that traditional American Indian stories have the power to make, remake, and unmake the world, I posit that so, too, do decolo-nial digital and visual stories.

Acknowledgments

I write this chapter with deep appreciation. First, thank you to Rose Gubele, Joyce Rain Anderson, and Lisa King for your hard work on edit-ing this collection and for supporting this project. I also appreciate each of you, our American Indian rhetorics workshop collaborators and par-ticipants, and the rest of the NCTE/CCCC American Indian Caucus for the intellectual, spiritual, and personal community over the years. This project is greatly informed by your smart work, as well as by the brilliant pedagogy of Malea Powell and Dànielle Nicole DeVoss, from whom I learned so much about responsibly teaching American Indian rhetorics, digital rhetorics, and visual rhetorics. Finally, I am also grateful for all that I have learned from the students in the American Indian, digital, and visual rhetorics courses I teach.

Notes

1.   My use of digital and visual manifest manners is inspired by the work of Anishnaabe writer Gerald Vizenor (2009), who uses postmodern theory and trickster rhetoric to tease out and respond to colonial "manifest manners" that have historically con-structed Native peoples as Indians in simulated, static "fugitive poses" that are more real in the colonial imaginary than are real Native peoples.

2.   Spurr's repertoire of colonial rhetorical tropes include surveillance, appropriation, aestheticization, classification, debasement, negation, affirmation, idealization, insubstantialization, naturalization, and eroticization.

3.   Specifically, Ridolfo and DeVoss (2009) explain that rhetorical velocity involves "strategic theorizing for how a text might be recomposed (and why it might be recomposed) by third parties, and how this recomposing may be useful or not to the short- or long-term rhetorical objectives of the rhetorician." Further, it requires "an understanding of how the speed at which information composed to be recomposed travels—that is, it refers to the understanding and rapidity at which information is crafted, delivered, distributed, recomposed, redelivered, redistributed, etc., across physical and virtual networks and spaces."

4.   Decolonial American Indian rhetorics pedagogy works to redress the ways in which centuries of imposed colonial educational systems—both formal and informal—have prescribed problematic ways for non-Indians and American Indians alike to engage with literatures and rhetorics about, for, and by people indigenous to the Americas.

5.   This pedagogy is also part of a larger digital and visual cultural rhetorics inquiry, which can be understood as a critical framework for looking, unlooking, and relooking at the cultural rhetorics and power dynamics therein that shape the ways in which we construct ourselves and O/others in relation to one another, to visuals and visibility, and to technologies (older and newer media).

6.   I understand that these influences play out on global indigenous peoples, and we do discuss this in relation to neocolonialism vis-à-vis global capitalism, economic imperialism, and so forth, but my courses tend to focus on primarily on people indigenous to the Americas (North and South), with particular emphasis on those currently living in what Western hegemonic discourse names the *United States of America* (US).

7.   As if history and the peoples living on this continent did not begin until the European invasion.

8.   Originally written for the *Muscogee Nation News* and then posted to her blog www.joyha rjo.com/news on December 28, 2006, but here I cite the reprint in Eric Gansworth's (2007) collection *Sovereign Bones: New Native American Writing.*

9.   According to Deloria (2004), more than one hundred films about Indians were released each year from 1910 to 1913, and instead of communicating the lived realities of well-educated and rhetorically savvy Indians of the time, such as Luther Standing Bear, Charles Eastman, and Zitkala-Sa, they worked to support the dominant understanding of Indians based on and perpetuated by stereotypes.

10.   Oftentimes rhetorics of technology remember only the favorable side of the cut edge (as determined by hegemonic culture).

11.   For more on the rhetorics of Western and indigenous technological expertise and advancement in relation to Gast and wampum belts, see Haas (2007).

12.   http://indiancountrytodaymedianetwork.com/.

13.   http://www.change.org/petitions/gap-discontinue-the-manifest-destiny-tshirt-and-issue-a-formal-apology.

14.   McNairy tweeted in all caps, just as he designed the GQ-Gap t-shirt with MANIFEST DESTINY in all caps. This layer of visual rhetoric would be worth assessing with students as well.

15.   http://nativeappropriations.com/.

16.   http://americanindiansinchildrensliterature.blogspot.com/.

17.   http://bradybraves.blogspot.com/.

18.   http://www.wipo.int/edocs/pubdocs/en/tk/933/wipo_pub_933.pdf.

19.   http://www.wipo.int/export/sites/www/sme/en/documents/pdf/marketing_crafts.pdf.

20.   http://www.un.org/esa/socdev/unpfii/documents/DRIPS_en.pdf.

21.   Due to the scope of this chapter, I cannot go into the issues related to video and institutional and personal access issues, but this recommendation—and all Internet-based recommendations—are provisional based upon the cultural and material contexts.

22.   For more on contemporary Indian humor, in addition to Deloria, read Amanda Morris's (2010) essay on American Indian epideictic rhetoric in stand-up comedy.

23.   http://www.youtube.com/watch?v=HyJNiIeJ054.

24.   http://www.thedailyshow.com/watch/wed-may-2-2007/trail-of-cheers.

References

American Psychological Association. 2005. APA Resolution Recommending the Immediate Retirement of American Indian Mascots, Symbols, Images, and Personalities by Schools, Colleges, Universities, Athletic Teams, and Organizations. http://www.apa.org/pi/oema/resources/policy/indian-mascots.pdf.

American Sociological Association. 2007. *Statement by the Council of the American Sociological Association on Discontinuing the Use of Native American Nicknames, Logos and Mascots in Sport.* http://www.asanet.org/about/Council_Statements/use_of_native_american_nicknames_logos_and_mascots.cfm.

Brown, Michael F. 2003. *Who Owns Native Culture?* Cambridge, MA: Harvard University Press.

Clifford, James. 1988. *The Predicament of Culture: Twentieth Century Ethnography, Literature, and Art.* Cambridge, MA: Harvard University Press.

Deloria, Philip J. 2004. *Indians in Unexpected Places.* Lawrence: University Press of Kansas.

Deloria, Vine. 1969. *Custer Died for Your Sins: An Indian Manifesto.* London: Macmillan.

Driskill, Qwo-Li. 2010. "Doubleweaving Two-Spirit Critiques: Building Alliances between Native and Queer Studies." *GLQ: A Journal of Lesbian and Gay Studies* 16 (1–2): 69–92. http://dx.doi.org/10.1215/10642684-2009-013.

Gansworth, Eric, ed. 2007. *Sovereign Bones: New Native American Writing.* New York: Nation Books.

Gast, John. 1872. *American Progress.* Originally commissioned by George Crofutt. Prints and Photographs Division, Library of Congress.

Haas, Angela M. 2007. "Wampum as Hypertext: An American Indian Intellectual Tradition of Multimedia Theory and Practice." *Studies in American Indian Literatures* 19 (4): 77–100. http://dx.doi.org/10.1353/ail.2008.0005.

Haas, Angela M. 2012. "Race, Rhetoric, & Technology: A Case Study of Decolonial Technical Communication Theory, Methodology & Pedagogy." *Journal of Business and Technical Communication* 26 (3): 277–310. http://dx.doi.org/10.1177/1050651912439539.

Harjo, Joy. 2007. "Comings and Goings in Indian Country: Spiraling from a Blog." In Vol. 1 of *Sovereign Bones: New Native American Writing*, edited by Eric Gansworth, 253–64. New York: Nation Books.

King, Lisa. 2011. "Speaking Sovereignty and Communicating Change: Rhetorical Sovereignty and the Inaugural Exhibits at the NMAI." *American Indian Quarterly* 35 (1): 75–103. http://dx.doi.org/10.5250/0095182X.35.1.75.

King, Thomas. 2005. *The Truth about Stories: A Native Narrative.* Minneapolis: University of Minnesota Press.

King, Thomas. 2007. *I'm Not the Indian You Had in Mind.* Short film. Big Soul Productions. Toronto: National Screen Institute; http://www.nsi-canada.ca/2012/03/im-not-the-indian-you-had-in-mind/.

Lyons, Scott. 2000. "Rhetorical Sovereignty: What Do American Indians Want from Writing?" *College Composition and Communication* 51 (3): 447–68. http://dx.doi.org /10.2307/358744.

Mignolo, Walter. 1995. *The Darker Side of the Renaissance: Literacy, Territoriality, and Colonization.* Ann Arbor: University of Michigan Press.

Mignolo, Walter. 2003. "Globalization and the Geopolitics of Knowledge: The Role of the Humanities in the Corporate University." *Nepantla: Views from South* 4 (1): 97–119.

Morris, Amanda Lynch. 2010. "Native American Stand-Up Comedy: Epideictic Strategies in the Contact Zone." *Rhetoric Review* 30 (1): 37–53. http://dx.doi.org/10.1080/0735 0198.2011.530108.

Morris, Kate. 2011. "Running the 'Medicine Line': Images of the Border in Contemporary Native American Art." *American Indian Quarterly* 35 (4): 549–78. http://dx.doi.org/10.5250/amerindiquar.35.4.0549.

Ohnesorge, Karen. 2008. "Uneasy Terrain: Image, Text, Landscape, and Contemporary Indigenous Artists in the United States." *American Indian Quarterly* 32 (1): 43–69. http://dx.doi.org/10.1353/aiq.2008.0004.

Powell, Malea. "Rhetorics of Survivance: How American Indians Use Writing." *College Composition and Communication* 53 (3): 396–434.

Powell, Malea. 2004. "Down by the River, or How Susan La Flesche Picotte Can Teach Us about Alliance as a Practice of Survivance." *College English* 67 (1): 38–60. http:// dx.doi.org/10.2307/4140724.

Reese, Debbie. 2008. "With Blogs and Children's Books: 'We Talk, You Listen.'" Presentation at the Annual Native Writers' Returning the Gift Conference, East Lansing, MI, March 14.

Ridolfo, Jim, and Dànielle Nicole DeVoss. 2009. "Composing for Recomposition: Rhetorical Velocity and Delivery." *Kairos: A Journal of Rhetoric, Technology, and Pedagogy* 13 (2). http://kairos.technorhetoric.net/13.2/topoi/ridolfo_devoss/intro.html.

Rosenstein, Jay. 1997. *In Whose Honor?* Blooming Grove, NY: New Day Films.

Smith, Linda Tuhiwai. 1999. *Decolonizing Methodologies: Research and Indigenous Peoples.* London: Zed Books.

Spurr, David. 1993. *The Rhetoric of Empire: Colonial Discourse in Journalism, Travel Writing, and Imperial Administration.* Durham, NC: Duke University Press.

Vizenor, Gerald. 1994. *Manifest Manners.* Lincoln: University of Nebraska Press.

Vizenor, Gerald. 1998. *Fugitive Poses: Native American Indian Scenes of Absence and Presence.* Lincoln: University of Nebraska Press.

Vizenor, Gerald. 2009. *Native Liberty: Natural Reason and Cultural Survivance.* Lincoln: University of Nebraska Press.

HOLY WIND[1]

Janice Gould

The Navajo say that wind enters us at birth, and when we die
it spirals up and out through the tops of our heads,
the whorls of fingers and toes.
Each spring, wind brings its shadows and troubles,
slitting wide the sky, whipping topsoil into clouds of dust,
corkscrews of red grit.
In summer, wind storms down canyons,
veers off rocks, shears snow from the face of mountains
shaking fire from the sky.
Wind nudges unfurled leaves and discourages sparrows
who perch tenacious amid tossing branches.
Rattling panes of glass at night, wind
flutes through cracks and under sills
while stars whirl through the dark depths,
heedless and distant. When sunrise shimmers
at the edge of the mesa, we wake to roads swept hard,
raked to a stony surface, and breathe
a common breath. Wind is relative to each of us—
animals, insects, earth, you and me.
It seems we are nothing but a vibrant residence
sheltering that cadenced force, that vast sigh.

Note

1.   This is reprinted by permission of the author. It originally appeared in *Understanding and Dismantling Privilege* 2 (1), published in 2012.

DOI: 10.7330/9780874219968.c011

THE STORY THAT FOLLOWS
An Epilogue in Three Parts

Lisa King, Rose Gubele, and Joyce Rain Anderson

That's the story that follows me everywhere. It sustains me through the tough distances.

—Joy Harjo, The Spiral of Memory

ROSE

I stood in front of an advanced composition class at Washington State University, numb, unable to speak, but knowing I had to say something. It was late September, and the Palouse was still hot and dry. I had been living in Pullman long enough to know the pattern, and I knew that soon the heat would give way to the cold dampness of winter. I was getting ready for my qualifying exams, which were scheduled for the following semester, and my mind was crowded with the multitude of worries that come to a PhD candidate at such a time. Those worries, plus the heat seeping into the classroom, were distracting me from the task at hand.

The task was proving to be more complicated than I had anticipated. I had been assigned two sections of advanced composition, and I had asked the director of composition for permission to teach the theme of American Indian rhetorics. He was happy to agree to my request, but I had begun to wonder if teaching American Indian rhetorics was such a good idea. The course was daunting, regardless of the course theme. My students came from a variety of backgrounds and had various levels of preparation. Some were already skilled writers, and some struggled daily with the course requirements. Adding to the difficulty, I had never taught a course that featured American Indian content, apart from the occasional Sherman Alexie essay in first-year composition classes. Some students dropped when they realized the course theme focused on American Indian issues. Some remained and openly displayed their prejudices. It was a painfully difficult semester at an already difficult time.

DOI: 10.7330/9780874219968.c012

LISA

I first began teaching American Indian literature/rhetoric as a master's student, sneaking it into the syllabus wherever I thought I could get away with it. I was so tired of cracking open anthologies and discovering so little that reflected indigenous writing or rhetorical practice, so I took it upon myself to start doing what I saw wasn't being done. It was a clumsy effort, though Sherman Alexie's electric and accessible writing made my job easier. The place I thought to begin was the big-name Native authors, as they were the most visible and most justifiable in a more traditional curriculum, and I was not comfortable discussing my own family's history and heritage in the classroom. Not yet. Neither the personal nor the historical made an entrance, or at least those histories made entrances only incompletely.

JOYCE RAIN

I had been teaching composition for ELL students during my graduate work. Because I had been reading Greg Sarris's and Leslie Marmon Silko's works, I continually thought about and used story in the classroom. Once I began research on American Indian boarding schools, I realized how the experiences of my students were linked to the experiences of American Indian children in as far as language learning and assimilation practices. Sarris's "Storytelling in the Classroom" became a guide for my developing composition courses, which engaged storytelling as a pedagogical tool. In those classes, students read from texts like N. Scott Momaday's *Way to Rainy Mountain*, Leslie Marmon Silko's *Yellow Woman and a Beauty of the Spirit*, Luther Standing Bear's *My People the Sioux*, and Polingaysi Qoyowama's *No Turning Back* along with letters written by children in the boarding schools. My students wrote their own stories as influenced by these authors, made comparisons to their experiences. But they also looked historically at how different groups of people treated others and why we must work together to make change in the world. This pedagogy always slips into my other courses and still remains at the heart of my teaching.

ROSE

On that first day, it was one of my students who gave me pause. She had grown up in St. Maries, Idaho, next to the Coeur d'Alene reservation. She had asked me a question I was having difficulty answering: "What do you want?" She continued by saying she realized from the course material and our discussions that I didn't want to be thought of as a stereotype, but she also realized I didn't want people to merely overlook my Cherokee identity. We had been talking about skin color and perception, and I had stated that, because I am light skinned, many people assume I'm white. "I'm not trying to be a jerk," she had said. "I really want to know." She went on to recount a youth filled with contact with American Indians. Still, she didn't believe she knew who we were. Complicating matters was the fact that the media is filled with stereotypical images of Indians. She said stereotypes were all she had.

I stood contemplating her question, realizing all of the students' eyes were on me. I couldn't help but acknowledge the fact that she was right. I didn't talk to non-Natives about my own experiences; I assumed they wouldn't understand. I knew many other Indians who did the same. Her question was valid. What *did* I want?

I remember I tried to salvage the situation. I remember I said something, though I am at a loss now to reproduce my words. I also remember that what I said was inadequate.

It took me another year to fully answer her question. The answer, I concluded, was that I wanted all Cherokees, and all Indians, to be seen as *aniyunwiya*, real people. But real people have to be *seen*.

LISA

Students have seemed perplexed at times that we cover American Indian writing in class—in some way, in any and every class I teach now—and I've had moments when I've second-guessed myself and wondered why I go to the trouble, why I make myself visible and therefore vulnerable over and over again. It doesn't always go smoothly. But here is the most frequent pattern: when students begin to see, to grasp, to understand there are larger stories at work that they have never heard, they struggle with the implications, yet they want more. In the words of some of my own students, "We need new words, and we need new stories." That's why this kind of effort is worth it every time. For me to remain silent is to be complicit with the stories that silenced my Lenape ancestors and the indigenous peoples of this continent; to speak now, and teach now, is to try to give all of us a new chance. All teachers can contribute to this work.

JOYCE RAIN

Over the years, I have taken my mother to visit the burial site of our relatives. We carefully offer flowers to each, choosing their favorites from wildflowers and our gardens. It can take us a while to gather these as we walk the yard and stop along the roadways. Not long ago, as I placed wildflowers in front of the stones and offered tobacco, my mother said, "Myra [my grandmother] must sit on your shoulder." It meant so much to hear my mother's words, and I am reminded of how our ancestors sit on our shoulders to keep us grounded.

I tell this story because I have been blessed to live in the territory of my ancestors and because I have been blessed with the responsibility to make their stories be heard. For the past few years, that responsibility has been carried out in my Native Writing and Rhetorics course, which is required for a majority of preservice teachers and also graduate students who are teaching in area K–12 schools. The students continually comment that the readings are "eye-opening." The inevitable question they ask is, "Why haven't we been taught these things before?" Indeed, as indigenous scholars and teachers, our work is not easy as we encounter curricula that needs to be decolonized.

LISA

As I'm witnessing this project come together, I am more and more grateful for my colleagues at the American Indian Caucus at CCCC, to all our contributors, and especially to my coeditors, Joyce Rain and Rose. Without this community, I would still be slogging by myself, trying to figure out how to do this teaching of American Indian rhetorics. I'm also thinking of other instructors out there who have taken this book up—out of curiosity, out of hope, out of despair—and may be wondering how they can begin to teach American Indian rhetorics, who feel a sense of obligation but worry that they might not be doing it right and that it might be better not to try at all.

JOYCE RAIN

During my graduate studies, I was pretty much working on my own until I went to CCCC in 1996 and met Malea Powell, Scott Lyons, and Janice Gould, who were also working in American Indian rhetorics. The next year, we got together to start the American Indian Caucus. Slowly, participation in the caucus grew as we sought out others who were engaged in this work. We began to present together and support each other's work, and finally to present workshops at the conference. It is through this circle that this project was born. Lisa, Rose, and I kept talking and finally pushed each other to bring this collection together.

ROSE

The year after that student's question, I worked with Joyce Rain Anderson, Lisa King, Qwo-Li Driskill, and Angela Haas coauthoring a proposal for a workshop on teaching American Indian texts for the Conference on College Composition and Communication. The workshop was accepted, and we conducted the first of many workshops in 2008. During that workshop and others, more questions came: How do I teach American Indian texts respectfully? What do I say to students' questions? What is the best way to be an ally?

Our workshops, and this volume, have attempted to begin the process of answering these questions and others. As many of the authors in this volume have stated, the process begins with storytelling. Students can understand stories. It is a way in for them. My own focus has always been stories about history. I find that understanding American Indian history helps students understand the anger they see in many of us and in American Indian texts. One student recently told me that now that she has heard a little bit about our history (which she was shocked to learn about because it wasn't taught to her in any other class), she can understand the anger. In fact, she asked me why we weren't angrier.

The specific Native texts a teacher assigns are also important. Students benefit from material to which they can relate, so many of us use material generated by local tribes. This helps students understand the history and context of their own area; they already have a personal connection to the material because they have lived it. But it helps them see their homes with new eyes as they begin to understand the history, a history often hidden from them.

LISA

If I had a chance to go back and talk to my grad-student self, besides telling her that teaching Native American texts and rhetorics is worth the risk, I'd also tell her to start small and local, to remember the land, the place, and the first peoples there. It is a habit I have slowly developed, especially since I have never had the pleasure of teaching on Lenape homelands (traditional or adopted), and my work has taken me to rural Illinois (and the historical Illinois Confederacy, the present-day Vineyard Shawnee Indians, and the Trails of Awareness Project), to Hawai'i (the Kingdom of Hawai'i, contemporary Native Hawaiian communities, and the larger network of Pacific communities), and now to East Tennessee (just over the mountains from the Eastern Band of Cherokee Indians). I am—or at least have been to this point—both indigenous insider and outsider. So to do my work well means that each time I am in a new place, by default I must to read up on the history, build relationships with the Native communities there, and make use of the resources available (Internet! Libraries! Native American organizations on campus! Local events! American Indian Caucus at Cs!). It means that each time I teach a Native author, I've done the legwork to provide some background and some history of the writer and the context they write from. It means I still worry that I'm not doing enough, but it also means results: my Native students see themselves affirmed, sometimes for the first time in their academic lives, and my non-Native students recognize histories and peoples and already-existing rhetorical practices they did not know existed. In this way, rhetorical power shifts, and alliances can be built.

ROSE

Clearly, being an ally is hard work. Allies must educate themselves. But as teachers, we already do this. For example, in literature classes I took as a part of my graduate degree, history and context were always discussed. In some classes, the teachers introduced texts with lectures; in others, teachers wove history and context into the course requirements by asking their students to present on various historical and cultural elements related to the texts. Regardless of their methods, it was clear to me that my teachers had studied the historical and social contexts within which our assigned texts were produced.

Non-Native teachers, especially, must realize that, in some ways, they have an advantage over Native teachers when they are teaching non-Native students. Their students are like them. When I teach non-Native students, I am the "Other," the outsider. I must begin by telling them it is okay to speak. An atmosphere of fear pervades the classroom. Non-Native students who take classes that feature Native content desperately want to learn, but they are afraid of saying the wrong thing. I have heard similar sentiments from non-Native teachers. I encourage teachers to talk to their students about their fear. It is also important to acknowledge the process. All of us hold onto stereotypical thinking. All of us have prejudices. All of us struggle to understand those who are different from us. All of us make mistakes.

JOYCE RAIN

Yet, a text doesn't always point someone in the right direction. So how do you start? My first response is "with your heart," for the teaching we are talking about is as much about heartwork as it is about anything else. You also begin by forming relationships, which are at the heart of any of this work. Current scholars such as Joann Archibald and Shawn Wilson discuss relationships more in depth—read them. But more important, create your own relationships to the materials you are using and the peoples they discuss. There are likely resources in your area you have yet to know—look for them. For example, we have a small museum about fifteen minutes from BSU that few people know. It's filled with artifacts from the people of this area. Make it a point to take your students to these places or ask them to visit on their own for a class assignment. Attend Native events in your area and meet people. Be careful to listen. Ask Native people if they would be willing to come to your classes, and find ways to pay them for their participation, whether it is through your department or through some other academic program. Understand the land you teach on is Native space, that there is a continued presence (not just a colonized past) and honor that. We offer a place to start here, a place to begin building relationships.

ROSE

Teaching American Indian texts is a community activity. I encourage teachers to connect with those of us who identify as American Indian. For those who have no Native connections, our book's associated website (http://www.survivancesovereigntystory.org) is an ideal place to begin. There, teachers can download materials, view updates and statements from those who contributed to this volume, and contact us with questions.

LISA

We invite you here, at the close, to join us in this work, to continue building the community of instructors and scholars who recognize and support the indigenous rhetorical traditions, past and present, that have been here all along, and to foster their growth.

Anushiik. Wado. Kutâputush.

ABOUT THE AUTHORS

An associate professor of English at Bridgewater State University, JOYCE RAIN ANDERSON traces her mixed-blood heritage to Algonquin, Wampanoag, English, and Irish ancestors. Her teaching includes FYW, Cultural Rhetorics, and Native Writing and Rhetorics. She is faculty associate for the Pine Ridge Partnership and coordinator of ethnic and indigenous studies. She serves on the advisory council for the Massachusetts Center for Native American Awareness (MCNAA). Her current book project explores indigenous rhetorical bodies in visual/written (mis)representations of Native peoples, material rhetorics, and embodied protest rhetorics. As Sassafras, she and her cousins present Native workshops around their homeland.

RESA CRANE BIZZARO'S research focuses on how language marginalizes contemporary indigenous peoples. Specifically, Resa examines rhetorical sovereignty, identity rhetorics, and indigenous peoples' health concerns. Resa has published in *College English, College Composition and Communication, English Journal,* and in edited collections and online journals. Resa works as a literacy consultant at the University of the Free State in the Republic of South Africa, where she studies and supports academic success of indigenous peoples. Resa is an associate professor at Indiana University of Pennsylvania, and she lives in western Pennsylvania with her husband, Patrick, and son, Antonio.

QWO-LI DRISKILL is a Cherokee two-spirit and queer writer, activist, and performer also of African, Irish, Lenape, Lumbee, and Osage *ascent*. S/he is the author of *Walking with Ghosts: Poems* (Salt Publishing, 2005) and the coeditor of *Sovereign Erotics: A Collection of Two-Spirit Literature* (University of Arizona, 2011) and *Queer Indigenous Studies: Critical Interventions in Theory, Politics, and Literature* (University of Arizona, 2011). S/he holds a PhD in rhetoric and writing from Michigan State University (2008) and is an assistant professor of queer studies in the women, gender, & sexuality studies program at Oregon State University.

Koyoonk'auwi (Concow) poet JANICE GOULD is the Pike's Peak Poet Laureate for 2014–2016. Her poetry has won awards from the National Endowment for the Arts and the Astraea Foundation. Her most recent book, *Doubters and Dreamers*, was a 2012 finalist for the Colorado Book Award. She earned her PhD in English at the University of New Mexico, and more recently a master's in library science from the University of Arizona. Janice is an associate professor in women's and ethnic studies (WEST), where she developed and directs the concentration in Native American studies.

ROSE GUBELE is a Cherokee mixed-blood. She is the director of first-year composition at the University of Central Missouri where she teaches courses in rhetoric and writing. She received her PhD in rhetoric and composition at Washington State University. Her research focuses on American Indian rhetorics, racism, and Cherokee rhetorics.

ANGELA HAAS is mixed-blood Eastern Cherokee and German-American and is an associate professor of rhetoric and technical communication at Illinois State University. Her research and teaching interests include American Indian rhetorics and literatures, cultural rhetorics, decolonial theories and methodologies, digital and visual rhetorics, indigenous feminisms, technical communication histories and theories, and transnational cyberfeminisms—and her work has been published in *Computers & Composition, Computers &*

Composition Online, JAC: A Journal of Rhetoric, Culture, & Politics, the *Journal of Business and Technical Communication, Pedagogy, Studies in American Indian Literatures,* as well as in other journals and edited collections.

JESSICA SAFRAN HOOVER is a PhD candidate in Illinois State University's doctoral program in English studies. Her dissertation topic is rhetorical sovereignty and trickster rhetoric in the works of Diné Laura Tohe. She teaches developmental writing, composition, and American ethnic literature. Her research focuses on cultural studies, Holocaust studies, rhetoric and composition, American Indian rhetorics and literatures, Slovak-American rhetorics and literature, and twentieth- and twenty-first-century American literature, with an emphasis on American ethnic literatures.

LISA KING is an assistant professor of rhetoric, writing, and linguistics in the Department of English at the University of Tennessee-Knoxville. Her research and teaching interests are interdisciplinary and include cultural rhetorics with an emphasis on contemporary American Indian and indigenous rhetorics, visual and material rhetorics, and rhetorical sovereignty. More specifically, her focus rests on the rhetorics of cross-cultural sites such as indigenous museums and cultural centers and theorizing cross-cultural pedagogy through the teaching of indigenous texts in rhetoric and composition classrooms. Her scholarship has appeared in journals such as (*College Literature, Pedagogy,* and *American Indian Quarterly.* Currently, her book project (*Legible Sovereignties*) continues to explore the rhetorical practices that surround and produce public representations of Native peoples within the United States in museums and cultural centers.

KIMBERLI LEE is a professor of English in the Department of Languages and Literatures and Cherokee and indigenous studies at Northeastern State University in Tahlequah, Oklahoma. She is the author of *"I Do Not Apologize for the Length of this Letter": The Mari Sandoz Letters on Native American Rights, 1940–1965.* Her current project, nearing completion (and coedited with Jan Johnson and Jeff Berglund), is about contemporary indigenous music of the Americas. She has also published articles on contemporary American Indian music as rhetoric of resistance. Other areas of interest include indigenous literatures, rhetorics, and pedagogies. She has relatives among the Lakotas (James and Eleanor Charging Crow) and Omahas (Coleen and Jesse Flores).

MALEA D. POWELL is a mixed-blood of Indiana Miami, Eastern Shawnee, and Euro-American ancestry. She is associate chair of graduate studies and associate professor of writing, rhetoric and American cultures at Michigan State University as well as a faculty member in American Indian studies. She is past chair of the CCCC and editor emerita of *SAIL: Studies in American Indian Literatures.* A widely published scholar and poet, her current book project, *Rhetorical Powwows,* examines the continuum of indigenous rhetorical production from beadwork to alphabetic writing. In her spare time, she hangs out with crazy Native women artists and poets and does beadwork.

ANDREA RILEY-MUKAVETZ is an assistant professor in the Department of English at Bowling Green State University. She teaches graduate seminars in contemporary rhetorical theory, decolonial theory, and cultural rhetorics. Currently, she is involved in a long-term oral history project with an Odawa elder. Her scholarship can be found in "Rhetoric, Professional Communication, and Globalization."

GABRIELA RAQUEL RÍOS is an assistant professor at the University of Central Florida, where she is actively involved in farm-worker organizing with Orlando's Youth and Young Adult Network of the National Farm Worker Ministry. Her research focuses on the material structures of knowledge production and civic engagement. Her current project looks to indigenous knotted recording devices called *khipu* to fill a gap in research on object-oriented rhetorics, offering an indigenous philosophical perspective for answering important questions about the roles that nonhuman actors play in the construction of language and society. Otherwise, she spends her time watching Korean novelas.

Sᴜɴᴅʏ Wᴀᴛᴀɴᴀʙᴇ (PhD) teaches in the University of Utah's Department of Rhetoric and Writing. Her scholarship advances theories and practices that positively influence indigenous students as they work to enact self-determination through self-education. Dr. Watanabe's work as a research assistant and writing mentor for the American Indian teacher-training program led to being awarded the Steffenson Canon Dissertation Fellowship. Her publications include a chapter, "Critical Storying: Power through Survivance and Rhetorical Sovereignty," in *Crafting Critical Stories: Toward Pedagogies and Methodologies of Collaborations, Inclusion, and Voice* as well as articles in the *Journal of American Indian Studies* and the *Western Humanities Review*.

INDEX

Battiste, Marie, 46
beading, 167
Beck, Jeff, 121
belief systems, 48
Berkhofer, Robert F., *The White Man's Indian*, 22
Beyond Buckskin: About Native American Fashion (Metcalfe), 26
Big Foot, 132
Bird, Gloria, 184
Bird, S. Elizabeth, 23
Birkenstein, Cathy, *They Say, I Say*, 47
Bizzaro, Resa Crane, 6
Blackbird, Andrew, 146, 172
Blackeagle, Kianoa, 165
Black Elk, Nicholas, 132
blogs, 199
"Blood and Scholarship: One Mixed-Blood's Story" (Powell), 110
Blu, Karen, 47
Blue Spruce, Duane, 168
Boas, Franz, 23
bodies, 57, 58, 167
borderlands, 94(n2); as spatial metaphor, 81–82
Borderlands/La Frontera: The New Mestiza (Anzaldúa), 64–65
Bosque Redondo, 182
Boudinot, Elias, 100, 113(n14), 113(n16), 113(n17); and *Cherokee Phoenix*, 101, 102–3, 104–6, 114(n21); as trickster, 108–9; trickster discourse of, 107–8, 110–11
Boyd, Jim, 117, 135(n5)
Bridgewater (Mass.), 160; history of, 161–62
Bridgewater Growing Spaces, 160; Indigenous Garden and Wetu Project, 167
Bridgewater State University, 164
Brooks, Lisa, 139; *The Common Pot*, 163, 166
Brown, Michael F., *Who Owns Native Culture?*, 199
Browne, Jackson, 121

Canada, environmental activism in, 20
Canandaigua treaty belt, 59, *61*
Candy, John, 102
Cantares Mexicanos (Nezahualcoyotl), 84, 85
Canyon de Chelly (Tséyi), 176, 177, 181
Carson, Kit, 177
Castillo, Ed, 99
Catholic Church, 19
Caucus for American Indian Scholars and Scholarship, 5

Cayuga, 20
CCCC. *See* Conference on College Composition and Communication
Cemanahuac, 85
chants, 12
Cher, *Half Breed*, 199
Cherokee, Cherokee Nation, 12, 109, 113–14(n19); advertising-analysis assignment, 27–28; double-woven baskets, 71–74; history, 99–106, 111
Cherokee language, 76(n7); and *Cherokee Phoenix*, 102, *103*, *104*, 106–7; immersion in, 67–68
Cherokee Phoenix (newspaper), 12, 99–100, *104*; Elias Boudinot and, 102–3, 107–8, 114(n21); and fight for sovereignty and land, 105–6; historical role of, 111–12; trickster discourse in, 110–11; use of Cherokee syllabary, 106–7
Cherokee Preservation Foundation, 68
Cherokee syllabary, use of, 102, *103*, *104*, 106–7
Cheyenne, Sand Creek massacre, 125
Chican@ rhetorical tradition, 85
Children of the Plains (film), 49
Chivington, John, 125–26
Chrystos, 146, 148; "I Walk in the History of My People," 99
CIC. *See* Committee on Institutional Cooperation
civic engagement, 81, 93–94
Clare, Eli, "Freaks and Queers," 89
classrooms, 11, 64; advertising-analysis essay exercise in, 27–30; compositional teaching in, 4, 10; as contested cultural space, 40–41
Clifford, James, 194
CLPCUSC. *See* Committee on the Literatures of People of Color in the United States and Canada
Cobb, Amanda, 181, 186(n4)
code-switching, 13–14, 175, 178, 186(n4); Laura Tohe's, 171, 183, 184, 185
collaboration, 45
colonial discourse, 176, 177, 189
colonialism, 61, 85, 99, 149, 196, 206(n2); educational systems, 14, 142, 188–89; global rhetorics of, 192–93; intellectual, 58, 190–91; settler, 64, 161–62
colonization, 11, 36, 48, 57, 140, 192
Color of Money, The, soundtrack for, 128
commercial products, images of Indians as, 189, 198
Committee on Institutional Cooperation (CIC), 139, 158(n2)

Huckabee, Anna, 72
human remains, in Cranbrook Institute,
152
humor, 199–200; Secola's use of, 122–24
Humphrey, Annie, 133
Hunt, Bonnie Jo, 129
hunting, as trickery, 178
Hwéeldi, 182
hyperabilities, of migrant workers, 90

"I Am Not a Mascot" (P. Deloria), 173
identities: indigenous, 64, 76(n6), 94(n4),
127, 200–201; scholarly, 143
ideologies, savage, 22
Idle No More movement, 20
imagery, 21; in advertising-analysis exercise, 29–30; of Indians, 193–94, 198–99;
rhetorical impact of, 30–31
I'm Not the Indian You Had in Mind (King),
200
imperialism, 192; rhetorical, 38
imprisonment, as theme, 122
Incident at Oglala: The Leonard Peltier Story
(film), 118
independence, 39
Indian, as representation, 22–24; as rhetorical construction, 27
Indianness, 23, 196; visualizing, 191–92,
193–94
Indian Removal Act, 105
Indians in Unexpected Places (P. Deloria),
194
Indians of All Tribes, 117
"Indians Today" (Deloria), 173
indigeneity, 36, 200
indigenization, with socioacupuncture, 36
indigenous peoples: knowledges of, 188–
89; representations of, 17–18, 21–25;
sovereignty for, 82–83
indigenous rhetorical practices, 5, 12, 68,
80, 141; decolonial skillshares and,
74–76; European political and legal
systems, 69–70; good heart in, 156–57;
knowledge making and, 85–86; mentoring and, 142–43; place in, 145–46;
resistance in, 66–67; survival in, 149–
50; teaching, 138, 139–40; teaching/
learning relationships and, 144–45,
147–49
indigenous rights, 20
indigenous sovereignty, 82–83
Indigenous Storywork (Archibald), 166
indigenous studies, scholarship in, 40
individual, in Western and Indian cultures,
49

in ixtli in yollotl, 11–12, 84–85; in writing
classes, 86–93
"Innocent Man" (Secola), 126
instruction, resistance to, 41
*Intellectual Property and Genetic Resources,
Traditional Knowledge and Traditional
Cultural Expressions: An Overview*
(WIPO), 199
intellectual sovereignty, 57, 83
intellectual thought, indigenous, 46
"Inventing the University" (Bartholomae),
79
in xochitl in cuicatl, 85–86
"I Walk in the History of My People"
(Chrystos), 99

Jackson, Andrew, 105, 106
Jewison, Norman, *Dance Me Outside*, 122
"Jini" (Tohe), 180
Jones, John Paul, *The Land Has Memory*,
161

Kashtin, 129
Kelly, Kevin, Cranbrook Institute collec-
tions, 151, 152
King, Lisa, 196
King, Thomas, 146, 192; *I'm Not the Indian
You Had in Mind*, 200; *The Truth about
Stories*, 3, 45, 48
King of Comedy, The, soundtrack for, 128
kinship, 120
Kipp, Darrell, 67
Kirkness, Verna J., 37
Kloss, Karlie, "Indian" costume, 29–30, 198
Knight, Eekwol, 133
knowledge, 88, 99, 173, 179; indigenous,
13, 188–89; knowledge-making, 85–86;
local, 162–63; Native, 13, 143, 163–64
knowing, indigenous ways of, 166–67
"Kokopelli's Blues" (Secola), 126–27
Kreisberg, Jennifer, 133
Kroeber, Alfred, 23

labor, collaborative, 63–64
LaDuke, Winona, 167
LaFarge, Peter, 121; "Crimson Parson,"
124–26
La Flesche, Susan, 172
Lake, Ricki, 198–99
Lakota Spoof video, 200
land, 10, 13, 20, 57, 140, 167; Cherokee,
100–101, 106; Diné, 177, 179; New
England, 161, 162
land claims, as song theme 122, 123–24
Land Has Memory, The (Jones), 161

language(s), 14, 57, 65, 171, 184, 188;
 indigenous, 10, 67–69, 76(n7),
 76–77(n8); Tohe's use of, 177–78,
 179–82; as Trudell theme, 120–21
language-immersion classes, 57; Cherokee,
 67–68
language play, and trickster discourse, 107
language revitalization, 135(n7), 153; as
 decolonial skillshare, 65–69
lasting, 161
learning, 41, 44, 57, 75, 89; indigenous
 languages, 67–69; and teaching, 91,
 144–45
Lee, Kimberli, 86
legal systems, indigenous rhetorics and,
 69–70
Lenape Nation treaties, 59
Leon-Portilla, Miguel, *Aztec Thought and
 Culture*, 87
Lepore, Jill, *Encounters in the New World: A
 History in Documents*, 166
Leyva, Yolanda, 86
Life Among the Piutes (Winnemucca), 175
Linking Arms Together, 58, 59–60
Lippmann, Walter, on stereotypes, 97–98
listening, 134–35, 143–44, 188
"Listening/Honor Song" (Trudell), 118–19
"Listening to Ghosts" (Powell), 133
literacies, 35, 44; alphabetic, 188; cultural,
 197; Euro-Western epistemological, 51;
 land-based, 94; multimodal, 45
literature(s), 134, 177; American Indian,
 4, 6, 201, 211–16; definitions of, 8–9; as
 rhetorical texts, 170–71
Llave Del Nahuatl (Garibay), 84
Lomawaima, K. Tsianina, 40
Lone Ranger (film), 174
Looking Hot video, 198
Lyons, Scott Richard, 5, 8, 20, 39, 197; rhetorical sovereignty, 6, 57, 83, 163, 172

Madness and the Moremes (Trudell), 121
"Making a Noise" (Robertson), 129
*Making a Noise: A Musical Journey of Robbie
 Robertson* (Coolidge), 126, 128
makings, 167–68
"Male Rain" (Tohe), 180–81
Mandvi, Aasif, 200
manifest destiny, visual rhetoric of, *195*–96
manifest manners, 24
Man Made of Words, The (Momaday), 121
"Many Horses" (Tohe), 176
mapping: Native and academic space,
 139–40; rhetorical project, 166
"Map to the Next World, A" (Harjo), 166

*Marketing Crafts and Visual Arts: The Role of
 Intellectual Property* (WIPO), 199
mascots, sports, 26, 200, 202–3
Massachusetts Center for Native American
 Awareness (MCNAA), 164
mass media, 189
McBride, Robin, wampum weaving, 69
McCarty, Teresa, 48
McClung Museum of Natural History and
 Culture, 29
MCNAA. *See* Massachusetts Center for
 Native American Awareness
McNairy, Mark, 198
McPherson, Robert S., *Navajo Land, Nava-
 jo Culture*, 177–78
memory, 70, 73
"Memory as Resistance: A Decolonial
 Skillshare" workshop, 63
mentoring, 142–43
Mestizaje rhetorical tradition, 85
metalanguage, 44
metaphor, spatial, 81–82
Miami regalia, in Cranbrook Institute, 152
Michigan, as Three Fires territory, 145
Michigan Indian Tuition Waiver, 142
Mignolo, Walter, *The Darker Side of the
 Renaissance*, 188
migrant workers, 93–94; Mexican, 90
Mihesuah, Devon, 36, 112
Miniconjous, 132
Minority Treaty. *See* Treaty of New Echota
Miranda, Deborah, 146
misinformation, and Indianness, 193
misrepresentations, 26
mission schools, Cherokee, 101–2
*Mixedblood Messages Literature, Film, Family,
 Place* (Owens), 178
Modern Language Association, 6, 65, 203
Modern Rhetorical Theory course, 64–65
Mohawk, 20
Momaday, N. Scott, 6, 211; *The Man Made
 of Words*, 121
Monberg, Terese, 81
Moorehead, Deborah Spears, 165
Moreno, Soni, 133
"More Than That" (video), 49
Morris, Kate, 196
multiculturalism, 10
multimodality, socioacupuncture and,
 50–51
muscle memory, and basket weaving, 72
museums: collections in, 151–52; cultures
 of, 194, 196; touring, 153–54
music, 10; Native American, 12, 133–34,
 173; as text, 134–35. *See also various artists by name*

Made in the USA
Monee, IL
18 March 2020

23466361R00143